AMERICAN SOCIETY
in transition

AMERICAN SOCIETY

in transition

CHESTER A. DAVIS

APPLETON-CENTURY-CROFTS

Educational Division

New York   MEREDITH CORPORATION

TO HELEN

PREFACE

Long experience in teaching college students has revealed that in fields dealing with American society they do not adequately understand the nature and functioning of American institutions, and that the conventional courses in the various areas do not permit time for including such materials. The purpose of this book is to try to fulfill that need, not only for college students, but also for the interested general reader.

I am primarily concerned with an accurate description of the American processes of social change, and the results of that change. For this reason both social theory and technical terminology have been kept at a minimum. Although historical materials are used to illustrate the transition of America from an agrarian to an urban-industrial society, this is not a history of American institutions. It is, instead, a study in historical sociology which attempts to picture the changes in the different areas of American society—its institutions. My aim is limited to a better understanding of the society in which we live through a clarification of social changes in our major institutions. Space limitations make it necessary to forgo needed voluminous historical details.

This is not an original research project, but one of synthesis. The materials available were so numerous that reading, selecting, and bringing together those that were pertinent constituted a major problem. Any claim to strict objectivity would, of course, be not only presumptuous but also untrue. Subjectivity obviously entered into the selection of materials as well as into their arrangement and interpretation. Generally speaking, it has been my intention that the reader draw his own conclusions from the facts presented. Occasionally I have not hesitated to inject value judgments, but I have tried to keep the facts and the judgments separated.

There are many excellent analyses of present-day institutions in all of the various fields. No one individual can, of course, be expert in all of them, and the attempt to do even an elementary synthesis of the whole range of major American institutions is justified only by its need. It is my hope that this book will be useful in the social science programs offered in many colleges, as a reference in American studies, and to the general reading public.

The arrangement of materials and the space allotments require some explanation. The first six chapters provide a background to the analysis

vii

which follows. The chapter on the economy is necessarily long because the economy is the most obvious fact in American social change as well as in our lives. It is also placed first for that reason. It is, however, impossible to discuss the economy without bringing in a great deal about government. For this reason and because government is an increasingly pervasive influence in our lives it is discussed next. The economy and government are the dominant dynamic forces in our society, and the family and education, and to some extent religion, must adjust to them. A great deal of use is made of materials on both the family and education in the discussions of the economy and government so that less space is required to deal with them adequately. The chapter on religion is rather long because the subject stands somewhat apart from the others and was not previously brought into the analysis to a great extent. Of course all topics could be carried to great lengths, but I have tried to keep them to a minimum consistent with clarity and the purposes of the book.

I am indebted to all of those teachers, authors, and students whose ideas over the years have become my own. To my former colleagues at Lamar State College of Technology, Dr. Claude B. Boren, Head of the Department of Sociology, for generously making available to me certain materials and facilities, and to Dr. Delbert L. Gibson, professor of sociology, for reading several of the chapters and for general consultation throughout the writing of the book, I am especially indebted. Professor William H. Matthews III, author of numerous books and articles on earth science, gave me many valuable suggestions regarding authorship and publication. To Dr. Elmer Lawson, Jr., formerly of Random House, for encouragement in undertaking a rather formidable task and for valuable suggestions in pointing up the approach to the whole undertaking, my debt is considerable. Miss Betty Duncan by her promptness, efficiency, and interest contributed materially to an earlier completion of the book. The patience and encouragement of my wife, Helen Barnes Davis, gave me an added determination to do this book. Her occasional pungent criticism no doubt made it a better book. Finally, I wish to thank my editor, Dr. Arthur J. Vidich, and the Appleton-Century-Crofts staff for their kindly consideration and helpfulness.

C. A. D.

Introduction

AMERICA at the turn of the century was still, despite the existence of some large cities, essentially rural in its outlook and way of life. Most people, except for the United States Post Office and the Rural Free Delivery, were scarcely aware of the federal government. There were no income or sales taxes, selective service, federal subsidies to farmers, Social Security, Medicare, or any of dozens of other ways in which the federal government touches every American today. Not many people traveled more than a short distance from home, and the majority lived and died in the community in which they were born. It was still the day of large families and the old party-line telephone, the harmonica, and the day when Mr. Edison's gramophone was a newcomer to the music world. Most people had only a family doctor who was called to care for serious illness or to deliver a baby. It was also the era of the medicine show, patent medicines, and medical fakers, who were permitted to swindle the sick and suffering with their fake nostrums that were mostly not only ineffective but often extremely dangerous. Hospitals were few, mostly in larger cities, and professional nursing and first-rate medical care were available only to the rich; and most of the contagious and infectious diseases were still specters that haunted especially the poor. There was little organized charity compared with today. Governmental aid programs and food and drug regulations were nonexistent.

The last quarter of the nineteenth century had seen the rise of the industrial era with growing cities and vast fortunes in the hands of a few enterprising enterpreneurs, called by their critics "robber barons." Labor was trying to organize to gain a fair share of the growing wealth of the nation, but had had little success. The results were extreme bitterness and violence. The rich and well-to-do were growing richer, the poor more numerous and worse off. European socialism had considerable influence on America at this time, especially among labor groups. Religion among the upper classes was challenging nineteenth-century evangelism, but the vast majority of the rural and lower urban classes were still believers in "hellfire and brimstone." Education in many areas, especially the rural South and Middle West, was still largely the one-room schoolhouse. It was still possible for a man to study and pass the state examinations for a teacher's certificate enabling him to teach in high school without ever having attended an accredited high school or college; and most lawyers, doctors, ministers, accountants, and other professionals had what today would be considered only meager professional training.

The turn of the century saw only a few automobiles, owned by the well-to-do, and they were mostly prestige symbols. As late as 1910 the automobile was still a "horseless carriage," and the Sears, Roebuck and Company catalog of that date indicates this by advertising the latest model as a "piano-box top buggy pattern" complete with side curtains and a fourteen-horsepower motor. These curiosities might attract attention, it was said, but certainly "nothing could ever replace horseflesh." Orville and Wilbur Wright were experimenting with a "contraption" called an airplane, but a lot of people agreed with the minister who said, "that if God had intended for man to fly, he would have given him wings." Radio, one of the most sensational and important innovations of the era, was still several decades in the future, as was the sound motion picture which so excited the entertainment world.

While the urban population in 1900 was around 40 percent of the total of 76 million, this is misleading as a representation of the degree of urbanization. A great proportion of those in the cities were newcomers who were driven from the farm by improved machinery or drawn to the cities by the promise of a better life. Furthermore, most of the immigrants from Europe, nearly a million a year, were from rural areas, but settled in American cities. The first decade of the present century was still very much in the tradition of rural America despite the great changes wrought by industrialization. Up to World War I, America was still in the era of the Chautauqua, the "bloomer girls," 10 percent illiteracy, the ravages of typhoid fever and smallpox, and the Saturday night bath. The tempo of life was slow. There were no refrigerators, air conditioners, supermarkets, televisions, radios, vacuum cleaners, or can openers. There was little specialization in the professions. Wages were low and hours long for almost everybody. Most people were against militarism, big business, and big government. Atomic energy, missiles, astronauts, and high-powered electric computers had not yet been dreamed of. Birth and death rates were high and divorce was still something of a disgrace to the family. Women were legally excluded from voting and holding office, and Negroes, although legally entitled to vote, were effectively disfranchised and left largely uneducated. About one-fifth of all Americans in 1900 had at least one immigrant parent. In 1910 in the eight largest cities more than one-third of the population was foreign born, and more than another third was second-generation. If all of this seems strangely unfamiliar to modern generations, it was but yesterday to many people still living.

If the latter part of the nineteenth century, with its transcontinental railroads, large corporations, and crowded cities, seemed far removed from early rural America, it was still a semi-industrial society whose way of life was essentially rural. Within the two-thirds of a century since 1900, it has changed from the simple, slow-moving, isolationist, horse and buggy society, to an urban, industrial, internationalist, sophisticated space-age society beset with all kinds of problems and anxieties, not only at home but also abroad. It is especially for those who are too young to remember the former, as well as those who lament its passing, that this book was written.

CONTENTS

AMERICAN SOCIETY
in transition

PART I

The backgrounds of American institutions

1

Social organization and social change

UNDERSTANDING SOCIAL CHANGE

FROM time immemorial a few individuals in every society have been concerned with understanding the purpose of society, its origin, and nature. In more recent times some have been concerned with how and why society changes. With the increasing complexity of modern industrial societies, many problems have arisen which demand a more complete understanding of the changing nature of society, and the advancement in social research in modern times has made it possible to attack this problem with a promise of some success.

Rapidity of change. A stable and smoothly operating society is one whose institutions are functioning in such a way as to satisfy reasonably well the needs of the individuals who make up the society. Because of the desire for social stability, people frequently go to war to protect these institutions—the family, the government, the church, the economic and educational systems—which are the very foundations of society. On the other hand, when a society's institutions become so outmoded that they do not change with the changing needs and interests of the people, reform is demanded, as was the case of the French Revolution or the civil rights of the Negro in the United States. If these demands are not met, ultimately some sort of violence is used to overthrow those whose efforts thwart the change. Those in power in most societies oppose change—at least rapid change—because they believe that their own interests, and probably the interests of the whole society, are best served by the status quo. This accounts for the fact that people of property and the well-to-do in general are usually conservative while the propertyless are likely to be more radical in their demands for change.

The recent industrial and intellectual changes in American society have created tensions and problems which challenge the very existence of our institutions as we know them. For example, does the instability of the family in America indicate a transition to a different kind of family of

3

the future? Again, what do the great changes in our American government and economic systems mean to the future of these institutions? It does not make much sense in a scientific era to say that we do not understand these changes, and even less to assume the fatalistic attitude that we can do nothing about them. It is necessary to do both. We, as well as other industrial nations, have developed so rapidly in the fields of science, especially in the areas of destructive potential, that we are in danger of destroying civilization because we have not at the same time developed the social intelligence with which to control these weapons of destruction. It is well that we are at present in a better position to understand the nature and processes of change through which American society is passing, and it seems imperative that we make every possible effort to do so.

Change and the institutions. How well the individual performs in his society depends largely upon his knowledge of the social systems within which he lives and works. The most important of these social systems are clusters of interrelated behavior patterns which we call *institutions*. Institutions are social organizations designed to meet the needs of the members of the society. There are numerous institutions, but we are concerned primarily with the major or basic institutions: economic, governmental, educational, familial, and religious. These institutions are universal: they are universal because each serves a basic human need. Besides the universal needs, each of these institutions also fulfills many other needs. The basic need that the family serves, for example, is that of reproducing the population, but it also provides for the protection, the physical well-being, and the moral and spiritual guidance of its young.

THE PATTERNING OF BEHAVIOR: SOCIAL ORGANIZATION

The idea of *patterned behavior* is most important to the understanding of social organization. It is patterns of behavior that make possible the prediction of what people will do; this predictability is the cornerstone on which social organization is built. Every individual must make many routine predictions throughout his life although he may not be conscious of making them. He will predict that getting married will give him a more satisfying life; that graduating from college will somehow help him to achieve the things he wants in life; that the profession or business which he chooses will be best for him; and so on indefinitely. Life without predictability is unthinkable, and predictability is possible only under recurring conditions to which the individual responds in recognizable patterns. We are all familiar with many examples. The college student is certainly familiar with such patterns as registration, college fees, class attendance, tests, grades, graduation, and so on. If these patterns did not exist, we could make no predictions concerning graduation or future employment. In fact, the organization of a college or university is possible only because both students and faculty follow predictable patterns of behavior. The same is true for all other areas of social organization. The most significant patterns of human behavior are, in fact, the concern of the field of sociology.

Culture and social organization: institutional relationships. Every society has a culture which is composed of all of the material things which man has made, as well as all of the non-material things he possesses such as attitudes, ideas, values, and technology. In other words, culture, which includes both the material and non-material, consists of the patterns of learned behavior and the products of learned behavior. It is the non-material culture with which we are concerned. Culture and social organization are man's devices for meeting his most important needs: culture provides his goals, ideas, values, techniques; social organization provides the structural means for carrying out action to achieve the desired goals. The chief social organizational structure through which a society functions we call its institutions. Institutions are the essential units through which individuals pursue most of their daily activities.

For purposes of convenience sociologists treat institutions separately. By dealing with them separately we can more clearly describe their social organization, their functions, and their various other aspects. This tends, however, to give the impression that institutions are more autonomous than they really are. It is obvious that all institutions cannot be discussed simultaneously and that for convenience, at least, they must be considered separately. We should not, however, be misled by this procedure because institutions are interrelated in many ways. In the first place, the same people are involved in all of them. Then too, a great deal of one's behavior may involve more than one institution, sometimes several. If, for example, Congress should pass a law granting funds to public educational institutions, this act of government would obviously involve the economic problem of taxes to provide the money, the educational institutions that receive the money, and indirectly, at least, the families who pay the taxes to support education, as well as their children who receive the benefits through the schools.

In simple societies the family is the one obvious institution. There, other institutions appear as functions of the family. We generally speak of such societies as highly integrated in comparison to complex industrial societies where the other institutions are said to be more differentiated, or set apart. While the institutions of all underdeveloped societies are highly integrated, they become increasingly differentiated as the societies become more urban-industrial. This can be observed from the fact that, as a society becomes increasingly industrialized, the functions of education, religion, economic activities, and government are more and more entrusted to institutions other than the family. As societies become more complex, their institutions become more autonomous. In primitive societies, most of the individual's life centers in the family, but as societies become increasingly industrial, the other institutions become more and more autonomous and occupy more and more of his time and attention. The most significant exception to this tendency to differentiation is the relationship between government and economic institutions whose functions have become so intertwined that they are inseparable, and this is true of all highly complex industrial societies. It is this transformation of American institutions from those of a simple agrarian society to a complex industrial society which is the subject of this book.

THE BASES OF SOCIAL ORGANIZATION

Social organization refers to the arrangement of individuals in groups to accomplish agreed-upon purposes. This involves placing individuals in positions called *statuses* and assigning the roles or responsibilities which go with the positions, such as the father in the family, the governor of the state, and so forth. These interrelated positions or statuses constitute the social structure through which groups, and ultimately society, carry on the activities of everyday life. In other words, social organization is the patterned relationships which exist between individuals within a group, or between individuals of different groups, or between the elements which make up an institution or a society.

Groups and associations. It is the factor of organization that enables people to work together in the pursuit of their common goals. It is organization that gives permanence to the group. Simple, small societies could carry on most of their activities on an informal or unorganized basis, but present-day industrial societies could not exist without formal organization. Groups may be either organized or unorganized. An aggregation of students at the union building carrying on a conversation would be a group, but it would not be organized. The family has a social structure, but it is not an organized group. A great deal of our behavior takes place within similar informal or unorganized groups.

Sociologists call organized groups *associations*. It should be noted that here we are not dealing with the organization of society, but with the organization of a group within the society. The concept of organization must be made clear. The group of students referred to above constitute an unorganized group until they appoint a committee or otherwise arrange some sort of more or less permanent relationship. At this particular point organization enters the picture. If they draw up a constitution and by-laws, elect officers, and proceed to carry out certain functions, they have ceased to be an unorganized group and have become an organized group or an association.

The concept of association, however, is not solely a matter of organization. It involves, in fact, a continuum ranging in size from the smallest organized group on the one hand to the extremely complex giant corporation on the other. But whether it is large or small, it is characterized by the fact that the members are conscious of belonging, and there is organization and social interaction among them. There are thousands of associations for as many purposes. The most important of these associations are in one way or another related to our institutions, as for example, the PTA, the ministerial association, labor unions, the chamber of commerce, or the organization of postal employees.

Social organization. Social institutions are organized, interrelated patterns of human behavior built around the stable and fixed needs of individuals and groups, and are best understood in terms of the needs and interests they are designed to satisfy. At the lowest level, the physical and biological, these needs are universal in regard to both time and place, and include food, clothing, shelter, sex gratification and the like. But modern man, with the ability to think and plan change, demands more than living at the animal level. In the psychological area the needs of man are almost endless in number because almost any human wish, aspiration, or ambition may be so designated. They are personality needs because they arise out of common cultural conditions and are common to nearly all members of the society. The higher the development of a civilization, the greater the number, and the more important these needs are in the daily lives of people. People want not just the necessary food, clothing, and shelter, but the best of these and many other things. These needs are elastic.

It is, at least theoretically, possible that the people of a society could be reduced to the level of mere physical and biological existence. If one can conceive of this kind of existence, compared with the affluent life in our society, he can realize something of the differences in the level of social life as well as the differences in social organization that can exist in different types of societies. These differences are something which man has created and which we call *civilization*.

Neither biological nor psychological needs necessarily lead to social change. It is in the solution to problems of meeting both physiological and psychological human needs that new patterns of behavior come into existence. When there is no known solution to a problem, the only obvious approach is one of trial and error. When, through trial and error, the people of a society find the solution to a problem, it becomes an accepted way to behave under these circumstances, a pattern of behavior. It is quite natural that different societies in different parts of the world with their extremely varied conditions would find different ways of meeting their needs, even in their solutions to the same problems. For example, the family everywhere fulfills the basic need for replacing the population, but the form or organization of the family is quite different in different parts of the world. This will also hold true for all other institutions.

There are certain basic requirements for the existence and operation of social organizations. The relationships of individuals and groups must be established and coordinated. Larger groups, especially whole societies, are composed of many different kinds of individuals and groups. Our concern is with the behavior which they have in common, such as the proper method of getting married, working for money, or electing those who govern them. In American society we have racial groups, ethnic groups, religious groups, and many others so that the effective operation of our society requires established and coordinated patterns of behavior. Without social organization, we could not provide so well for our needs and wants. These needs and wants are many and varied, ranging from the basic essentials of food, clothing, and shelter to those of the aesthetic and the spiritual. Social organization is essential to the stability and operation of a society. It is obvious that such institutions as our government and economic systems depend upon social organization. The highly developed division of labor which makes ours an affluent society is possible only because of it. And as we have previously stated, in order for individuals and groups to live and work together successfully, they must know what to expect of each other. Social organization is based on social action. It includes both processes and procedures. As persons interact over a period of time, mutual expectations develop and ultimately become *patterns* of behavior. In this way the framework of institutions grows out of action and becomes the mechanism designed to carry out the activities which are required to achieve the goals of the institution. An institution, then, is an organized procedure, a way of doing something.

PATTERNS OF SOCIAL ORGANIZATION: INSTITUTIONS

Institutions must be more specifically elaborated. Culture and social organization of which institutions are a part are the two sides of the same coin. Culture consists of knowledge, ideas, beliefs, values, goals, norms: it is the book you are reading and your reason for reading it; it is a belief in the hereafter as well as a system of philosophy. People cannot behave in an expected way or create a material object unless they first have ideas of how to do these things. Institutions are the mechanisms and social organization devised for the satisfaction of basic human interests and needs. Society recognizes five basic needs: (1) sex and the care of children, (2) the spiritual or religious, (3) social control or government, (4) material or economic, and (5) the transmission of the cultural heritage or education. Out of these basic needs have developed what we call our basic institutions. Of course all institutions serve other purposes than the basic ones stated above.

Institutions in operation include more than just organization. They must have: (1) an ideology, (2) a structure or organization for carrying out the ideology or purpose, (3) usages, rules, and laws to govern their actions, (4) usually some sort of facilities such as churches, school buildings, factories and so on, and (5) functionaries or people who carry out the actions involved. The Christian Church and public education are good examples. They have ideologies, the ways and means of achieving these, and a justification, or what they more likely call their social philosophy. The other four aspects mentioned above are too obvious to need clarification.

Origin and development. The origin of our major institutions is lost in antiquity. They probably have no origins apart from their development, but there are at least a number of theories about how they developed. Among the earliest in America, and still probably the most widely accepted, was that stated by William Graham Sumner. Sumner said that an institution consisted of a concept and a structure. The structure was the framework, or social organization, for carrying out the concept, or the idea, doctrine, or interest. They began as habits or customs which he called *folkways* and developed, at least the more important of them, into required patterns of behavior which he called *mores*. Perhaps the best known code of mores is the Ten Commandments. These are not laws, but some of them are considered so important that most societies have established laws to enforce them. But the enforcement of the concept "Thou Shalt Not Kill" requires a wide range of social organization such as legislatures to make the laws, judicial branches to interpret the laws, and executive branches to enforce them. These organizations and the procedures under which they operate bring into existence the institution of government. In the same way other institutions were supposed to have developed. From this the two basic features of the institution ought to be obvious: the concept or purpose for which it exists, and the structure or social organization for carrying out the concept or purpose.

Institutions in a society such as ours do not exist in an organized form in which an overall organization encompasses all of the institution's behavior. The federal government is an overall organization, but the institution of government includes state, county, and municipal governments as well as all other political subdivisions. The institution of the family has no overall organization in America society but is constituted of individual kinship groups. Education has a weak overall or national organization but has numerous state and local organizations which are more important. Religion in the United States, with the exception of the Roman Catholic Church, has very much the same kind of organization as education. Economic institutions are the most diffuse of all. There is

no overall organization of these institutions as such, but only a nation-
wide organization of certain economic subsystems such as the Federal
Reserve Bank, the National Association of Manufacturers, labor unions,
and so on.

The organization of our institutional subsystems, themselves generally called institutions, is more obvious, as for example, that of a college. Here an organizational chart could specify the various positions or
statuses along with their corresponding duties or roles. These statuses and
roles that provide the division of labor make it possible for the college
to perform all of the many interrelated activities involved in meeting its
total obligation, educating the student body.

Social institutions provide behavior patterns of a high degree of
stability, uniformity, formality, and generality. They are abstractions
which cannot be observed through the senses. They are inferred from
the behavior of people. Because we see students meeting in classes day
after day, we infer that there is a class attendance pattern—an abstraction
which we call a *behavior pattern*. There is a difference between "my"
family and "the" family. The first is specific, referring to a particular
family with a definite number of people of very definite characteristics.
The latter has no specific referent, and exists only as an abstract generalization derived by taking into consideration the common characteristics of families everywhere.

It is only by abstraction that we can consider institutions to have a
separate existence. Institutions grow out of the actions of people. Most
people, however, are not aware that their behavior is so classified. They
simply go about their daily routine unaware of the fact that in eating
breakfast with the family they are performing a family function; that in
working at the shop or office they are performing an economic function;
that in attending a PTA meeting or sending the children to school they
are performing an educational function; that in voting they are performing a governmental function; that in attending church and taking communion they are performing a religions function.

Interrelatedness of institutions. In modern industrial societies the institutions are more specialized than in pre-industrial societies. While the
school is the specialized agency for education, certainly a great deal of
education comes to the child from other sources—the family, the play
group, the church, television. In the same way the functions of other
institutions overlap and are interrelated. The division of labor which is
increasingly characteristic of industrial societies requires a high degree
of interrelatedness. Institutions are also influenced by factors which impinge on the society as a whole. Such factors include race, physical environment, population composition, and so on.

The interrelatedness of institutions may be further illustrated by
the fact that, in addition to its specific purposes, most people think of

education as a means to improve their economic opportunity, make them better citizens, improve their chances for a better life, and in some cases promote religious ends. In the case where people vote to raise taxes to support education, four institutions are involved: the family, education, the government, and the economy. In some cases functions are transferred from one institution to another, or at least shared with another. In early times education was largely a family function, but now we recognize it as a separate institution with a relatively high degree of autonomy. In the earliest times, no doubt, the family was the only well-defined institution, the others being only functions within the family. Even today, the family is the basic institution; the others exist to serve the needs of the members of the family.

Although institutions are usually discussed separately as though they were independent entities, it ought to be clear from the foregoing that they are only clusters of related behavior patterns built up around the basic needs of people, and that they are as interrelated as are human needs. Nor are institutions static. They change like all other parts of a culture changes. The development of our institutions can be fairly well traced, especially in more recent times. The social distance, however, is very great from that era of home-produced food, clothing, and most everything else the family needed, to our modern space age. But the difference in behavior patterns in government, family, religion, education, and economic institutions of that era and the present, although not so obvious as in the fields of science and technology, do represent a tremendous development in these institutions. Since institutions are mechanisms designed to meet the needs of a society, it is obvious that a simple society would in general have simple institutions, that a complex society would have complex institutions, and that a society in a process of rapid change such as ours would have rapidly changing institutions.

SOCIETY

Society is a functioning group that displays the following characteristics. (1) It involves individuals, who (2) are organized in the pursuit of some of their common interests, on (3) a more or less permanent basis, and who (4) ordinarily occupy a given territory. Societies, like institutions, are based on the recurrence of patterns of behavior which are related in definite ways. The relationships are obvious and they happen frequently enough to be recognized as patterns. Such patterns as marriage ceremonies, church communion, political elections, college classes furnish examples. These patterns have a continuity and they are definitely related to the larger institutional patterns. The individuals who enact them are born, live, and die, but the patterns, or in other words the institutions, survive them.

A society is the largest of the social organizations within a national state. It includes all of the individuals, groups, associations, and institutions among which an appreciable degree of regularity of relationship exists. Individuals in any society share many beliefs, values, and actions which recur in time and are related to other patterns. A society is made up of many social systems. The member units which comprise a social system are individuals and groups. A simple club is composed of its individual members. A federation such as the United States or the American Federation of Labor is composed of groups. A social system is composed of the interaction patterns of its members whether groups or individuals.

Some of the change in a society is inherent in the changing of its personnel: new members of a society are never exactly like the parent generation. In this respect, a society is undergoing a continuous process of change of which most of its members are unaware, but which, over a long period of time, is very significant. We usually think of this as progress.

Differences. It is easy to observe that societies throughout the world are different. These differences appear mostly as differences in their institutions. In classical China the institution of the family was dominant. Medieval society was predominantly a religious society. Some American Indian societies were highly competitive while others were cooperative. Our present American society is said to be a business society. In modern totalitarian states, political institutions are dominant. Not only are societies different, but there are great variations within the institutions of a given society. The upper class Boston or Charleston family is certainly different in many ways from lower class families wherever they are. It is only in the simplest, usually smallest and most isolated societies that a high degree of homogeneity can be found. Modern industrial societies tend to be more heterogeneous. This is particularly true of the United States. Any study that aims at an understanding of that society must, therefore, include a study of its institutions. But the understanding of a society requires more than the mere description of the structure and functions of its institutions. Some of the areas of concern are discussed below.

The proliferation of the many aspects of human relations in modern industrial societies has obscured the basic problems embedded in the social structure. When a society meets these problems satisfactorily, people are unaware of them, or take them for granted. Societies always face the recurring problems of adapting to their physical environment and to the problems of group living. These require not only meeting the elementary needs of food, clothing, and shelter, but also of providing for the care, protection, and training of the young who cannot do these things for themselves; meeting the requirements of individual members in the cultural areas; and meeting the requirements of coordinating the actions of individuals to avoid chaos and confusion. This requires rules for governing the actions of members, and the establishment of procedures for carrying out the rules. It is through these that the basic units of social organization are created.

Every operating social system must make some adaptation to its natural environment. Man continues to gain ascendancy over the forces of nature, but he can never ignore them. The population, its composition, age and sex structure, and distribution are all factors in social organization. The social institutions of a people must adjust themselves to the needs of the society whose population is undergoing change. If, as has recently been true of American society, the rural population is rapidly diminishing and urban areas are being overrun, rural institutions such as schools and churches are likely to decay while urban schools and churches may be unable to keep pace with the needs created by the shift. The structure of the family as well as that of the churches and schools will also be affected by the population shift. A large family of brothers and sisters who grow up in an urban environment will likely disperse, never having shared that intimacy which most characterized the early American farm family. These subsystems of the foundation on which society is built are factors in the determination of its social organization. The nature of culture and cultural change are likewise factors which enter into social organization.

Organization. Society may also be thought of as consisting of (1) primary groups, groups which have a structure but are not organized, (2) more formally organized groups which we have previously called associations, and (3) institutions. The primary groups such as the family, the play group, and the neighborhood are the very foundation on which society rests. In urban societies, especially in the United States, associations have become increasingly important as aspects of human behavior. Most of these associations are in one way or another related to our various institutions. All of these groups and institutions constitute the various communities which make up the society.

The factors mentioned in the preceding paragraphs are not the whole story concerning the nature of society: among other things, they do not explain what it is that holds the component parts of a society together. This involves an area of so-called "social imperatives." Among the most important of these are values, norms, ideologies, authority, and status and roles. These factors are closely interrelated in the operation of the social system, and each deserves a full explanation which we shall have to forgo. *Value* is the quality of something which causes it to be desired, such as individual freedom, or in our society the right to vote. Every society must have such a system of values. The American preferences for democracy, belief in the practical, worship of science, belief in progress, and humanitarianism are examples of values. Values concern the important preferences which represent the concensus of the group or society. Values are learned: they are a part of the tradition which we acquire simply by growing up in a society. It should be obvious that a common value system is a strong cohesive factor in holding a society together.

Another social imperative for a society is that it must have standards or rules which determine what action should be taken in any given situation. These standards for judging the conduct of individuals we call *norms*. Norms may state what action must be taken, or they may state what must not be done. For example, one must pay his taxes, or one must not commit murder. Norms are applicable to all areas of human behavior. They provide the basis for the fulfillment of mutual expectations and for the predictions of what others will do. The enforcement of conformity to social norms is brought about by (1) conscience, (2) group approval or disapproval, and (3) in more serious cases, the law. Norms are learned and transmitted from generation to generation. Authority is the social mechanism through which the legal norms are enforced. It is the accepted framework within which some individuals make decisions and impose their decisions on others. Authority is as essential to a democratic society as to any other, and without it chaos and confusion would reign.

An *ideology* is the blueprint for action as it is perceived by the members of a society. A society is integrated or held together by its ideology—its system of beliefs that offers an understanding of the social order as well as a justification for it. The individual interprets his environment in terms of his society's ideology. Through language and thought he gets his picture of reality. Most learning is verbalized, and through the use of language, rationalization gives meaning to the universe as well as to the behavior of people. Thus, ideology is the system of ideas which controls the actions of individuals, and the system by which they are judged. Every society has an ideological system over and above the particular ideologies of its component parts. This system consists of all the complex schemes whereby men interpret their world and adjust themselves to it. It consists of the attitudes, ideas, knowledges, theories, beliefs, traditions, myths, and so on, as well as the values and norms, ideals, conceptions of purpose, and goals that have accumulated through the decades of past experiences. In other words, it is an intricately interwoven fabric composed of all of society's interpretations, sentiments, faiths, doctrines, and hopes.

Status and role. At least two other related imperatives must be understood in order to understand the organization of a society—status and role. The fulfillment of the needs of the individuals in a society raises the problems, in Talcott Parson's terms, of who is to get what, who is to do what, and the manner and conditions under which it is to be done. The solution to these problems is found in the differentiation of the roles which individuals assume. *Status* is the position one occupies in a set of relationships among individuals. An individual has a status within each group of which he is a part and a general status abstracted from these specific statuses. He has a number of statuses as a member of the family. He may be a husband, a father, and a brother; he may also be a deacon in the church, chairman of his local political party, president of the Rotary Club, and secretary of the school board. These multiple statuses of individuals serve to relate not only the individuals to the group, but also the various groups and institutions to each other. In this sense, a social system may be thought of as a set of standard positions which interrelate the activities of members of a community.

Because one occupies given statuses, he acquires certain rights and duties. Thus, the husband's duties are to make a living for his family, help descipline his children, and so on, in other words, to play the role of the husband. The teacher should act like a teacher, the minister like a minister, the teenager like a teenager. This is to say that they should play the roles which these statuses lead us to expect of them. The role indicates the action which the individual should take because of the status he occupies. For analytical purposes the role is the most significant unit of social structure. Persons who occupy statuses and play roles change, but the statuses and roles continue.

All social organization is erected on statuses and roles. The statuses determine who shall occupy the positions, and the roles determine the manner and conditions under which the responsibilities of the job shall be carried out. Roles are complexes of customary ways of doing things. They establish the expected behavior of the individual in respect to the other person or persons involved. For example, there is a definite inter-relationship, based on status and role, among the members of the family, the personnel of a bank, or a college faculty. This network of interrela-tionships establishes the division of labor which makes possible the opera-tion of the various aspects of a complex society. People with different abilities and specializations occupy different statuses and perform differ-ent tasks at the same time.

Social cohesion. We have raised the question as to how a society is held together, and have indicated some of the ways. At least two other ways in which society is held together ought to be mentioned. In modern in-dustrial societies particularly, individuals produce practically none of the things they need. Thus a high degree of interdependence among indi-viduals exists. This interdependence is an important factor in the cohe-sion of a society. It is generally assumed that one gets what he wants by applying his effort within the social system and in behalf of the social system. How much of the cohesion of a society is based on the idea that the welfare of the society and that of the individual are the same is a question. Another factor, that of common values, ought to be mentioned.

It is obviously true that individuals who grow up in a society have similar values, which makes for cohesion in the society.

SOCIAL CHANGE

Since institutions are the chief mechanisms for meeting human needs, any study which aims at understanding a society must also understand that society's institutions and how they change. We must note the distinction between change in culture and social change. A change in culture is a change in values, attitudes, and ideologies; a social change is a change in the patterns of interrelationships. For general purposes the distinction is not usually made, and we shall use social change to refer to changes in both.

Rate of change. In primitive societies change is very slow. In fact, some societies have a concept of change entirely different from ours, or even no concept at all. This seems strange to us because we have experienced great change within our own lifetime. Of course there was always change, but in early times it was almost, if not completely, imperceptible. Change, which is an alteration in ideology, organization, or procedures, is cumulative in something of a geometric progression; the greater the number of traits, the greater the potential for change. This is because change in either the material or non-material culture is usually brought about by the combining of already known traits. The Selden patent, for example, combined six well-known pieces of machinery—the gas engine, the gas tank, the running-gear, the clutch, the drive shaft, and the carriage—to make the automobile. The United States Constitution, a social invention, was created from the concepts and principles of several sources. It is generally accepted that there has been more change in the past seventy-five or one hundred years than in all previous history. No doubt we can expect this progressive rate of change to continue.

Some older people in America today can remember when there were no automobiles, airplanes, refrigerators, talking pictures, discount houses, televisions, radios, or supermarkets; they remember when women could not vote, when there was hardly any divorce, when very few people had a high school education and still fewer went to college, when the family doctor who had comparatively little training was the only one most people knew, when most stores were general mercantile businesses, and when most of the American people still lived on farms. These are some of the changes within the lifetime of a single individual. But the changes go much deeper. If one can conceive of the differences in the way of life of a farm-oriented individual, and the more sophisticated way of life of an individual in our modern urban society, he can get an inkling of the deeper meaning of social change.

Theories of social change. Theories of social change are many: they include the "economic determinism" of Marx, the "geographic determinism" of Dr. Ellsworth Huntington, a "linear" as well as a "cyclical" conception of social and historical change, a conflict theory, and many others. Today it is recognized that the cumulative effects of scientific and technological developments are of special significance. Studies of both primitive and modern societies have reached the conclusion that social systems are functionally dependent upon technological systems. Some authors would go so far as to insist that social systems are determined by systems of technology.

Chain effects of social change. The various elements of a society are so interrelated that a change in one may create a chain reaction as in the case of the introduction of the farm tractor. The tractor was intended primarily as a more efficient form of power than the mule. But its effects reached much further than improved efficiency: it replaced the mule and most of the hired hands; the type of crops and the amount of land allotted to them changed because it was no longer necessary to devote a large part of the land to produce feed for the stock; share-cropping and, to a large degree, farm tenancy were virtually eliminated; farming became a more capitalistic and commercial enterprise; farmers became dependent upon the fluctuations of prices on the national and even the international market. Sometimes a purposeful change has some very unexpected consequences. Henry Ford intended to make a cheap mode of transportation. This he did, but much more. He changed the place and way of courtship: where it was formerly in the parlor, it now takes place at the movies, sorority dances, wherever cars will take young people. It helped to break down the isolation and provincialism of a great part of America, and it helped to promote the growth of cities.

BIBLIOGRAPHY

Bell, Earl H., *Social Foundations of Human Behavior: Introduction to the Study of Sociology.* New York, Harper, 1961.

Bredemeier, Harry C., and Richard M. Stephenson, *The Analysis of Social Systems.* New York, Holt, Rinehart and Winston, 1962.

Goldschmidt, Walter, *Man's Way: A Preface to the Understanding of Human Society.* New York, Henry Holt and Company, 1959.

Hertzler, J. O., *American Social Institutions: A Sociological Analysis.* Boston, Allyn and Bacon, 1961.

LaPiere, Richard T., *Social Change.* New York, McGraw-Hill, 1965.

Levy, Marion J., *The Structure of Society.* Princeton, N. J., Princeton, 1952.

MacIver, R. M., and Charles H. Page, *Society: An Introductory Analysis.* New York, Rinehart, 1949.

Mott, Paul E., *The Organization of Society.* Englewood Cliffs, N. J., Prentice-Hall, 1965.

Nordskog, John Eric, *Social Change.* New York, McGraw-Hill, 1960.

Williams, Robin M., Jr., *American Society: A Sociological Interpretation.* New York, Knopf, 1960.

2

The community in transition

IT is in the community that most of the basic needs of man are met. It is here that we have our homes, that we are born, get married, live and die; it is here that our children are born and go to school, that we work at our business, trade or profession, that we participate in church, service organizations, clubs, and other activities that make life meaningful and worthwhile; it is here that we have our warmest friends and our bitterest enemies, that we have our successes and our failures; and finally, it is here that our friends will lay us to rest.

In stressing the importance of the community we do not intend to minimize the significance of the nation as a community. Modern transportation and communication have obviously become important factors in changing the lives of people everywhere. Because of them, many forces outside the community impinge on all of us much more than in the past, and they will probably continue to do so at an increasing rate. This is especially true in the urban-industrial parts of the world. But there are still large areas where the local community is about the only world the individual knows, and this was true for even the urban-industrial areas in the not too distant past. No doubt the influences of the extremely community-centered way of life still pervade our modes of thought and the way we feel about many things. History is replete with ideas that the major virtues reside in the local areas of our lives, especially the rural areas; and a great deal of present-day thinking reflects the idea that big government is bad because it is big, and that the big city is still the den of vice and iniquity. They are obviously centers of a multitude of serious problems.

While it is the community that makes the person the kind of adult he will be, the influences of the greater society cannot be denied. There are many culture patterns that all Americans have in common, but these are also an intrinsic part of community behavior. There are also many things which give the community distinctiveness. It is certain that the community life of an individual in Boston or Chicago is different from that of an individual on a ranch in the Southwest or on a farm in the Mississippi Delta. But regardless of size or heterogeneity, the quality of community institutions is most important to the individual. They are his home, his church, his job and so on, and any change in them is a change which directly affects his life.

THE MEANING OF THE COMMUNITY

The term *community* has been used as a synonym for society, social organization, group, and social system. While these definitions are many and varied, most of them do have certain areas of agreement. Among these are: area or place, people, shared interest and values, and social interaction. For our purposes we shall consider a community as (1) a place or area with (2) people who (3) through their common interests and shared values (4) interact through (5) common organizations and institutions. The term has frequently been used to apply to rural areas, towns, and villages, but it may also be applied to metropolitan areas.

Modern definitions of the community tend to ignore the area, and to extend the community to include large cities, or even the nation. This raises the question as to the degree to which people share values and interests and reciprocal communication in order to constitute a community. The community can be considered in terms of the satisfaction of the individual's needs, most of which must be served at places easily accessible; places where one works, trades, worships, and educates his children. Usually most of these services will be found in a village or town, or in a suburban community center. The area within which most of the basic needs are satisfied is generally what we mean by the community. The real community is composed of the relationships of the people who live within the area. The idea of the community as the focal point of the individual's interests goes back to Ferdinand Tönnies' concept of Gemeinschaft. Tönnies recognized in descending orders of "area" the country, the province, the town, and the village. In more familiar terms these might be compared with the nation, the region, the community, and the neighborhood. It was the town community and its surrounding territory within which Tönnies found the feeling of intimacy, the feeling of belonging, the feeling of wanting and being wanted in all the aspects of community life: the social, the spiritual, and the economic. It is the contrast between this type of society and the modern industrial society which has largely superseded it that is the theme of this study.

In the traditional or older conception of the community, the individual shared the common interests and way of life of the whole community. Social cohesiveness was achieved through participation. In modern industrial societies the individual's participation is not in the community as a whole but in segments of it: industrial organizations, labor unions, professional associations, fraternal orders, and service organizations. These organizations are of a different order: the common interests and shared values, the interaction among the people, and the organizations and institutions of the community have been transformed into a different kind of social order.

This transformation has rendered the idea of an isolated, self-sufficient community inadequate for urban societies. The newer conception of community is much more complex. Within the older type of community, the individual could largely satisfy all of his needs. He was almost compelled to be reasonably self-sufficient. In present-day industrial societies, individuals are dependent upon areas far removed from their communities for both material goods and services. The degree of specialization of service that one demands determines the geographical area required to meet his demands. Simple, everyday needs can be provided largely in the immediate community. If, however, one needs the services of a very highly trained brain specialist, or services in any other highly developed technical fields, he may have to go several hundred miles for them. The same is true in the field of material goods. Some things are produced only in certain areas, and in some cases things will have to be imported from abroad. Modern societies are becoming increasingly interdependent because of the division of labor and specialization. That this trend tends to break down the traditional type of community is obvious.

The result of this trend is to expand the limits of the community and to turn its attention outward both in regard to its needs and its outlook. Some of the consequences of this change are: a dispersal rather than an intensification of relationships; emphasis on occupational rather than neighborhood development; sectional specialization in economic development; increasing functional groupings to represent all vital economic interests; reduction of social relationships to an impersonal level; and fragmentation of community experiences.

It is not too difficult to conceive of a city of forty thousand people, and its surrounding sub-communities as constituting a community, that is, of more or less meeting the requirements of our definition. But what of New York City which is composed of five boroughs, each a separate county with what was formerly a large number of more or less independent communities and large enough to be considered a metropolis in its own rights? Such large metropolitan areas indicate not only the degree to which we have moved away from the traditional community, but they also raise the question as to whether the community is disappearing, or whether a rather completely new definition of the community is necessary. Thus, the traditional idea of a community as a well-defined geographical area with people who were a self-governing unit with interrelated economic activities and a sharing of interests and values has given way to one largely based on special interest groups whose characteristics do not conform to the traditional concept of the community.

Primary group dominance. The neighborhood is the first grouping beyond the family. It is the simplest form of community. Several neighborhoods usually make up a community. A neighborhood can be based on a combination of factors: geography or natural resources, nationality or ethnic composition, religious groups, and economic or social status groups. A neighborhood is a geographic unit in which people know each other, where visiting, borrowing, and mutual aid are common practices. It is the area outside the family where the greatest intimacy is to be found. It is where we find our warmest friendships and bitterest enmities.

The neighborhood is founded on primary groups whose relationships are direct and intimate, the modern community on groups whose relationships are secondary and impersonal. The neighborhood provides a very limited number of the goods and services, the community satisfies most of the individual's needs. The neighborhood is usually built up around such basic institutions as the school, church, or store, or a combination of these. The relationships within the neighborhood are based on tradition and sentiment, those of the community on the social and economic needs of its residents and the organizations and institutions that satisfy them.

The neighborhood is the place where primary groups are dominant. In it the informality of contacts, the similarity of status levels, the homogeneity of ethnic background and so on are conducive to the development of close personal relationships. The family and the other neighborhood groups are the ones within which the young grow up. It is here that a society either succeeds or fails in producing the kind of citizens it desires.

Decline of the neighborhood. In addition to the types mentioned above, neighborhoods may also be urban or rural, rich or poor, mining, manufacturing, religious, and their characteristics may be as varied as the factors which make them up. But one thing they have in common: as they grow, their institutions grow and become more neighborhood-centered in order to satisfy as many needs as possible. Also, as they grow, segregation and specialization in business, industry, and social cliques take place, thus altering the old neighborhoods and creating new ones. They also lose their unity—the situation in which the individual was a part of practically all the experiences of the group—and tend to expand their demands for both goods and services beyond the neighborhood. Their relationships tend to become segregated into special interest groups which are rarely based upon locality, but rather upon members who are widely dispersed; where contacts are more formal and more impersonal; and where tradition and sentiment have little place. It is generally recognized that the shift in interest and association away from the neighborhood to functional interest groups has brought about a great decline in the relative importance of the former.

GROUPS AND ASSOCIATIONS

Nature and importance of groups. We spend most of our lives in groups of one kind or another—the family, the play group, the work group, the recreational group, and so on. The number of groups is probably greater than the number of people. Groups are the units through which society carries out most of its business. We not only live in groups, but we are continuously creating new ones. It is this extensive complex of groupings which comprise the patterns of the social structure. The essence of the group is the social relationships of its members.

We are not particularly concerned with the classification of groups, but some explanation of different kinds of groups is necessary. A social group is generally said to be an aggregate of persons who are conscious of each other's status and who are in reciprocal communication. Sometimes a number of people are classified together, such as teenagers or men of draft age, as purely statistical aggregates. These do not constitute a group because they are not conscious of each other and are not in reciprocal communication. The group is the most pervasive social unit in society. It is through groups that most of the business of society is carried out. Officials of larger social organizations such as corporations may formulate policies, procedures, and regulations, but it is the smaller groups that eventually carry out the work. All of us are almost constantly involved in the activities of many groups. Our participation in groups may be by chance or it may be purposive, and it may be either organized or unorganized. If a social group becomes formally organized, it is called an *association.* That some social groups are not organized does not mean, however, that they have no social structure. The family has a social structure, although it is not formally organized.

A distinction is often made between primary and secondary groups. A primary group is any number of persons, usually a small number, who meet on intimate and personal terms and whose relationships are more ends in themselves than means to ends. The latter is a characteristic of secondary groups. Secondary groups are those in which the contacts are more casual, segmental, and infrequent, and where lack of intimate acquaintance leads to matter-of-fact or impersonal relations. In some cases the individual ceases to be a person and becomes a mere functionary, such as the personnel in very large firms where one does business. We seldom know anything intimate about them, their families, or their friends. In fact, a machine might replace them without much concern to the customers.

A society based on primary groups (Gemeinschaft) would encompass most of the life experiences of the individual. It would be a society in which most of the concern and conversation would be about people. In secondary groups, occupational interests in particular take precedence over people. That the latter is true of modern urban-industrial societies is evident from the unconcern of people for those among whom they live. In such cases people may live in the same apartment building or near each other on the same street and not know each other, and in fact not want to know each other. They have little or nothing in common. There are reports in recent years of cases in our large cities where people have watched others being murdered, beaten, and robbed without even calling the police. This would be unthinkable in a society which was primary-group oriented.

Primary groups in a secondary group setting. It is not that primary group relationships have been eliminated in modern societies, but that secondary group relationships have become dominant. More and more in churches, schools, the government, and the economic activities of the individual, the very size tends to make the relationships more impersonal, more formal, and more goal-oriented. More and more, in all of the activities in which the individual participates, the control is by those whom he does not know and who are largely beyond his power to influence. The primary group is still, however, the nucleus of social organization. Any large organization—religious, educational, or economic—will have within it a network of primary groups. In every organization the individual will find his place within the group of his associates. These groups within groups have their own leadership, status and roles, and become integrated into the secondary group setting.

The main primary group is, of course, the family, and in spite of the dominance of secondary group influences, it is probably more important than ever before. With the vast array of influences competing for the attention of the family, it has never been so important for parents to give attention to family matters, especially to the rearing of children. Modern societies have responded to this challenge, especially in regard to children; they have never been so child-centered. Other primary groups are also important. We are members of many of them in our lifetime: play groups when we are very young; athletic, social clubs as youth; occupational, civic, church when we are adults. Membership in all of these except the family are more or less transitory. It is only the family that remains intact and of course it changes with time. As a social unit, it is within the primary groups that people find fulfillment of their needs for affection, outlets for their frustrations, and the satisfaction of their common ideals and values.

Associations: nature and functions. While primary groups continue to play a strong role in the intimate life of the individual, the affairs of the society are increasingly dominated by formally organized groups. These groups are generally called *associations* and are characterized by consciousness of kind, social interaction, and social organization. Associations are groups of people who, conscious of common interests, organize themselves in order to achieve those interests. The purpose of the organization may be as specialized as an African violet growers society, or it may be as broad as the United Nations. The number of associations and the purposes for which they are organized are among the most amazing phenomena of modern times. Their importance in our lives can hardly be overemphasized. A university for example, has clustered around it dozens of subsidiary associations. It has hundreds of athletic and recreational associations. The same is true of business and professional associations, religious associations, manufacturing associations, banking associations, as well as labor, welfare, political, and artistic associations. An astonishingly large number of these can be found even in small towns.

An association may be distinguished from an institution because it consists of individuals who are grouped together for a certain purpose, while an institution is a set of social relationships. It differs from an institution also in having more limited purposes, such as to promote a tax reform or to prevent cruelty to animals. The institution pursues more general purposes. Institutions have many associations attached to them to promote one or more of their purposes. The school has its PTA and alumni associations, the church has its youth groups and ladies' guilds. Some associations, however, are not connected with any institution. Most recreational groups and hobby clubs fall into this category.

Each association is organized to promote one or more specific functions. Labor unions promote the interests of laborers through efforts to secure higher wages, better working conditions, and better fringe benefits; merchants' associations attempt to increase trade and to improve profits; teachers' associations try to increase salaries and improve tenure. Besides these specific functions, associations play many other roles. They tend to distribute the power in the community through their different purposes. In a highly industrial area the business associations and the labor unions tend to counter-balance each other. This counter-balancing recurs throughout our society for there are always two or more associations with conflicting needs and desires.

Associations separate special groups from the rest of the community, but at the same time they tend to integrate the basic institutions into the larger society. Each association is not a little island unto itself. Some people belong to a dozen or so different associations and most people belong to several. These overlapping and interlocking memberships create an intricate network of contacts which tie the community and ultimately the society together. This gives cohesion as well as stability to the society. As on-going concerns, associations also provide the mechanisms whereby desirable changes are planned, promoted, and sometimes tested.

Prior to the industrial revolution, the community through the family and church largely satisfied the human needs for fellowship, personal security, and an explanation of the supernatural. As geographic mobility, urbanization, and secularization advanced, the individual was increasingly involved in impersonal, secular activities, and the family and church lost a great deal of their hold on him. One of the important functions of associations is to reintegrate the individual into the broader community and society.

Associations weaken the unity of the traditional community because they are composed of interest groups which encompass only small fragments of the community, not he community as a whole. Many of these associations are functionally related to and frequently controlled by authority at a regional, state, or national level. Also, they are formally organized and operated by explicit rules and codes, whereas the community has no organization and operates on a more or less informal and implicit basis. Thus the community has become a collection of more or less autonomous organizations the relationship of whose members are increasingly functional, impersonal, and goal-oriented. In the Yankee City study W. Lloyd Warner found in a community of 17,000 people, over 800 such associations.

THE COMMUNITY AND ITS INSTITUTIONS

Place in the community. Since we have discussed institutions in a more general way, our purpose here is to explain the place of institutions in the community. Community institutions are related to societal institutions both vertically and horizontally. In small and extremely isolated cases, the neighborhood and the community institutions may be the same; there may be few vertical or intercommunity ties. In such cases the institutions are highly integrated. At the opposite extreme, such as a suburban community, the institutions are related both vertically and horizontally in many ways and are much more distinct from the more broadly based societal institutions.

The functions of teaching and learning, making a living, bringing up children, government, and religious worship are universal. When the behavior patterns dealing with these functions become regular and recognizable, when they are performed by certain designated persons—teachers, ministers, governors—usually at designated places and under more or less standardized procedures, the patterns have become institutionalized. Teaching and learning take place almost everywhere, but it is only within the school that they are institutionalized. In other words, one may become a member of an educational organization which is an association, but he cannot join "education," which is an institution. Or again, one may belong to *a* family, but not to *the* family, which is a universal institution, an abstraction.

The community consists mainly of its subsystems, its institutions. If the family, the church, the school, the government, and the economic institutions and their satellite groups and associations were removed from the community, what would be left? There are numerous factors which determine the nature of the institutions and in turn the community. In the case of the Amish, for example, the dominance of religion may in a large way influence all other aspects of the community. A community composed of retired people would have little need for schools or strong economic institutions. There would not be much need for a curfew or many police officers, and the churches would likely be well attended. Farming, mining, ethnic, university, and Bohemian communities would each be largely dominated by any one or any combination of these or dozens of other factors. It is true that these same institutions constitute our total society, but within the society the communities display an amazingly varied and colorful array of characteristics.

Differentiation and specialization. The main components of a community as units of study are the institutions—the subsystems. As societies move from simple to complex, rural to urban, the institutions become more autonomous and more specialized in their functions. One example will suffice. In primitive societies, families were almost exclusively responsible for teaching their children the things they needed to know. In industrial societies this function has been largely removed from the family and placed in a separate institution called education. As a society becomes more and more complex, the educational function becomes more confined to the institution, which in turn becomes more differentiated and specialized. The early American college, for example, was mostly devoted to general education. With the exception of the old professions of law, medicine, and theology, education did not prepare people for jobs. College training has become preponderantly job training and any large university will offer degrees in seventy-five to one hundred different fields, and the number and degree of specialization continues to grow.

In summary, it may be concluded that to the ordinary individual it is the community about which he is most concerned—the immediate family, the local school, the local church, the local government and economic institutions. In most respects, it is the efficiency of their operation that determines his well-being. This is true despite the growing welfare programs of the federal governments. In other words, no community whose family life, religious life, education, government, and economic activities are unsatisfactory is a place where anyone would want to live.

Meaning and origin. Institutions as well as societies are more than just social structures: they also embody values, beliefs, and ideologies. It is impossible to understand institutions without understanding the concept of value. The community is comprised of people acting together to attain certain common goals. It is their values that govern their behavior in their efforts to attain these goals. A value system, then, is comprised of the goals to which people aspire and the means of achieving them. In other words, values determine the purposes of life and the means of achieving them. It is value which gives more prestige to the status of physician than to that of truck driver. The process by which the physician is given preference over the truck driver is an evaluation, not a value. Value is the standard or criterion by which the evaluation is made.

All values arise in and have reference to the patterns of organized behavior. Their existence may be exhibited by social research, but neither their validity nor their justification can be empirically established. For example, the customer who chooses a prime steak over either goose liver or a pork chop shows a preference—he places a higher value on one than on the other—but this does not validate or justify the choice. The choice is a psychological one and may depend, for example, on whether the customer is a Christian, Hindu, or Jew. The reality is in the human mind and not in the material object. The Rhodesian chieftain who said to Lillian Russell, a famous beauty of her time, "Miss Russell, had Heaven made you black and fat, you would be irresistible," displayed the subtlety with which values are determined by one's culture.

Values or shared judgments may be common to all societies, peculiar to one society, or to a subsystem of a society. As implied by the example of the Rhodesian chieftain, values grow out of the experiences of the people involved. They are the conclusions arrived at in the solution of problems. Some are advantageous, some are not. Values are acquired by the individual through the simple process of growing up in a community or society where they prevail. They determine why the Chinese dislike milk, why the Japanese commit hara-kiri, why the Hindus will not kill a cow, why the Jews will not eat pork, why we send missionaries abroad. Values are in the traditions of the society and they are mostly acquired and often held without awareness by the individual who possesses them.

Since it is impossible for individuals, groups, or communities to have everything they want, goals and ends have to be ranked in some order of importance so that efforts may be directed toward achieving those considered most important. Values are the criteria or standards by which the choices are made. Values, however, do not exist as separate entities. They are a part of what has been called value orientation. Just as customs are what people do, value orientations are the ways they see life in general.

Value orientation. Understanding a community depends upon understanding its value orientation. Community and even national value orientations are of numerous kinds. One of the most common concerns human nature which may be conceived as evil, good, or neutral, changeable or unchangeable. Conceptions of society generally rest on some assumption or assumptions concerning the nature of man. If a society holds that human nature is unchangeable, then it would consider any effort at reform not only useless but also foolish. If a group or society holds that human nature is evil but changeable, then it would not suppress any attempt to reform it. Modern American society is increasingly accepting the idea that human nature is good and that efforts to reform should not be suppressed.

There are many conceptions of the nature of a supreme being. The spiritual beliefs of individuals in a society and their form of worship depend upon their particular conception of man's relation to the deity. Some societies have been oriented to the past. Medieval society, with its predominantly Christian orientation, was such a case. Religions in general are oriented to the past in varying degrees. Modern industrial societies are more likely to be oriented to the present. All communities stress in varying degrees the past, the present, and the future. A community stressing the past will be traditional and resist change while one oriented to the future will work for improvement or change. American society is obviously oriented to the future. Latin America has been characterized as a "mañana" society in contrast to our bustling business society.

There are still other ways of looking at the differences of communities and national societies. Tribal societies are based on kinship, and the goals are more group goals than individual goals. American society is more individualistic. The individual is freer from restricting relationships, and individual goals take precedence over group goals.

It should be understood that such classifications as the above are only theoretical formulations to be used in the study of the community or society. Any single study must be a cross-sectional view at a given time. Since change is continually taking place, in the long run any given analysis will be outdated. Significantly, a restudy of the same community or society is the best method of determining both the rate and direction of change. The study of a community or society is essentially a problem of determining the relative importance of different values. For this purpose it is necessary to know something of the degree to which the value is accepted and whether it is temporary or more or less permanent. It is also necessary to know how important the value really is; whether it is something to which people only give lip service, or whether it is something meaningful in everyday life. These things can be empirically established by social science research.

Functions of a value system. Every on-going society, or community has a value system which dominates all individuals and groups, who may or may not look upon it as essential to the kind of society they wish to preserve. Because there is a common value system in the community or the society, people are able to agree on the things which they want as well as on the means of acquiring them. Values are also a major reason for the activities in which people engage themselves, as well as the goals for which they strive. In other words, the value system is the chief basis for cohesion or unity in a society.

As we have indicated above, values are psychological; they are qualities of personality. The values by which people live become symbolized, and the symbols and the reality become so intertwined and unified in the thoughts of people that they are not easily separated. In our society financial success usually brings the acquisition of large cars, pretentious houses, and other gadgets which become symbolic representations of achievement, sometimes called status symbols, and may even be equated with personal worth. Symbols are powerful motivating factors in channeling individual behavior.

Values and social change. One of the chief functions of a value system is to provide the bases for concrete forms of social life. For example, the value placed on education gives form to the educational institutions; the value placed on marital fidelity acts to preserve the family structure; religious beliefs give form and stability to religious institutions. Value systems, however, always operate within the reality of a society in which social change is always present. As modern industrial societies become increasingly complex, the rate and degree of social change increases, bringing in their wake changes in the value system. For example, when America was rural, it was a virtue to rise early in the morning; in fact, failure to do so was looked upon with disapproval. Today those who have to get up at four o'clock in the morning to go to work are looked upon with sympathy. The previous reference to the introduction of the farm tractor and its effects is a more pervasive example of social change which has had a powerful influence on our whole value system.

THE COMMUNITY AS A JOB AND SERVICE CENTER

Change in the nature and place of employment. The community is not only a place or a collection of people, it is the service center where people have their jobs. This is especially true of the rural and small town communities. Services and jobs cover everything from shoe repair shops, beauty shops, and automobile repair shops to public utilities and the professional services of doctors, teachers, and ministers in addition to those employed in agriculture. In metropolitan communities people frequently live in a "residential" community and work and have many of their services met outside this community, or they may live near a "community center" where most of their needs are met, but work in the metropolitan area. With the present metropolitan growth, jobs are increasingly removed from immediate home environment.

One of the amazing developments of modern times is the change in the nature of jobs and work and the degree to which division of labor and specialization have taken place. At the end of the colonial period there were the three professions of law, medicine, and theology, and a dozen or so services available to the average individual. Today even the professions are becoming highly specialized. A century ago the family doctor did everything for the average family. Today the areas of specialization in medicine are so numerous that the average person knows little about them. In the other services specialization is even more extreme. In comparison with the dozen or so jobs that were open to a boy when he was grown, say in 1800, today the United States Census lists over 15,000 occupations and 12,000 industries, and the Dictionary of Occupational Titles lists 39,000 occupations with 35,000 job descriptions.

A comparison of the employed in a Latin American agrarian community with an urban industrial community shows the change in the nature of jobs when a society becomes industrialized. A study by Irwin T. Sanders reported in his book, *The Community*, showed that of the 16,000 people employed in Oshkosh, Wisconsin, 8,200 were in manufacturing which included metals, woods, textiles, and foods. Construction employed 500 people; commerce employed 5,500, of which 2,800 were in services, 300 in wholesale trades, and 2,400 in retail trades; transportation accounted for 1,300; and others, 200. In contrast, in San Luis, Guatemala, with 1,535 employed, the distribution was as follows: agricultural wage workers, 1,341, or 87 percent of all; landowners, 100; skilled and semi-skilled workers, 94, including woodworkers, carpenters, ironworkers, stoneworkers, masons, roofers, and shoemakers. Then there were many part-time workers such as musicians, midwives, dressmakers, school teachers, pottery workers, and bakers.

The degree of specialization in both goods and services varies with the size of the community. In a rural community with a village center, one finds things like staple groceries, working clothes, and simple repair shops. If one wanted exotic foods, an expensive wedding gown, stocks or bonds, or a racing car, he would have to go to the larger service centers. The small community would have few men's shops, women's hat shops, large department stores, or shoe outlets. The same is true in the areas of professional services. The doctors in such a community would likely be general practitioners, but if one needed a serious operation, he would have to go to a larger center.

The community and specialization. The functions which community organizations serve are still numerous and are usually grouped around the major institutions. Today the economic factor has become the dominating one in determining where the individual will live and to a large extent the kind of life he will have. In a small community persons with little education are more likely to remain while those with a greater degree of specialization are likely to leave. All of this tends to complicate what used to be a simple occupational structure and way of life. It also robs the rural areas and small communities of their youth, especially the better educated ones, leaving mostly older people and young children.

In the United States in 1790, boys and girls had little choice as to their life's work—95 percent of the boys would be farmers and a like number of girls would be their wives. The remaining 5 percent comprised the professions, businesses, and other services. This was the basis for a strong community. It provided few services and job opportunities, but it did provide security and a basis for an individualism which present-day society has largely lost. The whole trend raises the question as to whether we can have the warm glow of the life so nostagically referred to by older people and, at the same time, the affluence to which we have become accustomed. Since it is life in the community and the neighborhood which shapes the destiny of individuals, there are those who view this trend with alarm. There are also those who blame this loss of local contact and control on some pernicious theory, rather than on the changed conditions under which people live. Any analysis of this question would have to take into account those factors which brought about the changed conditions. Change in technology is recognized as the most important of these factors.

Change in work environment and values. The family head in the traditional, rural American community was an individualist, not so much because he followed some theory, but because of the conditions under which he lived; his well-being depended on it. He was mostly self-sufficient: he was his own boss; he usually owned his land, his tools, and his livestock; he went to work when he wanted to, quit when he wanted to, worked the way he wanted to, and in the end he owned what he produced. This does not mean that he had greater freedom than he has today. He was, in fact, a slave to hard physical work. The conditions under which he lived required that he be independent and self-sufficient. The contrast of the present-day urban community is very sharp, indeed. America today is essentially an employee nation—over four-fifths of those who work outside the home work for some other individual or corporation. In contrast with rural America of a century ago, the present-day employee's working hours are short and his physical labor light, but he does not own the place where he works, the machinery with which he works, or the products he makes; he cannot go to work when he wants to, do the work the way he wants to, nor quit when he wants to; and he can be fired or retired against his will. The only claim most people have today for their work is their periodic paycheck. This is the sole basis of their well-being and their security. The billions of dollars spent on various kinds of insurance is an effort to buy back the security which has been lost. These are some of the consequences of the changed conditions under which we Americans live today.

This rather complete transformation in the bases of American life is the dominant factor in the rapid transformation of the whole society. The new industrial environment in which the American finds himself has changed not only the conditions of his life and work, but also his attitudes concerning both, and new ideas and values dominate the American scene. No longer does the Puritanical concept of hard work and abstinence govern the behavior of Americans. Summer and winter resorts and all other kinds of recreation and amusement facilities are always crowded; weekend traffic always takes its toll in killed and maimed—some 53,000 killed and several millions maimed annually. In fact, work is becoming just something which must be done to acquire the means to more satisfying pursuits. "Creature comfort" and self-gratification have become a fetish: homes, businesses, and the family's two cars must be air-conditioned; all but the very lowest income families must have travel vacations; and the money spent on liquor, tobacco, and other luxuries would adequately support a program to relieve our disgraceful poverty, including a first-rate education for all children.

Increasingly Americans take long weekends and some week days off despite the inconvenience to the public. This includes professionals such as doctors, bankers, and public officials whose work or service is necessary for the convenience or well-being of society, as well as teachers and dock workers who maintain the right to strike even at the expense of the education of the children and the health of the community. These and many other conflicts between the self-interest of individuals and groups and the well-being of the community have arisen because of the rapidly changing conditions within the society. Americans are apparently coming to accept the idea that the most important thing in life is living it in a satisfying and worthwhile way and are relegating materialism to the position of being a means to that end. Dr. Ashley Montague, an outstanding British anthropologist, contends, however, that American parents still press upon their children materialistic values, which many of them do not accept, to the point that the pressure becomes a main cause of frustration to modern youth.

If older generations seem perplexed and see only purposelessness, confusion, preoccupation with materialism and sex, the breakdown of law and order, the loss of personal integrity, and the lack of patriotism in the new way of life, it is because the extremely rapid rate of change has created a much wider gap between the generations than was formerly the case. Because of this tremendous gap between the ideas and values of the generations, youth sees the behavior of the older generations as archaic and are neither impressed by it nor sympathetic to it. Obviously the old "community" way of thinking is gone, and we have not yet formulated an adequate set of new ideals and values to replace those that are being discarded. Whether in the end this will be accepted as good or bad only the future can tell. But based on past history, we should expect that later generations will approve.

BIBLIOGRAPHY

Goldschmidt, Walter, *Man's Way: A Preface to the Understanding of Human Society.* New York, Henry Holt and Company, 1959.

Hausknecht, Murray, *The Joiners: A Sociological Description of Voluntary Association Membership in the United States.* New York, Bedminster Press, 1962.

Hertzler, J. O., *American Social Institutions: A Sociological Analysis.* Boston, Allyn and Bacon, 1961.

Loomis, Charles P., and J. Allan Beegle, *Rural Sociology: The Strategy of Change.* Englewood Cliffs, N. J., Prentice-Hall, 1957.

Nelson, Lowry, Charles E. Ramsey, and Coolie Verner, *Community Structure and Change.* New York, Macmillan, 1960.

Rose, Arnold M., *Theory and Method in the Social Sciences.* Minneapolis, University of Minnesota Press, 1954.

Sanders, Irwin T., *The Community: An Introduction to a Social System.* New York, Ronald, 1958.

Stein, Maurice R., *The Eclipse of the Community: An Interpretation of American Studies.* Princeton, N. J., Princeton, 1960.

Sussman, Marvin B., *Community Structure and Analysis.* New York, Crowell, 1959.

Tönnies, Ferdinand, *Community and Society.* New York, Harper, 1957.

Warren, Roland L., *The Community in America.* Chicago, Rand McNally, 1963.

3

Urbanization and urbanism

URBANIZATION can be described as a process, urbanism as a way of life, a set of circumstances. Through urbanization urbanism is achieved. There are two aspects of urbanization: the first is the shifting of people from country to city and from agricultural work to urban types of work; the second is a change from one way of life to another. As a process, urbanization is characterized by the movement of people from farms and villages to cities, and this normally involves moving from farm or farm-related jobs to any of a great variety of other kinds of work. As a change in place of living, urbanization represents moving from an environment in which man's life is intimately bound up with the forces of nature to one in which natural forces have little part. The farmer is in competition with the forces of nature and his welfare is in large part dependent upon them. The urbanite lives in a man-made environment, his competition is with people and his welfare depends upon manipulating them. There is not much communing with nature in the big city nor much place for the high-powered advertising agencies, insurance companies, or brokerage firms in an agrarian society.

The change in the way of life in America is represented in part by the change in place of living and change in types of work, but it is not necessarily so. One may move from farm to city and retain his rural behavior patterns, or he may live in a rural area and acquire urban ways of behaving. Nor is urbanization a one-way movement. Between 1920 and 1950 in the United States, some 50 million people left the farm for the city, and about two-thirds as many left the city for rural areas. This reverse movement alone would tend to urbanize rural America. But there are even more compelling forces: modern transportation and communication have brought most of rural America within the orbit of our cities. It is from our urban centers that the forces of change and progress largely emanate. In fact, the way of life in rural America is largely dominated by our urban centers.

This domination, however, should be accepted with some explanation. The city is the political as well as the commercial and cultural center of the community. The fact that this domination is far from complete is shown by the former power of the so-called "farm bloc" in Congress and by the domination of some state legislatures by rural representatives, even though they represented a minority of the total population. This is the center of the recent controversy over the reapportioning of representation in the state legislatures under the decree of the United States Supreme Court. It is obvious that the correlation between the degree of urbanism and the degree of dominance is not sharply defined.

Urbanism, as a way of life, is not confined to the cities. The individual in a rural area may be very urban in his way of thinking and conduct. In recent years thousands of our urban elite have bought farms and rural cottages—refuges from the tensions of urban life—but this should not be mistaken for a reversal of urbanization. These people may seek retreat in a rural environment, but they have made sure that all of the conveniences of urban life have been transplanted to their "rural" domiciles, and they would resist vigorously any effort to change their urban patterns of behavior. They do not really want rural life: they want urban life in a rural environment and, like those who move to the suburbs, they immediately start making their rural environment more urban. In the United States, the urban population is approximately three-fourths of the total, and the rural population is increasingly becoming urbanized.

Although there were large cities in the earliest times, they had a level and style of life very different from that of the rural peasants. The rural populations were in no sense urbanized as they are in Western society today. Pre-urban societies, sometimes called folk societies, never reached a high degree of civilization. It was only when industrialized cities came into existence that new patterns evolved and change or progress became significant. Especially since the end of the Middle Ages, urbanization has gradually encroached upon folk societies. In America today "folk society" has all but disappeared. Urbanization is a stage of civilization, and as a product of industrialization will, no doubt, invade the present underdeveloped countries as they become industrialized. In the United States in 1960 the farm population was approximately 15 million or about the same as in 1860. In 1960 this was 9 percent of the total population, whereas in 1790 the rural population was 95 percent of the total. By 1967 it was reduced to 12 million and was only 6 percent of the total. In the eight years prior to 1967 the number of farms declined by almost one-fourth to 3,176,000.[1] Furthermore, the remaining rural population was fast losing its distinctiveness; a more homogeneous American society

[1] From a report by the U. S. Department of Agriculture, quoted by Beaumont Enterprise in a bulletin of November 20, 1967 (Beaumont, Tex., Beaumont Enterprise, 1967).

was in the making. The traditional concept of community was in eclipse, and a community on a society-wide basis was replacing it.

It should be kept in mind that we are not here discussing the growth of cities, but the process of urbanization of which urban growth is a component. An industrial society involves much more than industrialized cities. The bases of the whole society were changed and the development of science and technology, which made possible the industrial revolution, were responsible for this transformation. "Industrial Revolution" is a very inclusive term. It is used to cover the technological innovations of the eighteenth and nineteenth centuries which completely altered the production process, replacing households and small shops with the factory system. For the first time in history, national economic systems produced food and material goods in excess of the needs of the members of that society. In fact, the concept of material well-being of all its members has become the accepted norm in the new industrialized societies. In many non-industrialized societies, however, the status of the poor is still accepted as inevitable.

Before urbanization could really get under way, it was necessary to improve production in agriculture. The Industrial Revolution brought the improvement in farm technology and farm machinery. No society can develop a high civilization as long as it has to expend all of its energies on providing the basic material needs of its members. This is the case of the underdeveloped countries today where vast numbers are always hungry. This is the vicious circle in which they find themselves trapped: they cannot take from their production the necessary capital with which to build industries, and because they cannot do this their production rates can be improved only very slowly, if at all. Even Russia, and especially China, is still plagued with the problem of producing enough consumer goods while at the same time building up its industries. The Western world underwent the process of industrialization over a period of three centuries and it was so gradual that a minimum of civil disorder and other problems of social disorganization were apparent. Present-day societies are in a bigger hurry. Beginning in the third quarter of last century and profiting by Western experience, Japan was transformed from a feudal into an industrial society in about twenty-five years. In 1917, Russia was a peasant society. Today it is fairly industrialized. China is speedily making the transformation. The extent to which technology in the United States has improved farm production is indicated by the fact that in 1790, the 95 percent rural population produced only a surplus for the 5 percent urban, whereas in 1967, less than 12 million people produced enough for the 200 million population with large quantities for foreign aid, and with still large troublesome surpluses.

The Industrial Revolution is generally said to have begun in England with the inventions of the spinning jenny, water-frame, and power-loom which transformed production in the textile industry. Improvement in the processing of iron and steel played an important part in industrial progress. The early source of industrial energy was water power. Beginning in the early part of the nineteenth century a new source of power, steam, was to revolutionize industry and make possible a much higher degree of industrialization, and of course urbanization. The application of steam not only revolutionized the factory, but also brought about a new era in transportation.

The United States soon became a veritable network of transportation systems with steamboats crowding the inland waterways and the frenzied development of railroads making the West Coast only a few days from New York. The addition of the telegraph and the telephone completed the necessary transportation and communication requisites to rapid industrialization and urbanization of the whole country. The development of electricity as a major source of power and, more recently, atomic power, added immeasurably to the dynamic force of the industrialization process in transforming American society. This transformation is thus a direct result of the changes in the kind of energy used to do America's work. In 1850, the sources of energy were: human, 13 percent; animal, 52.4 percent; and inanimate, 34.6 percent; by 1950 human energy accounted for only .9 percent; animal, .6 percent; and inanimate, 98.5 percent. The energy required in 1950 was 38 times greater than in 1850.[2]

An indication of the degree of industrialization can be drawn from the number of patents registered in the United States Patent Office. Before 1850 the number registered annually was under 500; by 1860 it was nearly 5,000; and at present it is around 40,000. The telephone was invented in 1876. By 1900 there were some 1.3 million telephones in the United States; by 1910 as many as 7.6 million, and in 1963 some 84.5 million or 44.42 percent of the population.

The influence of the circulation of millions of daily newspapers, and weekly and monthly magazines of all sorts, and the tremendous number of books published, as well as the 224 million radio sets and 93 million television sets in 1967, cannot be overlooked. With the thousands of other inventions and improvements, including the supersonic airplane, space technology, and computerized business and industry, we are obviously on the threshold of the most fabulous era imaginable.

THE MASS SOCIETY

The transformation of the material bases of American society is also the transformation into a mass society. A mass society may be thought of

[2] Harold A. Phelps and David Henderson, *Population in Its Human Aspects* (New York, Appleton-Century-Crofts, 1958), p. 323.

as mass production and mass consumption along with mass communication, especially advertising, and mass transportation. But much more is involved. The division of labor and specialization on which a mass society is built make necessary an almost unbelievable degree of interdependence of the individuals in the society. If one checks all of the items in a large department store, a large jewelry store, or supermarket, and if one then checks where all of the articles came from and the transactions necessary to place all of these thousands of items at his disposal, he will get an inkling of the degree of interdependence in modern mass societies. It even goes beyond national boundaries. A drought in Brazil may make the price of coffee go up all over the United States, even all over the world. Problems in one area of our economy have their repercussions throughout the whole society, and a general strike by the teamsters or the railroad workers could paralyze the whole country.

Significance. Mass society has been through a leveling process. The standards of an elite which once governed the arts, manners, and customs are reduced to the standards of "the common man." The control of the mass society has passed from the hands of the educated and "cultured" elite to control by the masses. Historically, society has passed from the domination of the aristocratic ideals of Alexander Hamilton to those of Andrew Jackson. The nature of higher education has changed from that of the cultivated mind for a select few to that of vocational or job preparation for almost everybody. Art and music have become popularized, they have become "folk" art and music. The leveling process also had a standardizing effect: hamburgers and Coca Cola pervade every corner of the United States, and, more important, the daily newspapers, radio, and television serve the same fare to all throughout the country every day. National sports champions have their followers everywhere and all American women follow the current fashions. It is not so easy to prove that our thinking is likewise standardized, but it is obvious that to some degree this is true.

Mass societies represent the dominance of urban society. The family and primary group relationships have been minimized. Social control by custom and group approval has given way to written contracts, laws, and court systems. The participation of the individual in the total experience of the community has given way to the experiences which are limited to small interest groups. Living close to nature and in competition with nature has given way to a way of living in which the individual is utterly dependent upon others.

Mass production and advertising. The basic factor in mass society is mass production, with its standardization, interchangeability of parts, and synchronization of men and machines. With these and the assembly line, increasing productiveness has come to depend more upon the efficiency

of the machine than the skill of the worker. Mass production has brought
the cost of most products within reach of the masses. It has changed the
nature of industry from being almost entirely small scale to a situation
in which increasingly a few giant corporations largely dominate the field,
especially in production. Such examples as the automobile industry, communications, transportation, the meat packing industry, electric appli-
ances, farm machinery, the oil companies and a few score others come to
mind. Along with mass production goes mass marketing. Increasingly
chain stores and large discount stores take over the field from small retail
businesses.

One of the most phenomenal aspects of this whole change has been
the growth of advertising. From a society in which advertising played
little part, we have come to the point that it is a dominant feature of
everyday life. In 1968, newspaper advertising in this country amounted
to over $5.5 billion, television advertising over $3 billion, and enough
from other sources to total $17.5 billion, as compared with a gross na-
tional product of some $56 billion in 1933.[3] Not too long ago advertising
was based on the idea that people needed certain things and knew what
they needed. Its purpose was to make the product attractive. The buyer
could be reasonably expected to know the value of the product. Today
there are so many new products that people cannot know about most of
them, and know even less about their uses and values. The result is that
at present the big job of advertising is to create new wants and needs so
that people will want to buy the products. This amounts, of course, to
the manipulation of the tastes of the society. If this creates flexibility, and
a degree of instability in the area of tastes, it probably does so in other
areas also.

Installment buying and insurance. The old-fashioned "good sense" of not
buying until one had the money to pay for a product has given way to
an extravagant mortgaging of the future. Installment buying, although
ancient in origin, was relatively insignificant until recently. In fact, going
into debt of any kind was thought to be bad business. That that day is
gone is shown by the fact that in 1968, installment credit in the United
States amounted to about $79 billion as compared with only about $3
billion in 1929. Charge accounts for the same period rose from $1.5 to $21
billion, and the total consumer credit from $6 billion in 1946 to $100
billion in 1968. The mortgage debt in the country in 1964 amounted to
$278 billion, while the gross public debt in 1968 amounted to $350 billion, or $1,766 per capita.[4] Not only does private business encourage

[3] *Information Please Almanac for 1969* (New York, Dan Golenpaul Associates,
1968), p. 706.
[4] *The U. S. Book of Facts, Statistics and Information for 1966* (New York, Herald
Tribune, 1965), p. 407.

credit operations, but government does as well. All of this brings up the big problem of keeping the economy in equilibrium, and it increasingly involves the government in economic affairs. One of the best examples of the government's efforts is the Federal Reserve Bank.

Another factor in the change from a community style of life to a mass society is the growth of the field of insurance. Traditional community life provided its own security. It was a kind of self-sufficient, mutual-aid type of life. When ill, one did not go to a hospital, for example. A man's family and neighbors took care of him. In rural America, neighbors even worked a man's crop for him when he had an extended illness. Today we expect a man to go to the hospital when he is ill, and we expect him to have insurance to take care of the expenses. The change from a self-sufficient, mutual-aid society to a mass society has brought an insecurity which the individual has tried to buy back with all kinds of insurance. The result is that insurance has become one of our greatest industries, and middle-class people often have a dozen kinds of insurance to stave off possible calamity. The growth in all kinds of insurance has been phenomenal as represented by the change in the amount of life insurance in force from about $15 billion in 1910 to over $984 billion in 1966, or a 6,500 percent increase.

URBANIZATION AND PEOPLE

Urban growth. The most obvious thing about urbanization is the movement of people. The change from a nation 95 percent of whose population lived on the farm in 1790, to one in 1967 with only some 6 percent of the population living and working the farm tells a remarkable story in itself. It means the transformation from a simple agrarian society to a highly complex urban one. This movement is characteristic of what has happened in other industrialized societies. In addition to this transition, for the same period the United States admitted some 40 million immigrants, the majority of whom settled in the cities. Some other nations have grown rapidly, but the growth of the United States from 3.9 million in 1790 to 200 million in 1967 is a rather amazing phenomenon. From 1790 to 1865 the population doubled approximately every twenty-five years. From 1865 to 1900 is doubled again, but it took from 1900 to 1950, or fifty years, to double again. This slower rate of increase was accomplished in spite of the rapid increase in immigration, especially after the Civil War and up to World War I.

The shift in population from rural to urban has been great in numbers and just as great in its impact on both rural and urban institutions. In 1790, there were only twenty-four urban areas in the United States; that is, areas with over 2,500 people. New York had 33,000 people; Philadelphia, 28,500; Boston, Baltimore, and Charleston had between 10,000 and 25,000 each; and the other nineteen were less than 10,000 each. In

1950, there were 4,284 urban areas, 18 with over a half million people each, and 232 with over 50,000 each. In 1960 the United States was 70 percent urban, and by 1966 there were 224 "standard metropolitan areas"—areas with a central city of 50,000 people or more—containing 70 percent of the total population, or 140 million people.[5] The decline in farm population is just as astonishing. The greatest farm population was reached in 1932 when it was 32.5 million. By 1940, it was down to 25.5 million; and by 1967, to a low of 12 million, or about 6 percent of the total population. Not only did the farm migration swell the city population, but the total increased from approximately 75 million in 1900 to 150 million in 1950, and this in spite of a decrease in the number of foreign-born in the country from 15 percent in 1910, to only 5 percent in 1960.[6] Another indication of the enormity of the rural to urban movement is the decline in farm workers from 71.8 percent in 1820, to only 3.8 million or less than 6 percent in 1968. A part of the significance of this change is told in the change in the labor force. By 1960 approximately 22 million women were in the labor force along with 48 million men. During the decade of 1940 to 1950, the number of men in the labor force increased only 8 percent while the number of women increased 35 percent; men in farm jobs decreased 40 percent while those in professional and technical jobs increased 51 percent. By 1960, government employment at all levels had become one-eighth of all employed workers.

Immigration and change in population composition. The number of immigrants to the United States was not recorded by the Census Bureau until 1820, but in this year it was small, only 8,385. Between 1821 and 1840, only 742,562 immigrants were admitted. The number began to take on important proportions during the 1840s and 1850s, when many Irish and Germans came to this country. The decade prior to 1860 saw some 2.8 million arrive on our shores. By the 1880s the numbers were increasing and coming from a different source. Up to this time most immigrants came from Northwestern Europe.[7] This "new immigration" which reached 3.75 million for the decade ending in 1890, came mostly from Central, Eastern, and Southern Europe, and continued in increasing proportions to the outbreak of World War I. From 1900 to 1914, the number approached a million a year, the largest number being 1,285,349, in 1907. World War I stopped most of the immigration temporarily, and after 1920 the immigration laws reduced the numbers to around 150,000 annually.

It is interesting to note the change in composition of the American

5 *Time Magazine* (July 28, 1967), p. 10.
6 *Information Please* . . . , p. 701.
7 Nelson Manfred Blake, *A Short History of American Life* (New York, McGraw-Hill, 1952), pp. 473–477.

population due to the "new immigration." In 1790, American population was about 77 percent British and Irish, about 7.5 percent German, 4.5 percent Irish Free State, 3.3 percent Dutch, 1.9 percent French, and all others combined about 5 percent. By 1950 the percentages of foreign-born in the United States were distributed as follows: from Italy, 14; Canada, 9.8; Germany, 9.7; USSR, 8.8; Poland, 8.5; England and Wales, 5.8; Ireland, 5.2; Mexico, 4.4; Austria, 4.0; Sweden, 3.2; Czechoslovakia, 2.7; Hungary, 2.6; Scotland, 2.4; Norway, 2.0; and others with smaller numbers. The percentages by major regions in 1950 were: Northwestern Europe, 22.8; Central Europe, 29.0; Eastern Europe, 12.0; Southern Europe, 16.7; and Canada, 9.8. In 1870 foreign-born in this country from Northwestern Europe were 55.8 percent of all foreign-born, but by 1950 this was reduced to 23 percent. The white population of English descent amounted to approximately three-fourths of the total in 1790, but was reduced to approximately one-third of the total by 1950.[8]

While it is true that all immigrants to this country have been in varying degrees assimilated into our culture, it is also true that the assimilation has in some degree altered our values and way of life. It could not be otherwise when 49 percent of the population by 1920, were descendants of immigrants who arrived after 1800, mostly after the Civil War. Some of these influences have gone unnoticed but others have caused problems. The rise of Know-Nothingism of the middle of last century was one of them. Most of the "new immigrants" were from countries with a Latin-based culture and Catholic religion, while the early Americans were largely Anglo-Saxon and almost completely Protestant in religion. Also, most of the new immigrants settled in a concentrated area from Philadelphia to Boston, especially in the New York area. The influence of this immigration change on American culture is not easily evaluated, but it is without doubt of great significance. It is particularly significant that all immigrants shunned the South, and that a large proportion of the "new immigrants" settled in the large Eastern seaboard cities. Another difference is that most of the early immigrants settled as individuals and families in rural areas, many on the frontier, and were rather readily assimilated. The "new immigrants" came in greater numbers and were confronted with both language and culture barriers which encouraged them to settle in "colonies"—Little Italys, and so on—thus making assimilation more difficult. The past several decades, however, have seen many of the descendants of these immigrants taking their places among the highest ranks in business, industry, and politics.

One of the amazing facts of population growth in the United States has been the decline in the rate of increase. From about 35 percent for the decade ending in 1800, the rate varied little until after the Civil War,

[8] Warren S. Thompson, *Population Problems* (New York, McGraw-Hill, 1953), p. 112.

but by 1900 it was only 20.7 percent, and by 1920 only 14.9 percent, and reached the lowest point of only 7.2 percent for the decade 1930-1940. For the decade ending 1950, it was up to 14.5 percent, and for 1960 up to 17.5 percent.[9] This reversal of rate of growth was due largely to the change in the birth rate. From the end of the colonial period, the birth rate had established a downward trend with no exceptions, and then abruptly, the trend was reversed. Statistics show that in 1800, there were 1,281 children born for every 1,000 women. In 1910 there were only 609, and in 1940 only 400. But in 1950 there were 551 children born for every 1,000 women. The birth rate has not varied greatly since 1950. The rapid increase in population has been due to the fact that the death rate, especially among infants, has decreased more rapidly than the birth rate; it is also due to immigration. There are those who argue that immigration has not added to our total population because it caused a rise in the status of native Americans whose values were so affected that a rapid decrease occurred in their birth rate, off-setting the immigration, and that this would not have happened otherwise

Influences of the American frontier. No attempt to describe the American population can neglect the influence of the American frontier. The westward movement or westward expansion is common knowledge to all Americans, but the significance of the frontier as a factor in shaping the American way of life is not so well understood. The frontier was brought to public attention in 1893, when Frederick Jackson Turner, a young professor from the University of Wisconsin, read to his colleagues a paper on "The Significance of the Frontier in American History." He spent the remainder of his life elaborating this theme.

The frontier was a given place at a given time only temporarily. The frontier was ever-moving; it was a recurring experience as the waves of migration moved westward, a way of life which influenced the ideals, values, beliefs, and attitudes of those who grew up on it. It began with the first settlements and proceeded systematically across the whole continent, ending about 1890. Every part of the United States was at one time a frontier.

Early events which give expression to the significance of the frontier on American social and political philosophy are numerous. Bacon's Rebellion in Virginia in 1676 was an expression of a conflict between the frontier demand for "a real democracy" and the ruling Tidewater planters' aristocratic rule. More than a hundred years later, in 1786, Shay's Rebellion in Massachusetts was a test of strength between the prosperous commercial and business interests of the coastal area and the small farmers of the interior who found it impossible to pay their debts and taxes.

[9] Paul H. Landis and Paul K. Hatt, *Population Problems* (New York, American Book, 1954), p. 28.

The so-called Whiskey Rebellion in Western Pennsylvania in 1794 was only a symbolic expression of the general opposition of the small farmers and landholders to the policies of Alexander Hamilton, which favored the merchants, manufacturers, shipbuilders, and commercial interests of the cities. The controversy between Jefferson and Hamilton was largely one of differing conceptions of a society. Jefferson believed that a nation of small farmers was an essential for a democratic society. This was a reversal of the European ideal of the rule by the aristocracy. It is one of the strange turns of fate that the democratization process which Hamilton so feared, and the urbanization process which Jefferson feared have coalesced into our great democratic, urban civilization.

As indicated above, the frontier movement began with the earliest settlements in America and ended only with the closing of the frontier around 1890. This arduous and sometimes dangerous task has been told by our historians. We are concerned only with its social implications. While many aspects of Frederick Jackson Turner's thesis are not now acceptable, in a broad perspective the great influence of the westward movement on American ideals and institutions is undeniable. The abundance of free or cheap land, the possibility of "moving on" when conditions changed, and the general open society of the frontier promoted an individualism which elsewhere would have been considered excessive, and which developed something less than a desirable respect for constituted authority. The frontier was always a kind of leveler of social distinction and, whether or not it promoted democracy, it certainly discouraged the kind of aristocracy which prevailed in Europe at the time. The first inauguration of Andrew Jackson as President, "the common man" in Washington, was a celebration of the rescue of the government from the hands of "the aristocrats." This "common man" was a frontiersman, a hero with muddy boots, rude manners, and excessive zeal. "The Revolution of 1828" represented something of the distrust in which rural America had come to hold the more sophisticated, or the more urbanized, areas. Rural people's distrust of the cities, their idea that virtue, honesty, and manliness prevailed in greater degree among themselves than among the more sophisticated people of the cities has carried over in lessening degree even to the present. Most of the accusations made against the city were unfounded, or only partly true, but this was unimportant as long as they were believed.

After 1890 the frontier as a significant historical force had ceased to be important. It had played its role in the shaping of American ideas, but not so much in the way it has too often been pictured. The romantic picture of the West was largely imaginary. The portrayal of the West and its heroes in dime novels and in the "Wild West" shows, the presentation of Buffalo Bill to Queen Victoria, all built up an aura around the West which was about as realistic as the legend of King Arthur. The real influence of the frontier was the re-orientation of the way of life of individuals, especially family life, due to the conditions under which they lived. On the frontier they could not escape the conditions of loneliness, self-sufficiency, and the impact of the immediate environment. The frontier was an equalizing force because it was as difficult for the upper as for the lower classes to succeed. Hard work and self-assurance were ingredients of success and these bred a rough-and-ready way of life, even including manners, entertainment, and religion. Obviously the old ties with Europe and even with the more urban part of this country were weakened. The culture that developed was something different. It had little need, and even less respect, for education. Its religion had little in common with the Puritan or Episcopalian churches of the East, but was wide open to evangelism. Its individualism was rampant, and it developed a kind of ruthlessness as shown by its treatment of the Indians and the public domain.

Westward expansion began with the settlement of the first colonies, but the "winning of the West" occurred in the eighteenth and nineteenth centuries. This was largely a three-stage development. First came the adventurers, traders, and miners, then the cattlemen, and finally the farmers. A later stage of urban-industrialism has followed. Although the West had its influence on the American way of life, more realistic assessment by scholars indicates that such other factors as immigration, technology, urbanization, sectionalism, and the interplay of European and American ideas all had an influence on American social development. Along with these, the frontier had a prominent place. Its great impact is largely due to the unusual conditions of the frontier to which American institutions had to adapt themselves. This was a long process with the frontier repeating itself every twenty-five years or so, and its heroes represent not only the romantic figures of the imaginary West, but also at one time or another Jefferson, Jackson, Lincoln, and Bryan.

URBANIZATION AND WORK

Work is always related to the needs of the people of a society. In agrarian societies, work is related directly to the needs of the people. That is, people largely consume what they produce. It is easy to see that one's income and welfare depend upon one's effort and, in large degree, that they are proportionate. In highly urban-industrial societies this relationship is not apparent and actually exists only in that the value in one's work is exchanged for the things he needs. Because the ends of production and consumption have become so widely separated, with so many intermediate steps, the relationship between work and the returns on work is not so obvious in modern urban societies. As mass society grows, the distance and number of operations between the producer and consumer become greater, and the machinery of production and distribution becomes more intricate and complex. This increasing interrelatedness of work of all kinds has produced a situation in which serious problems in one area are likely to affect several other areas, and possibly the whole society. If the production of automobiles and automobile parts, for example, were to be stopped over a long period of time, the whole American society would feel the effects. The problems that arise from this kind of unstable equilibrium give rise to general welfare demands which did not exist in the agrarian society. The result is a much clearer recognition of the fact that the welfare of the society supersedes that of the individual. In other words, the rampant individualism of early America is not compatible with the modern urban way of life.

The division of labor and specialization, which is the foundation of mass society, gave rise to problems of coordination in the field of industry and business and produced the "managerial revolution." The magnitude of this change is indicated by the change in employment and the change in the numbers of people involved. This kind of specialization could not exist in agrarian societies. The United States Bureau of the Census tells the amazing story. In 1820, 71.8 percent of the population were farm workers and 28.2 percent were non-farm; in 1860, 58.9 percent were farm and 41.9 percent non-farm; in 1900, 37.5 percent farm and 62.5 non-farm; in 1967 less than 6 percent farm and 94 percent non-farm. Another significant aspect of this change involves the number of women employed outside the home. In 1870, women employed were only 13.3 percent of all women and 14.8 percent of all employed; in 1900, the percentages were 18.8 and 18.3 respectively; and in 1963, 37.0 percent and 33.2 percent respectively. This 94 percent employed in non-farm jobs in 1967, involved over 75 million people employed in some 30,000 more or less specialized jobs. This is a far cry from the small number of possible job classifications in agrarian America.

Those who look back on our agrarian era with nostalgia could justify their feelings because of the loss of a certain amount of individualism, self-sufficiency, and meaningful human relationships. This is not to say that they have not gained more than they have lost.

The convergence in American history of a number of factors has caused work to be looked upon as a virtue, and the earning and saving of money as good, right, and proper. The many maxims on the subject attest to this fact. Among the most important factors were the possibilities of unusual material rewards, the Puritan tradition, and the fact that most early immigrants were working-class people who knew little of the luxuries of a leisure class. Work became an end in itself and many Americans still hold in low esteem those who do not work, whether they need to do so or not. One of the problems today of those who are retired while still able to work is that they cannot feel comfortable living a "useless" kind of life. This is because our society has insisted that all people work. There is a feeling of moral deficiency about not working. In our modern urban-industrial society, work as an end in itself has lost a great deal of its standing. The causes for this change are many and complex; but among them, no doubt, are the rise of a stable upper class, the general high standard of living, the removal of the direct relationship between work and the ends it serves, the softening of the Puritan tradition, the rise of technology, and the secularization of American society.

BUREAUCRATIZATION

Converging processes. The period of modern history has seen three proc-esses interwoven into the fabric of Western societies, bringing about an undreamed of transformation. The first two, urbanization and indus-trialization, are common knowledge; but the third, bureaucratization, is not so well understood. Bureaucracy is a form of social organization, a division of labor and specialization. Specialization leads to the establish-ment of a hierarchy of statuses because jobs carry differing degrees of prestige. The bank, factory, college, labor union, and professional organi-zation all have some organizational plan more or less resembling a table of organization of the army. Each position carries with it specific duties as well as a ranking in the organization. Both prestige and authority increase as one ascends the hierarchy.

Without attempting to answer definitively why bureaucracies came into being, certain conditions which promote them can be stated. The growth of technology, the rise of a money economy and a capitalistic system, and the resultant growth of all kinds of organizations, are factors. The growth of the giant corporations, no doubt, promoted the develop-ment of bureaucracy in business, labor organizations, and government. This has caused some controversy as to whether bureaucracy in govern-ment came about because of pressures from business on government for services, or because of efforts on the part of government to regulate busi-ness. Regardless of the cause, the trend toward bureaucratic organization in all large organizations is an established fact, and it is not likely to be reversed. The prospect of continued growth in most all kinds of organi-zations presents a challenge which must be understood if we are not to develop a kind of corporate feudalism. This means that bureaucracies must be controlled, and a prerequisite to control is understanding.

An evolving system of social organization. Mass production as a function of industrialization is a new development; bureaucratic organization has ancient roots. The degree to which it exists or has existed in the past varies. Some ancient societies were bureaucratically organized for purposes of government. This, however, always involved only a very small minority of the population and was not a matter of economic organization. In contrast, in our society it is vast and pervasive. Associations, as discussed in Chapter 2, tend to become bureaucratic in organization. Almost all types of organizations—business, labor unions, bankers associations, educational associations, bar associations—tend to grow from local to district, to state and regional, to national, and sometimes to international proportions.

In folk culture the dominant organizational principle was that of kinship. Leaders in other areas such as the priesthood and the military were chosen from the kinship groups. Kinship in the Middle Ages gave way to a dominant form of social organization known as feudalism. In the feudal organization, the social structure encompassed the lowest serf to the first lord of the realm or king, and it was the system of land tenure with its privileges and obligations which bound the society together. While the feudal society was hierarchical, the relationship of the overlord and the vassal at all levels was a very personal one. With the rise of modern urban-industrial societies, bureaucracy replaced feudalism as the dominant organizational principle. Today it is characteristic of virtually all public and private organizations, especially the large ones.

Bureaucracy is a system of organization in which all jobs are defined and their duties and privileges specifically stated, usually in written form. Officers in the hierarchy carry specified salaries, normally increasing with advancement. Those who occupy the offices hold special qualifications, and make their jobs a "career." There is an increasing demand for greater and greater specialization and, of course, this requires an increasingly higher level of preparation, such as college degrees and professional certificates. Operating a large corporation under this type of organization requires a tremendous amount of paper work—forms, files, vouchers, rules of procedure, documents, and correspondence—what we call "red tape." In a bureaucratic organization, authority is vested in the office, not the man. This makes doing business an impersonal matter—personalities are not supposed to have anything to do with decisions. Subordinates carry out the orders of the superiors, usually unknown individuals from headquarters somewhere else. Men in office are transferred from place to place because of promotion or maybe a policy of rotation. They come and go, but the organization and the authority vested in the office remain, and business goes on as usual.

Efficiency and the "experts." The purpose of bureaucratic organization is efficiency in the performance of the work of the organization. Its advantages derive from the specialization of individuals, from its predictability, from its rationality, and from the uniformity within its operation. The specialization that characterizes bureaucratic organizations eventuates into a system of professional managers at the top. Based on the principles and rules of operation, a high degree of predictability produces a stability which is conducive to efficiency. The large corporation or other organization is a rational or objective approach to a problem and there is little room for emotions or personal whims. Furthermore, the uniformity in rules and procedures in large corporations today make the handling of transactions more efficient than they would be if handled on individual merits. In other words, the goal of bureaucratic organization is efficiency.

The degrees of specialization and bureaucratization go hand in hand, and most people are not generally aware of the extent of this development. This is the age of the "expert." Cities have their managers and other experts; colleges have their presidents, comptrollers, auditors; public schools have their superintendents and other experts; banks have their presidents, department heads; labor unions have their officials and staffs of experts. The experts in these organizations are the ones who know the facts of the inner workings of the organization, and the average individual or stockholder must rely on them for his knowledge. Members of city councils, government administrators and legislators, school boards, bank directors, and most other governing bodies, both public and private, must rely upon their paid professional experts for the necessary specialized knowledge about their organizations. The public in general is a third step removed from the main source of knowledge in highly developed bureaucracies. It is the contention of some authorities that these "experts" attempt to keep secret the knowledge of which they largely have a monopoly. Whether this is true or not, it is true that the average layman or stockholder, and frequently the board member, is in a poor position to argue the case against the "expert."

An evaluation. Bureaucracy is a powerful instrument for those who control it. Who has ever known of the case of the large corporation stockholders' meeting where the officers in charge did not get the things they wanted adopted, or defeated as the case may be? Individual stockholders may ask a few questions for information, and occasionally one dissents vigorously but he soon finds himself unable to secure enough support to challenge the hierarchy. This in no way implies that the action of the bureaucratic officials is not in the best interest of the organization, only that they have the power to get what they want. In modern mass societies the fate of the masses more and more depends upon the proper functioning of bureaucratic organizations. The welfare of the masses and employees, as well as of the officers, stockholders, and experts, as the case may be, are all tied up together in these organizations. Any idea of eliminating them is absurd.

It is necessary to distinguish between bureaucracy in private corporations, government, political parties, and bureaucracy in the military. Nobody expects our large military establishment to be run on a democratic basis, but we do expect it to be kept generally subject to policies made by our elected civilian officials. In like manner no one expects the high corporation officials to be elected by the employees, but it is expected that they be ultimately responsible to the stockholders. In neither of the above cases is the operation of bureaucracy questioned. But what about the area of government? The significance of bureaucracy in the administration of government is illustrated by the case of France where, until De Gaulle came to power, prime ministers and cabinets changed in rapid succession, but the everyday affairs of government were carried out in an orderly way almost as if the cabinet crises were not a part of the same political order. The federal government of the United States operates very much in the same way. Its everyday operations are carried out without very much regard as to whether one party or the other is in power. The elected administration may make new policies or change old ones, but it can neither eliminate most of the bureaus nor change many of their functions or personnel. To do so would be to wreck the machinery through which the functions of government which they are sworn to administer are performed, and require that they establish others to perform precisely the same functions.

The tendency for bureaucracies to expand has been facetiously called Parkinson's Law. The efforts of deans, department heads, and others around colleges to expand their functions and personnel has sometimes been called "empire building." That this effort goes on is well known, and it is no doubt just as true, and even more intense, in economic and governmental organizations. This is in keeping with the American values of work, competition, and expansion, which we generally call "progress." Actions based on these values are important to our way of life, but that there must be some limitations on the resultant bureaucratic development is obvious. The development of a bureaucratic "power elite" in government, or in industry, in a democratic society, must always be subject to regulation by the representatives of the people. In other words, the interests of bureaucracy run counter to the interests of the general public, at least in some areas. Bureaucratic power in government, unless regulated, is inimical to the democratic process. Excessive bureaucratic power in the economic area would also be dangerous to the democratic process unless regulated, otherwise those who control the wealth of the society would also control the government.

By way of summary we may say that our American way of life is largely dependent upon bureaucratic organization. It makes possible a standard of living and an economic security unparalleled in history. It offers almost unlimited productive outlets for individual talent. On the other hand, it promotes the type of society in which the individual is a rather insignificant entity whose life is in considerable part scheduled by the organization and/or the machine which he attends. Lest he become further dehumanized, regulation becomes a necessity. The one area which must not become a prey to bureaucratization is politics. The political process is the means through which democracy functions and must never be a prey to a "power elite," regardless of the name under which it operates.

Change in the expected norm. As societies develop, they not only change in size and complexity, but also in their social organization, organizational functions, value systems, and social processes must continuously make adjustments. The rate of this change varies from one society to another, but is especially rapid among highly industrialized societies. In American society change has become the expected norm, and we usually think of it as progress. Throughout the whole of American history, the rapidly changing environment has so conditioned us that we are mostly unaware of the changes which are taking place all around us. It is not difficult, however, for older people today to remember when there were few automobiles, no airplanes, sound motion pictures, radios, televisions, safety razors, beauty parlors, fountain pens, refrigerators, supermarkets, or paved roads. A very perfunctory review of changes in American society during the past hundred years reveals a transformation which staggers the imagination. It is our purpose to point out a few general aspects of that transformation.

We do not mean to imply that the changes which we indicate are due to urbanization alone. As we have previously stated, they are largely the results of the converging forces of industrialization, urbanization, and bureaucratization, although this is not the whole story. The value system of the society into which these forces are introduced give them direction. In other words, these forces in themselves are neutral and are given direction by the people of the society. Like education, which may be fostered as a means of protecting the society's institutions, but which ultimately becomes a powerful force in their change, the results of industrialization, urbanization, and bureaucratization become largely the controlling factors in many areas of the lives of the individuals in the society. It is not too much to say that the whole way of life of a society is affected by them, some areas vastly changed and others changed little.

As stated in Chapter 1, change in a society may involve a change in the interrelationships of the individuals and groups, or a change in the material or non-material aspects of culture. Change in some areas is obvious. Proof that families are smaller than they used to be is a simple matter of statistical records; that people use automobiles instead of horses and buggies is a matter of simple observation; but whether present-day urban-industrial societies are depriving the individual of his freedom and making him an obsequious conformist or whether they are actually offering him for the first time an opportunity for self-fulfillment is not so easy to determine. We shall deal with only a few of the more obvious changes for purposes of illustration and orientation.

Institutional adjustment to new needs. Along with other changes, our basic institutions have been, and are now being, modified to meet the needs of a modern society. We have all heard out-moded ideas castigated as "horse and buggy" ideas. Instead of a more or less self-sufficient agrarian society, we have developed a commercial, capitalistic economy with a high degree of specialization. Jobs have changed; hours of work have changed; working conditions have changed; many women work outside the home; people work for money; income from agriculture is only a small part of the national income, and so on. In the field of government, growth and complexity have become astounding. We have gone from a society in which only a few people were employed in government at each level to a situation in which one out of eight people employed is employed by some level of government—an alarming change. In rural society, people largely sustained themselves, with occasional aid from their neighbors, and with no thought of help from the government. Today government at the several levels touches us from the day we are born until the day we die. Public welfare has to a large degree replaced private charity, and through social legislation, government has taken over a great deal of what was once considered largely the responsibility of the family. These facts only faintly hint at the degree to which our economic and political institutions have changed in their functions.

In like manner, great changes have taken place in the family, as well as in our educational and religious institutions. The recent changes in these institutions, as indicated above in our economic and political institutions, would never have occurred in a rural society. This is understandable if we keep in mind that institutions are originated and continue to exist because they meet needs of people in the existing society. The changes in education are a good example of this point. Rural society needed little education except as a matter of personal gratification. Education was naturally general in nature. Urban society, however, demands more education and more highly specialized education.

An even more dramatic consequence of urbanization is the rise of new and specialized institutions and services. Earliest among these are the fire and police departments in our cities. To get some idea of the enormity of these areas of change, one must check the number of public health agencies, public welfare departments, employment offices, civilian defense establishments, labor union halls, workmen's compensation offices, urban services such as streets, water, sewer, transportation, and recreation, public housing, and veterans services in any large city. These new agencies are only a few of the more obvious consequences of urban-industrial development.

Other consequences of urbanization, less obvious but just as important, include new roles for government. We have come a long way from the idea that the people who are governed least are governed best. One of the questions that has to be answered is: Where does it stop? Another result of urbanization is the opportunity for individual self-expression and fulfillment. Rationalization itself, which is the basis of modern secular society, is also an urban phenomenon. One of the baffling aspects of modern industrial societies is the increasingly technical character of urban problems. This is not only true in the fields of government and economics, but in the area of personal problems as well. We are at the mercy of the experts in everything from mental health problems to our income tax returns.

BIBLIOGRAPHY

Anderson, Nels, *The Urban Community: A World Perspective.* New York, Henry Holt and Company, 1959.

Bell, Daniels, *The End of Ideology: On Exhaustion of Political Ideas in the Fifties.* New York, Collier, 1961.

Bensman, Joseph, and Bernard Rosenberg, *Man, Class, and Bureaucracy: The Evolution of Contemporary Society.* Englewood Cliffs, N. J., Prentice-Hall, 1963.

Blau, Peter M., *Bureaucracy in Modern Society.* New York, Random House, 1956.

Bogue, Donald J., *The Population of the United States.* Glencoe, Ill., Free Press, 1959.

Crozier, Michael, *The Bureaucratic Phenomenon.* Chicago, University of Chicago Press, 1964.

Gouldner, Alvin W., *Patterns of Industrial Bureaucracy.* Glencoe, Ill., Free Press, 1954.

Hauser, Philip M., *Population Perspectives.* New Brunswick, N. J., Rutgers, 1960.

Katanga, George, *The Mass Consumption Society.* New York, McGraw-Hill, 1964.

Martindale, Don, *American Society.* Princeton, N. J., Van Norstrand, 1960.

Merton, Robert K., et al., *Reader in Bureaucracy.* Glencoe, Ill., Free Press, 1952.

Rogers, Everett M., *Social Change in Rural Society.* New York, Appleton-Century-Crofts, 1960.

Rosenberg, Bernard, Israel Gerver and F. William Howton, *The Mass Society in Crisis.* New York, Macmillan, 1964.

Stein, Maurice R., *The Eclipse of the Community: An Interpretation of American Studies.* Princeton, N. J., Princeton, 1960.

Vidich, Arthur J., and Joseph Bensman, *Small Town in Mass Society: Class, Power and Religion in a Rural Community.* Princeton, N. J., Princeton, 1958.

Weber, Max, *From Max Weber: Essays in Sociology,* ed. and trans. by H. H. Gerth and C. Wright Mills. New York, Oxford, 1958.

4

Institutional backgrounds

THE social system is the highest level of social organization. It is made up of parts that are arranged so that it functions as a whole. The automobile, for example, is composed of many components such as the ignition system, the cooling system, the braking system, the differential, and so on. An analysis made of the automobile as a whole would include the ease of steering, smoothness of ride, quickness of acceleration, and gas consumption. But if this is all we know, we are far from any substantial understanding of the functioning of an automobile. An adequate understanding would require that we break the automobile down into its subsystems, such as the ignition system or the cooling system, and study them separately. This is also the most productive approach to an attempt to understand a society. For the purpose of study we break the society down into its subsystems such as the economy, government, education, and religious and family systems.

SOCIETAL SYSTEM AND SUBSYSTEMS: A PROBLEM OF EQUILIBRIUM

The structure of society consists of primary groups, associations, and institutions—the basic institutions with which we are concerned. These institutions, of course, have their subsystems which have their subsystems. A large university, for example, is a subsystem of the larger educational institutional system, but has its subsystems in schools of arts and sciences, engineering, and business, and they have their subsystems in divisions and departments which operate as social units in a definite relationship to the whole. The economy has its subsystems of banking, manufacturing, distributing corporations. The relationship of the various economic subsystems may be less observable than those of an educational institution, but they are equally important. Our purpose in this study is to gain an understanding of institutions as the basic machinery through which society carries on its daily routine. But because we treat these subsystems separately, we should not be misled into believing that they function independently. They are in continuous interaction.

In a smoothly operating social system, all the parts or elements are in a state of equilibrium. This does not mean they are static; "static" would mean, over a long period of time, stagnation. They are instead ever-changing, a condition described as "unstable equilibrium." A social system is said to be in equilibrium when it is able to react to change by making the necessary adjustments at the same time it carries out its functions effectively. An example or two will illustrate this process. The rise of labor unions brought about a change in the relations between management and labor. It took a considerable length of time and at times a great deal of disorder before the necessary equilibrium was re-established in 1935 through the recognition of the right of labor to organize and bargain collectively. In the case of women working outside the home, at least two institutions were directly affected—the family and the economy. It should be obvious that the re-established equilibrium can never be that of the status quo because it has incorporated changes into the institutions. Changes, large and small, are continuously taking place throughout our institutions in order that they may adequately serve the present and anticipated needs of society.

The problem of institutional change is a problem of the direction of change and the degree to which it should go. Sometimes institutions are unable to absorb change and a disruption of the institution takes place. This was the case of the Protestant Reformation. The Roman Church was unable to accommodate itself to the demands for change and it was disrupted as an institution.

If the changes in a society were so all-inclusive that the institutions could not adjust to them, then the institutions as we know them would disintegrate. This, however, is difficult to perceive because change at any given time seldom involves more than a small area of one institution. The change in pattern of courtship would hardly disrupt the family system, or the extension of voting to women the political institutions. The violence of the French Revolution caused modifications in French institutions, especially government and the class structure, and it took years for a new equilibrium to be established. The Russian Revolution of 1917 created very forceful impacts on Russian institutions. The Russian family has probably been least changed. The economic, political, and educational institutions have been profoundly changed. Americans usually think of the American Revolution as creating great changes. Its immediate impact on American institutions, however, was in fact relatively small, mainly in the areas of government and trade. It is important to remember that institutions may undergo great change, even a complete change of personnel, and still survive. This, however, should not surprise us if we keep in mind that institutions exist to fulfill certain needs. If anything should destroy our present institutions, we would have to invent others to serve the same purposes.

The medieval system. The findings of anthropologists during the past hundred years have thrown much light on the nature and development of institutions. They have emphasized the importance of the historical setting in which institutions have developed. The ancient civilizations were based on agriculture, as was medieval society. These were largely subsistence societies. The basic difference between subsistence and capitalistic economies is that one produces for direct consumption and the other for sale and profit. The nature of the economy in all societies has a profound influence upon the nature of other institutions.

At this point it seems advisable to turn to a brief discussion and analysis of the salient features of the society of the late Middle Ages for the following reasons:

1. The roots of Western civilization lie deep within its cultural heritage and the complex of ideas and institutions of that period have greatly affected the civilization which has followed.
2. It brings into perspective the nature of society's institutions and their interactions.
3. It shows how institutions, in the course of time, adjust to the needs of society.
4. It pictures in a small way a type of society which is in vivid contrast with our own.

The feudal system which largely encompassed every aspect of medieval society was a system of relationships: political relations centered in the relations of the landlords or nobles to each other and to the monarch; economic relations centered in the relations of the lord of the manor to the serf or peasants; and to a high degree the Church was an integrated part of both. We shall limit our discussion to the economic, political, and religious aspects of the period.

The Barbarian invasions from the North and the later Saracen invasions from the South brought the Roman Empire to an end, and from 500 to 1100 there ensued what historians have called the Dark Ages. With the decline of Roman central political authority and universal law came a period of confusion and disorder out of which the feudal system developed. Roman roads were abandoned, trade was curtailed, bands of criminals and organized vagabonds lived by pillage. All business was carried on at great risk. Under these conditions individuals gave up their lands and became vassals to a noble or a monastery from which they received protection and security. In return for this protection, the vassal rendered military service, a certain number of days work per year, and a part of what he produced. The basis of the feudal system was property in the form of land, and feudal society was completely organized through the medium of land tenure. From the king down to the lowest serf, all were bound together by the obligations of service and defense. Feudal society was based on a subsistence economy whose emphasis was on production. It produced almost all of its goods and services, goods were exchanged for labor or by barter, and money as a medium of exchange was relatively unimportant. By about the twelfth century, this transformation of Western societies into the feudal system was complete.

The decay of commerce, industry, and city life reached its lowest point in the ninth and tenth centuries. The backbone of medieval society was the peasant who worked the soil. The society was controlled by the military nobles. A third social class was the clergy. The fall of the Roman Empire brought the old economic and political institutions into ruin. The Catholic Church grew and became the dominant institution in the Middle Ages. From this situation a class structure developed in which the clergy assumed first rank, or "first estate," the nobles were the "second estate," and the peasants, vagabonds, and other commoners, the "third estate."

By the beginning of the eleventh century, town life with its interest in commerce and industry was being revived. With the growth of town life and its increased development of business, industry, and commerce, a new class known as "burgers" came into prominence. This class of merchants and artisans was outside the purely medieval pattern of society described above. It functioned in terms of secular values, outside the estates system, and the burgers were generally disapproved of by the Church. It was said that medieval society was composed of "those who work, those who guard, and those who pray." The town with its merchants and artisans did not fit into this social arrangement. This is the beginning of the middle class which played a great part in the final destruction of the medieval system and which eventually came to dominate all of the societies in Western Europe.

The medieval church. No understanding of the institutions of the Middle Ages is possible without a consideration of the position of the Catholic Church, and its peculiar nature at that time. It was a superstate which exercised not only spiritual power, but also extensive political, economic, and administrative authority. As a proprietor it owned one quarter to one third of all the real property in Western Europe; it collected rents and imposed taxes; it produced material goods and employed labor on a large scale; it was involved as merchant, tradesman, banker and mortgage broker; it had its own system of courts; and it was the most significant educational institution outside the family. Through its secular involvements, the Church had become a rather completely feudalized institution. The Protestant revolt of the sixteenth century was by no means a purely religious movement. The statement that the Church had become "worldly" was only a generalization from the specific involvements listed above. A critical attitude had developed toward the tremendous material wealth and economic power which the Church enjoyed. Furthermore, these were points of contact which cannot be overemphasized in the Church's conflict with the rising national states.

The functions of the Church and the state were hopelessly confused. Church officials were lords who held fiefs, controlled their inhabitants, and exercised their feudal rights as did any other lord of the manor. As lords they also exercised the political authority which went along with their positions. It takes very little imagination to see the potential for conflict between the Church and the state when the force of nationalism began to assert itself. The continued acquisition and exercise of power by the Church reached its height about the year 1300 when the Church declared that all power belonged to the Pope as the representative of God on earth, and that the prince or political ruler derived his authority by delegation from the Pope. With the growth of the national state and the consolidation of secular authority, the conflict became critical. Even the most devout rulers determined that the Church should not interfere in the internal affairs of their realms. This was also the period of the early stages of the capitalistic system, with its money economy and urban ideals and interests. The restrictions of the Church became intolerable to the rising middle class. The Church's effort to make salvation the main purpose in life ran counter to the purposes of the new bourgeoisie with its motive of profit. The Church uniformly condemned the taking of interest for the use of money, and the theory of "just prices" was designed to make competition impossible. The theory of "just prices" was that prices should be fixed so that the individual should have a fair return for his labor, materials, and other costs. While these ideas expressed a greater appreciation for the social welfare and social responsibility than did the doctrine of laissez-faire which finally susperseded them, they were to be doomed by the economic changes which were to follow.

From the beginning, the Church was beset by heresy from within and an almost continuous struggle for power with the secular rulers. In the end, it found itself with a strong organization with unity and vitality, which made it possible to accomplish the task of curbing the anarchy of the Middle Ages with which the secular powers were unable to cope. But the story of the future was to be different. The beginning of the Protestant Reformation by Martin Luther in 1517 touched off a bitter and bloody conflict which did not end until 1648. Its reverberations were sufficient to cause the makers of the American Constitution in 1787 to include a provision separating church and state. The recent acrimonious controversy over decisions of the United States Supreme Court indicate that the issue is still with us.

The rise of nationalism. The idea of nationalism, or the national state as a political unit, superseded the older idea of "the empire." It is still the dominant force in the lives of modern nations. Nationalism is expressed through political institutions. All other institutions in modern societies are subservient to the national interests.

Between the eleventh and fourteenth centuries, England and France developed strong central governments. Many of the outstanding events of this development in England are common knowledge. The origin of the national or King's Court, the petit and grand juries, the common law, the Magna Carta, and the rise of Parliament are only a few steps in the institutional development of the modern state. Germany and Italy did not become unified until after the middle of the last century.

Institutions and change. Questions are frequently raised as to the causes of such drastic institutional changes as in the transformation from medieval to modern societies. Historians have recorded that this transformation consisted on the one hand of the decline of feudalism, the manorial system, the guild system, and the medieval Church, and on the other the rise of the European Renaissance, the rise of the national state, the Protestant Reformation, the commercial revolution, the rise of capitalism, the influences of Moslem culture, influences deriving from the Crusades, the alliance of kings and the middle class, and so on. While it is probable that no satisfactory empirical answer can be given to such a broad question, the most fruitful approach is an analysis of the changes which derive from the revival of trade, commerce, and industry, and the resulting growth of towns. This raises the question as to why trade, commerce, and industry were revived. It requires an analysis of such factors as the results of the Crusades, the influences of Moslem culture, and the causes of secularization. The increase in trade, commerce, and industry brought into existence the bourgeoisie whose interests were opposed to the feudal restrictions. It also brought into existence a money economy with which to escape them. Through the use of money, vassals bought their freedom, burgers bought their town charters, the wealthy bought exemptions from feudal law and from jurisdiction of the feudal courts, kings raised their own armies and were relieved of dependence upon their nobles for military service.

THE ECONOMY AND MERCANTILISM

The revival of the town economy. It is largely out of the nature of the economy that economic organization, economic theory, and the class structure develop. For this reason it seems desirable to sketch the story of the development of Western commerce and industry, the latter stages of which we call the Industrial Revolution. With the passing of Roman control in the West, towns with their thriving commerce became empty shells, trade was limited to local regions and was not revived until the twelfth and thirteenth centuries when merchant and craft guilds as well as the Hanseatic League (founded in 1267) came into existence. The guilds frequently controlled the political as well as the economic affairs of the towns. The Hanseatic League maintained an army and navy and held its own with the national monarchs. By the time of the first English American colonies, vast trading corporations such as the Muscovy Company (1552), the English East India Company (1600), and the Dutch East India Company (1602), had spanned the known world. These widespread commercial operations give some idea of the significance of the rising business, trading, banking, and professional class which was to become the bourgeoisie, and which later contested the older classes for both economic and political control in all Western societies.

Along with this vast expansion in business and commerce came a revolution in the European price system, the rise of commercial capitalism, new methods of banking, insurance, joint-stock companies, stock exchanges, and a new economic theory called *mercantilism*. With their kings' ability to raise money for armies, the bourgeoisie gained both power and prestige. By the sixteenth and seventeenth centuries, many of them became very powerful, especially in England, Spain, and France. This development of the national state brought in its wake a long period of colonial and dynastic rivalries which lasted until the beginnings of the nineteenth century and resulted in complete regulation of all economic activities by government. This policy was common to all large states of the West.

The mercantile system—colonies. All policies are based on assumptions of some kind. The body of ideas about the relation of the state and the economy was collectively called the mercantile system. The basic assumptions of mercantilism were: that the wealth of a nation was determined by the amount of gold and silver it controlled; that trade was the best means to acquire this specie; and that a "favorable balance of trade" was necessary. This policy looked upon colonies as commercial enterprises and their trade as a justifiable monopoly of the mother country. Colonies were maintained for the purposes of furnishing the mother country with raw materials and markets for manufactured goods. Manufacturing was forbidden in the colonies. Shipping was restricted to trade that was in the interest of the mother country. Not only was mercantilism a national commercial policy, but stringent control was extended over economic activities at home. In England, the government controlled labor, prices, and the guilds. This policy flourished throughout Europe from the sixteenth to the eighteenth century, and some of its vestiges lasted much longer.

The commercial revolution and the rise of capitalism. Along with the commercial revolution came the rise of commercial capitalism. Every society has some kind of economic system or economy which is definitely organized and regulated and which has definite technical knowledge and procedures. We have previously, in various ways, touched on the nature of pre-capitalistic economies. They had no competition or profit motive in the modern sense, and they were dominated by other than the materialistic concept current in the industrialized world. These beliefs, no doubt, derived from the way in which people got their living. When the methods by which people get their living change, it is reasonable to expect that their economic beliefs will also change. This is saying that people whose economic interests are promoted by high import duties believe in high tariffs while those whose interests are harmed by such import duties are opposed to high tariffs. There is probably no better illustration than the tariff controversy in the United States where the industrial and commercial North favored tariffs and the agricultural South opposed them.

The ideology of capitalism is dominated by three distinct but related ideas: the profit motive, competition, and rationality. Rationality is the idea of using the best suited methods of production for the continuous increase of profits. These ideas constitute the basic theory of capitalism. For any set of assumptions or theories to be effective, it must, of course, be formulated into policies and then put into practice. The dominant idea in the formulation of capitalist policies is that of freedom from government restrictions except where absolutely essential, or put in another way, that the economy is a private matter and that those who control it should take responsibility for its success or failure. This is why the bourgeoisie who came to dominate the rising capitalistic economy vigorously opposed the theory and practice of mercantilism. The capitalistic system took centuries to evolve and did not reach maturity until the nineteenth century. It was applied first to finance, then to commerce, and finally to industry. Today, especially in the United States, even agriculture is becoming a highly capitalistic enterprise.

We should not assume that because mercantilism came under attack and eventually lost out that it was wrong. It had served a very useful purpose and had become out-dated because of the changes in the societies in which it existed. Let us return at this point directly to the struggle of the middle class to gain supremacy.

THE EVOLUTION OF MIDDLE-CLASS SOCIETY

The bourgeois revolution. The bourgeois revolution was economic, commercial, and industrial; it was also a social and eventually a political revolution. The social aspects of the revolution included not only the rise of the new classes in the towns but also the emancipation of the serfs and the demise of the manorial, or feudal, system. The political aspects are represented by the rise of the bourgeoisie to control of the towns and into an eventual struggle for control of the national state. But it was even more than this: it was the townsmen who instituted and sustained the Renaissance. The first sponsors of the Renaissance were the rich bankers and merchants, mostly Italian. The most significant outcome of the Renaissance was a new outlook on life, which was essential to the final success of the bourgeois movement. The Renaissance ideal was the "Renaissance Man" with a strong sense of individualism. The ideals of the Protestant Reformation were very much the same. It was this "new man" who burst upon the scene of modern history to direct the struggle to bring medieval institutions up to date so that they might better serve the needs of the changing society.

The bourgeoisie is characterized essentially by the fact that it derives its income from investments of capital in a competitive market economy. Profit is essential, but it is by no means the only motive. Desire for power, personal recognition, and pride in achievement may be even stronger motives. Somewhere in this complex of motives we would probably find the reasons for the drive of the bourgeoisie to free itself from the restrictions of mercantilism. As this class gained in economic strength, it demanded a greater share in political power and social prestige. While this movement has a long history, the most serious aspects of it began in England in the seventeenth century. It led to the movement for independence in the American colonies, and eventually to the American Revolution.

The rise of economic liberalism. The idea of economic liberalism implied the removal of mercantile restrictions from the economy, but the bourgeois movement included social and political aspects as well. Since the mercantilist used political power to achieve his economic ends, the bourgeois was forced to use political power to remove governmental restrictions on his financial enterprises. The accession of Henry VII to the throne in England in 1585 had marked the beginning of modern history and the beginning of "absolutism." The absolute monarch had become the symbol of arbitrary and unlimited use of power. Thus the struggle against the interference of the state in the economic life of the individual was also a struggle against interference in his private life.

A few examples may clarify this brief description of the struggle of the middle class for supremacy. The struggle of the American colonies against England began with the opposition to the Navigation Act of 1651. It became especially bitter with the policies of George III in the 1760s, its restrictions on manufacturing, money and banking, and taxation. In England, the middle class led the long struggle against the King which ended in the limited monarchy and the supremacy of Parliament as established by the Bill of Rights, and under which it was increasingly easier to assert its claims. The late eighteenth and early nineteenth centuries saw the rise of the Industrial Revolution based on technological inventions and the factory system. The Industrial Revolution hastened the middle-class movement, and the final success came in the nineteenth century with the growth of free trade and such other achievements as the abolition of restrictions on the political rights of Catholics and Dissenters, the extension of suffrage through the Reform Bills of 1832 and 1835, the abolition of slavery, the Poor Law of 1834, a more moderate criminal code, and a more liberal imperial policy. Other European powers went through a similar process and ultimately every vestige of the medieval system was removed. The new ideal which we call *laissez-faire* was to develop an economic system free from everything which might hinder the operation of the forces of supply and demand. Harold Laski in *The Rise of Liberalism* states that the middle class needed the principles of liberalism: religious tolerance, limited monarchy, a controlled aristocracy, abrogation of medieval restrictions, and the secular state; and that a state was built which corresponded to the wants of the new men of power.

The French Revolution, 1789–1795, and the European revolutions of 1830 and 1848 were in the manner of the seventeenth-century English revolutions and the American Revolution. They were largely directed by the middle class and, although they depended upon the support of the lower classes, were not much concerned with true democracy. They intended to destroy the "old regime" in order to gain more freedom and power for themselves. Despite their democratic protestations, all these revolutions are significant mainly in bringing the middle class into a position from which it would gain control of the state.

Economic liberalism and the triumph of laissez-faire. As stated above, a long struggle had gone on with the new middle class trying to gain political control and to remove the out-dated mercantilist restrictions on the economy. For any movement to endure, it must somehow produce a set of ideas that explain and justify it. The first such body of doctrine to come to the aid of capitalism was that of the French Physiocrats and was known as *economic liberalism*. The Physiocrats advocated the immediate removal of all restrictive legislation and the introduction of laissez-faire individualism. Adam Smith, a Scottish philosopher, took laissez-faire as the central theme of his great work, *The Wealth of Nations*, published in 1776. He emphasized commerce and industry rather than agriculture as the chief source of wealth. Smith's economic principles were just what the middle-class manufacturers needed to justify their policy of government non-interference in business. He said that the productive base of the nation, not the amount of money held, was the basis of its wealth. Money facilitated the distribution of goods, the degree of specialization of labor determined productivity, and the specialization of labor depended on the size of the market. This led to the idea of free trade and world markets. The economy was seen as self-regulating through competition in the market. Smith's work was the first significant comprehensive economic theory and became the basis for classical economic theory. As such it served not only as an explanation of the economic system, but, even more important, as a justification of it. A large number of later economists made significant contributions to the doctrine of economic liberalism, but the basic ideas of laissez-faire governed not only economic theory but also the economic policies of the nineteenth century. The laissez-faire or classical theory of economics has in great part been made obsolete by the drastic changes in the economy since the theory was formulated in 1776. It is still used, however, as a justification for a policy of non-interference of government in business.

Forces resulting from the loosening of feudal restrictions, the development of science, and the liberation of the individual resulting from the Protestant Reformation and the Renaissance were all prior to the Industrial Revolution which dates from about 1790. Every economic and social trend was intensified by the Industrial Revolution, which in its early stage was essentially an English movement. It became, however, a European movement, a culmination of forces whose roots were centuries old. During this period demand was greater than supply, and the desire for greater production did exist. Men of those times were probably not conscious of their condition as it appears to us in historical perspective. Most of the inventions and discoveries of the Industrial Revolution were made by ordinary men who were trying to find answers to problems which had a direct bearing on their immediate lives, such as how to improve spinning or weaving or how to grow more turnips per acre.

Originating in England in the sixteenth century along with the introduction of capitalism, and culminating in the last half of the eighteenth century, was what has become known as the Agricultural Revolution. The most important aspects of this revolution were the introduction of new and better tools, experiments with new crops, improvement in stock-breeding, drainage, and fertilization, and the establishment of scientific societies for the improvement of agriculture. The significance of this movement is attested to by the names connected with it: in England, Lord (Turnip) Townshend, the Duke of Bedford, Lord Summerville; in America, George Washington, Thomas Jefferson, John Taylor of Carolina. Washington introduced new crops, applied fertilizer of different kinds, and improved his livestock. Making the transformation from feudal to modern agriculture in England was difficult. It involved educating the most backward element in society to new ideas, and, perhaps more difficult, a complete revision of the system of land-holding inherited from the manorial regime. This transformation was the consolidation of small holdings into large farms, known as "enclosures," completed between 1760 and 1830. The introduction of new methods in America were more difficult and more delayed. In England land was scarce and labor plentiful, in America it was the reverse. There were many journals and books, but the "dirt farmers" did not read books, and would not have believed them if they had. The eighteenth-century American plows were crude wooden affairs, requiring eight or ten oxen to pull them, which scarcely scratched the ground. Even so, when Jefferson demonstrated mathematically the greater efficiency of the moldboard plow, and when an all-iron plow was invented in 1797, the farmers still clung to their wooden plows. It was the popular opinion that the iron plows poisoned the soil. The second quarter of the nineteenth century finally saw the arrival of the American agricultural revolution.

With the improvement in agricultural production, urban-industrialization became possible. The Industrial Revolution is usually dated from the opening of the first steam-run textile factory in England in 1785. By 1820, England had made great strides in industrial development. She dominated the trade and commercial world until 1914. It was not until the middle of the nineteenth century that the United States got off the ground, and only after the Civil War that the intense business activity which has come to be characteristic of American life came into being. The Industrial Revolution had created the greatest era of material well-being in the history of the world; but industrialization has not been an unmixed blessing. Critics have said that the price has been too high. Society has been split into economic classes, millions have been exploited, a few men have piled up huge fortunes, men have lost their pride of workmanship; there is the psychological strain of urban life and the loss of individualism. Even if these problems remain unsolved, the industrial societies of the present appear to have greater vitality than ever before, and the prospect is for still greater change.

The period from the end of the Napoleonic Wars to World War II was the heyday of economic liberalism, laissez-faire. Its triumphs were magnificent. It made England into a workshop and the greatest commercial nation in the world. During the last half of the nineteenth century, America approached the liberal ideal. But liberalism was more than an economic doctrine, it merged with the democratic idea in the promotion of individualism, civil liberty, extension of suffrage, religious toleration, and other areas of freedom of thought, and transformed the way of life of the Western world. The old conservative classes who had been the opponents of liberalism largely disappeared. Capitalism under laissez-faire had triumphed, but it had acquired its enemies along the way. They ranged from those who, through mild reforms, would have softened the cold brutality of capitalism, to the communists who would have totally destroyed it. Fortunately, its success in the production of great wealth had made possible concessions to the masses which have blunted the attacks. Although many concessions have been made in the doctrine and practices of laissez-faire, in most of Western Europe and America the belief in the validity of the private ownership of the means of production has been sustained.

The connection between European institutions discussed above and early American institutions needs little elaboration. American institutions were transplanted European, especially English, institutions. The American political system grew from its British beginnings, and religious institutions were transplanted to America intact, problems and all. The American economy developed somewhat differently during the colonial period due to its peculiar environment; and the American class structure also became something somewhat different. America was always middle class in the sense that it never had a feudal tradition or an aristocracy.

BIBLIOGRAPHY

Ayres, C. E., *The Industrial Economy: Its Technological Basis and Institutional Destiny.* Boston, Houghton Mifflin, 1952.

Bensman, Joseph, and Bernard Rosenberg, *Man, Class and Bureaucracy: The Evolution of Contemporary Society.* Englewood Cliffs, N. J., Prentice-Hall, 1965.

Chambliss, Rollin, *Social Thought: From Hammurabi to Comte.* New York, Dryden Press, 1954.

DeRuggiero, Guido, *The History of European Liberalism,* trans. by R. G. Collingwood. Boston, Beacon Press, 1959.

Ferguson, Wallace K., and Geoffrey Bruun, *A Survey of European Civilization.* Boston, Houghton Mifflin, 1947.

Geise, John, *Man and the Modern World.* New York, Hinds, Hayden and Eldredge, 1947.

Heilbroner, Robert L., *The Making of Economic Society.* Englewood Cliffs, N. J., Prentice-Hall, 1962.

Laski, Harold J., *The Rise of European Liberalism: An Essay in Interpretation.* Barnes & Noble, 1962.

Shaw, Charles Gray, *Trends in Civilization and Culture.* New York, American Book, 1932.

Von Martin, Alfred, *Sociology of the Renaissance,* trans. by W. L. Leutkens. New York, Harper, 1963.

5

Economy in transition

AN agrarian society is one in which agriculture is carried on for purposes of consuming what is produced rather than for purposes of marketing. It is a way of life in which land is the chief asset, as well as the sole source of livelihood. The feudal society discussed in the last chapter was agrarian in a collective way. American society in its earlier stages, however, was a society in which most families were largely self-sustaining.

AGRICULTURAL DEVELOPMENT TO 1860

Rural America commercial-minded. America as a rural society was composed of people who had no intention of settling down to a subsistence way of life. If this existed, and in most areas it did, it would be only temporary. Although sectional variations in the early American economy make generalization difficult and often misleading, it can be said that all areas did have a large degree of forced self-sufficiency. As farms improved and more people settled the areas, the production for sale of some goods developed: tobacco, rice, indigo, grain, tar, pitch, turpentine, cotton, furs. In the South the development of the great staples promoted an almost entirely self-sufficient system on the plantation. But even the plantations needed things they could not produce, or could import more cheaply. Trade with England provided them with furniture, table services, wallpaper, fine clothes, and books. While this trade was limited to a small part of the population, its advantages pointed the way to a commercial-agrarian society. New Englanders were more self-sufficient, but even they could not supply all of their needs. To procure such things as salt, sugar, and iron, they needed money, and for this they turned to fur trapping, especially beaver, shipbuilding, and lumber-jacking. Even the frontier families who at first struggled for a bare subsistence soon produced a surplus for sale of corn, deerskins, and beaver furs. American society was never strictly agrarian, but was from the beginning a middle-class society bent

on making money. The general exception to this rule was the few Southern planters who developed an aristocratic style of life and a corresponding
social philosophy and attitude. The Civil War put an end to this way of
life, and there began a period of general commercialization of life in the
South.

Stages of development. It was only the decade before the American Revolution that hunters and speculators pushed their way across the Appa-
lachians of Western Virginia and North Carolina into the Kentucky-
Tennessee country. Most notable of these was Daniel Boone, agent of
North Carolina land speculator Judge Richard Henderson, who in 1775
marked the trail through the Cumberland Gap into Tennessee and then
northward into Central Kentucky. In this area, wild life was abundant and
hunters sought the finer furs of the mink, the otter, the fox, and the
beaver, and the more utilitarian deerskins and buffalo hides. Deerskins
were widely sought and were worth about a dollar each. The hunters
usually banded together into groups of ten to forty for convenience of
transportation and for protection from the Indians. After the hunters
came traders and squatters with their families who built cabins and
cleared a patch of land for corn. Another route to the West was across
Western Pennsylvania to the headwaters of the Ohio River at Pittsburgh,
then by "flatboat" down the Ohio to West Virginia, Kentucky, or Ohio.
Through these trails caravans poured as the beginnings of the westward
movement that ended at the Pacific Coast about 1890. The squatters cut
and burned the virgin forests with little regard for the future. But it was
not a complete loss as potash and pearl ash had a ready sale when they
could be moved to the market. The squatters were mostly indifferent
farmers, preferring to hunt and trap or gather beeswax or ginseng for
marketing. Next came cattlemen. In the Piedmont and the Great Valley,
wherever natural pasture land was available, vast herds ranged during
the eighteenth century. The first "long drives" were not to Dodge City,
but to Philadelphia, Baltimore, and Charleston. The hunters, traders,
missionaries, and cattlemen did not develop the wilderness. It remained
for the sturdy pioneer families who pushed out from the older communities to establish homes and churches, to make permanent the conquest, and bring the refinements of civilization into the life of the West.

Commercial development. The first task of the new settlers was to find a
place to settle. If it turned out to be a good one, others settled there and
the vacant areas began to fill up. As the numbers grew, they set up grist-
mills, sawmills, and blacksmith shops. Soon stores were established to
supply the needs of the community; buyers of the goods for sale appeared,
and innkeepers established themselves. As agriculture improved, surpluses
grew, as did the demands of the community for goods from outside the

area. As this process continued, the towns grew and town life became more sophisticated, civilized, and organized.

Farming became more and more mechanized and commercialized, so much so that increases in production far surpassed the needs of society. The large surpluses became an immense problem in itself. A few statistics tell the story: in 1935, the farm population was 32 million, or 25 percent of the total; in 1940, there were 6.1 million farms producing $11 billion in income; in 1967, there were only 3.2 million farms producing about $50 billion in income.

THE END OF AGRARIAN SOCIETY

Aftermath of the Civil War. It has been said that the Civil War separated the agrarian democracy from the era of industrial domination in the United States. While this may be true politically, we should be cautious about such inferences regarding the economy. Certainly the foundations of the American industrial economy were well laid before the Civil War, but the "embattled farmer" fought a losing rear-guard action until the political campaign of 1896. The social upheavals of the last third of the nineteenth century can be seen as failures of our institutions to adjust rapidly enough to the changing conditions of their social environment.

The Civil War had completely destroyed the economy of the South. The completeness of this destruction of property of all kinds, including cities, homes, farms, railroads, and livestock, has had few parallels in history. Not only was the South compelled to start from the very bottom, but for a decade it was handicapped by the Reconstruction policy which limited the activities of the only class which was capable of initiating the recovery. A great deal of the trouble with the economy of the South, not only before the Civil War but even to more recent times, derived from its dependence on one crop, cotton. Any society or region that depends solely on one commodity is subject to serious trouble when the market is unfavorable or when some natural disaster overtakes that crop. The early colonists of Virginia who made tobacco the basis of their economy were troubled with overproduction and low prices; they resorted to price-fixing, production quotas, destroying surpluses, and encouraging diversification. The South was subject to this same problem until very recent times.

The South did recover rather rapidly after the Civil War, considering the circumstances. "The New South" was "new" mostly in the ownership of land and in the methods of working it. It did not change its dependence on cotton, whose production was the surest immediate means of sustaining life, and, at this point, a necessity. Cotton promised money for food, clothing, tools, work animals, and the rebuilding of homes and cities. The textile industry that did invade some areas of the South did not materially change the rural and agricultural nature of the South.

The Civil War affected agriculture in the North in a different way. Since the war was fought in the South, agriculture in the North actually prospered. The relentless march of the American farmers with their livestock and grains moved ever westward as it had done throughout American history. This final movement, ending before the turn of the century, differed only in detail from the earlier ones. Between 1860 and 1900 the number of farms increased about two and a half times and the amount of land in cultivation increased at about the same ratio. The grain grower could produce in the 1890s as much as twenty times the amount he could have produced a half century earlier. It was argued that the great surpluses in farm products were due to improved machinery. The great surpluses in the grain belt, however, were no greater than those in the cotton belt where most of the labor was still done by hand. But whatever the cause, the great increases in agricultural production tended to strip the farmer of his land and to turn both him and his children into wage earners. The number of share croppers more than doubled during the last quarter of the century. As the agricultural surpluses grew, the farm population continued to decline. In 1790 it was 95 percent of the total, in 1850 it was 85 percent, and in 1900 only 60 percent. Of course this has continued on until in 1967 the farm population was less than 12 million or about 6 percent of the total of 200 million.[1]

Agricultural expansion: the trap. The agrarians were caught in a trap of increasing production on the one hand and of decreasing prices on the other. Farms expanded and production continued to increase, but each year the bushel of wheat or corn or the pound of cotton was worth less. The forces which made the massive farm increase possible also created giant financial and industrial corporations against which the farmer could not compete. Since agriculture was now almost solely production for sale, the farmer had to compete in a national or even an international market. He also had to buy back many, in fact most, of the things he used, especially farm machinery. He was thus caught in another trap in which he controlled neither the prices of the commodities he sold nor those of the goods he had to buy back. Mrs. Mary Elizabeth Lease of Kansas advised the farmers "to raise less corn and more hell." They could not do the former and succeeded none too well at the latter.

Ever since the Civil War, with the exception of the decade beginning in 1896, and the periods of the world wars, the American farmer has been in trouble. The farm population up to World War I was sufficiently large to control the government and to control the economic policies. Had it been able to organize or vote as a unit, it might have succeeded. The period down to 1900 was the last desperate effort of the declining agrarian

[1] Paul H. Landis and Paul K. Hatt, *Population Problems* (New York, American Book, 1954), p. 350.

society to survive. The difficulty of organizing the farmers, plus the antagonisms between the South and the West, and the robust individualism of the American farmer, made even temporary success impossible. It is ironic that the government was fostering policies such as the establishing of agricultural and industrial colleges and other means of increasing production when this was and still is one of the most insoluble problems of the farmer.

Agricultural needs and efforts at solution. The banks made money, the factories made money, the railroads made money. The farmer did not. He was in debt and needed cheap interest rates, but this was controlled by the big Eastern bankers; he needed low freight rates, but they were exorbitant; he needed ready markets, but they were beyond his control. The farmer, particularly of the Midwest, organized the Granger movement and turned to the state legislatures where some laws were passed regulating railroads and warehouses. They also established cooperatives, particularly for the manufacturing of farm equipment and for buying and selling, but both of these efforts were in the end unsuccessful. Their lack of success came largely from inexperience and mismanagement. This movement was followed a few years later by the Farmers' Alliances, which had some success in state legislatures but little at the national level. The farmers entered the political arena at the national level with the Granger movement, the Greenback movement, and the later Populist movement. The campaign of 1896 with Bryan and the Democratic Party taking over most of the Populist program was the crowning defeat of the "agrarian crusade." From this time on agriculture became less and less influential in both the economy and the politics of the nation.

AGRICULTURE IN THE TWENTIETH CENTURY

Capitalistic and commercial agriculture. Increasingly, the twentieth century has brought the farmer into the capitalistic-commercial arena. No longer do the rural people of America milk their own cows, make their own bread, can their own fruits and vegetables, or make their own clothing. Giant corporations now produce all of these. Rural people and urbanites both have the problem of securing the money with which to buy the products that flood the markets.

The invasion of the farm by tractors, gang-plows, harvesters, and automobiles has completely transformed American agriculture. The American farmer increasingly produces himself poor. In spite of all of the efforts of government credit and subsidies, the farmer has fared badly. He has received parity only during periods of war. His parity ratio in 1940 was 81 percent[2]; in 1955, only 84 percent; and in 1968, only 74 per-

---

[2] *The U. S. Book of Facts, Statistics and Information for 1966* (New York, Herald Tribune, 1965), p. 634.

cent. This fact, plus the fact that food and fiber are essential to the society, increasingly tie agriculture to the apronstrings of politics.

The introduction of farm machinery caused an increase in the size of farms and a decrease in the number of tenant and other farm workers. Between 1910 and 1959, the average size of farms in the United States grew from 138 acres to over 300 acres, while the number of tenant farmers decreased from 2,355,000 to 376,000, and in the South from 1,537,000 to 366,000. The number of farms continues to decrease and the size to increase. In 1966 there were 3,286,000 farms, a decrease of nearly one-fourth since 1959, and the average size was 350 acres. The machine not only replaced the farm hand, it also replaced horses and mules. Since the farmer no longer needed to feed his stock, he planted different crops. Nor did he grow his own fruits and vegetables or produce his own dairy products. Farming became almost totally devoted to a crop-for-sale system. But the total net farm income declined between 1949 and 1960, while the national income rose by 86 percent. For this period, non-farm income per person rose 51 percent and farm income per person rose only 29 percent, and most of that increase came from non-farm jobs.

Consolidation, increased production, and surpluses. American farm production is the envy of the world. During the 1950s the average annual increase in production per farm worker was above 6 percent, compared to about 3 percent for non-farm increases. In the United States about 7 percent of the labor force produces food and fiber; about 25 percent in Western Europe do, and about 40 percent in Russia. At the end of 1960, the capital investment for each worker in agriculture was $21,300, compared to $15,900 in other industries. In 1960 the American farm worker produced enough food for 26 people, in 1940 his efforts would feed only 11. But with all of this productivity, the average farm family income in 1959 was $2,875, compared to $5,911 for urban families; 18 percent of all farm families had total incomes of less than $1,000 annually compared with only 3 percent of urban families in this class. In fact, the top 3 percent of all farms produce more than the bottom 78 percent.[3] In 1946, 41 percent of farm families were in the lowest fifth of all families in the United States on the income scale; this increased to 50 percent in 1953, and to 55 percent in 1957. The consolidation of farms is evidenced by the fact that in 1930, farms of 1,000 or more acres comprised 28 percent of the farm land, and in 1959, only 3.7 percent of all farms were over 1,000 acres, yet these farms comprised 49 percent of all farm land, with an average size of 4,048 acres. Obviously the small farm, like the small factory, store, and service industry, is passing from the scene.[4]

[3] Edward Higbee, *Farms and Farmers in an Urban Age* (New York, The Twentieth Century Fund, 1963), pp. 3, 11.

[4] *Ibid.*, p. 3.

Many of the remaining farms are small and unproductive. More than half of all farms produced less than 10 percent of products for the market. In fact, in 1959, 24 percent of all farms were classified as "part-time" and another 11 percent as "part-retirement." These two groups combined produced only 3.5 percent of farm sales. Still another 9 percent of small farms produced only 1.5 percent of total sales. In other words, the lowest 44 percent of all farms produced only 5 percent of all farm sales.[5] These groups can hardly be classified as commercial farms. Rural slums today, especially in the South, are among the worst in the country. These areas are among the most difficult to improve because increasing production, even if it could be done, is no long-term answer since we already have such tremendous surpluses. There are about one million people in this country on subsistence farms who add little to production, and who are woefully underemployed. This group is concentrated in three segments of the population: farm operators in the low-income areas, hired farm workers, and older operators on small farms in commercial areas. The obvious answer to this problem is to move more and more of these inefficient farmers off the farms. This problem is complicated because these people are mostly ill-prepared to move to other jobs, and their low level of education makes retraining difficult and sometimes impossible.

The government and farm policy. The long-time American farm policy has been, at least in part, responsible for the critical situation in agriculture today. Given the natural resources, the two most important factors in production are education and technology, both of which the state and federal governments have supported vigorously over the past hundred years. The land-grant colleges created by the Morrill Act in 1862, with their extension divisions and experiment stations, have blanketed every corner of the United States. The vocational programs of colleges and high schools, reclamation programs, soil conservation programs, farm credit programs, and dozens of others have been responsible for much of the improvement in agriculture. In the light of history, these programs were both desirable and commendable. It has become very ironic that we should now be spending billions of dollars to try to curb agricultural production, and when there is still much poverty in this country and terrible poverty in most of the world. Our efforts should be on trying to find a better distribution. A great deal of so-called over-production is nothing but poor distribution.

There is no doubt that farmers are entitled to parity for what they produce, that farm poverty should be liquidated, and that the net income per person in farm families should be raised. This should be in special consideration for the poor on the farms who have reaped little of the

5 *Ibid.*, pp. 52, 155.

benefits of the billions of dollars of past government programs. The government already supports such programs for the farmers, even if they have not worked well, and both the government and the farmers have a responsibility to the whole American community, to the future, and possibly to the underprivileged peoples in other areas of the world. While major crop surpluses increased tremendously between 1955 and 1960, by the end of 1965 government acreage control plus foreign aid and trade had shrunk the foodstock pile by $1.3 to $6.7 billion. The cost of the storage of these commodities amounted to around $400 million a year.

The government began assuming responsibility in the field of agriculture with the enactment of the Agricultural Marketing Act in 1929, and it has become increasingly involved. The farm commodity programs for the decade of 1952–1961 cost the taxpayer over $22 billion and the total price support, 1933–1967, $54 billion. The commodity program has three categories: first, basic commodities which include cotton, wheat, corn, tobacco, rice, and peanuts; second, non-basic commodities which include dairy products, wool, mohair, tung nuts, sugar beets, and sugar cane; and a third, which is a non-mandatory support group. Only 44.7 percent of all farm commodities come under price support. In 1961 the net farm income reached nearly $13 billion but the Department of Agriculture contributed nearly $6 billion to support that income, and the Congress authorized an estimated increase to over $7 billion for 1962. According to the Congressional Record, two of the ten biggest lobbies in Washington in 1961 were farm organizations. The American Farm Bureau Federation and the National Farmers Union combined to spend more in that year than did the American Medical Association which led the field in spending for lobbies. At the time agriculture was receiving these billions out of the taxpayers pocket, these organizations were crying that they were being tortured on the rack of state socialism.[6] A closer look at the matter reveals that they were obviously not opposed to receiving these billions, but only to the public's right to know where its money went, and whether or not it was well spent. This would be a strange sort of socialism and the worst kind of business practice. Wherever Congress appropriates money, it has not only a right but also a duty to see that the money is well spent.

COMMERCE AND INDUSTRY TO 1860

Early commerce. We have already noted how the British mercantile policy affected the American colonies adversely. But despite any limitations that British policy may have had on colonial commerce, its extent and diversity are surprising. By 1760, New Englanders owned some 2,000 ships. Some 300 ships and 4,000 sailors were engaged in whaling at the outbreak

6 *Ibid.,* pp. 140–141.

of the Revolution. Lest we get the idea that trade was limited to New Englanders, let us note the following data valued in British pound sterling, in 1770:

Tobacco exports	900,000	mostly from Virginia and Maryland
Rice exports	340,000	mostly from South Carolina, Georgia and North Carolina
Indigo	131,000	mostly from South Carolina, Georgia and North Carolina
Wheat, bread and flour	636,000	mostly from New York, Pennsylvania, and New Jersey
Dried fish	375,000	from New England
Pickled fish	400,000	from New England

Total exports (1769)	North	1,195,275
	South	1,657,150
Total imports (1769)	North	1,154,821
	South	1,468,583
Total exports to England (1769)		1,531,514
Total imports from England (1769)		1,604,981

Source: Table constructed from information in Edward C. Kirkland, *The History of American Economic Life* (New York, Appleton-Century-Crofts, 1951), pp. 104–111; Fred Albert Shannon, *America's Economic Growth* (New York, Macmillan, 1951), p. 32; Howard U. Faulkner, *American Economic History*, 6th ed. (New York, Harper and Brothers, 1949), pp. 79–84.

It will be observed that the five Southern colonies of Maryland, Virginia, North and South Carolina, and Georgia shipped more than half of the colonial exports and received more than half of the imports. Only about half of the total exports went to England, and about three-fifths of the imports came from England. There was half as much trade in both imports and exports with the West Indies as with the mother country, and the American colonies exported more than one third as many goods to Southern Europe as to England. This seems surprising in view of the British mercantile policy and of the general complaint of the colonists against British colonial restrictions.

By 1790, 90 percent of both American imports and exports were carried in American ships. American shipbuilders had gained preeminence during the colonial period and they retained it until the middle of last century. By 1800, both foreign and domestic trade were increasing rapidly, and as commercial and industrial centers grew the amount of subsistence farming in America continuously declined.

Hamilton's policy and industrial development. A good illustration of the significance of industrial development, as well as of the attitudes of those involved, is found in the events of Washington's first administration. The really great political battles of the First Congress were fought largely over economic issues. Of course this had been to some extent true of the Constitutional Convention. One of the first acts of the new Congress was to pass a tariff law. It was called a revenue act, but it was intended to be protective. The assumption of the national debt, the funding of the state debts, the National bank, and the excise tax were all designed to stabilize the government and promote commerce and industry. The arguments over the issues were not academic. Hamilton's Report on Manufactures in December 1791 is most revealing. That his efforts in behalf of industry had only minor success was due to the fact that the interests of the country were still largely centered on commerce. The first economic survey in American history was made by men sent out by Hamilton in the summer of 1791. These reports can be found in Hamilton's papers in the Congressional Library, and they are considerably more extensive than would generally have been expected. One interesting case contained an item by Drury Ragsdale, Inspector for Survey No. 3, King Williams County, Virginia, which showed 310 persons, including slaves, in twenty families making 2,914 yards of cloth, and 260 pairs of stockings valued at 501 pounds sterling; one furnace in Philadelphia produced 230 tons of steel annually; Maryland had a productive glass factory. Hamilton's Report mentioned the following industries: leather and leather goods, iron manufacturing, shipbuilding, flax and hemp manufacturing, brick and tile, spirits and liquor, paper, hats, sugar, oil, copper and brass, tinware, carriages, tobacco products, starch and hair powder, lampblack and painters' colors, and gunpowder. These industries had, no doubt, developed to a point beyond the local markets.

The seaboard areas were teeming with activity and Hamilton's efforts, including extensive letter-writing, agitated them still more. But even before the First Congress met, some states had granted aid to the development of industries. In November 1791, a factory was chartered at Paterson, New Jersey, which had exemptions from state taxes, authorization for a $100,000 lottery, and other provisions that would gladden the heart of any enterpriser today. There were also other compelling reasons for promoting industry. It was argued that Connecticut, for example, must have manufactures because, although the state had a population of only 200,000, she had lost 100,000 in ten years by migration. The westward movement was seriously affecting many areas adversely.

Hamilton set forth the arguments for a protective tariff in the most effective way. He listed a dozen or more methods of promoting industry, including not only tax exemptions but such things as bounties, premiums, drawbacks, building of roads and canals, and the specification of types of taxes to be avoided. The Southern opposition to the tariff was expressed by Tucker of South Carolina, who (shades of John C. Calhoun) said it was calculated to oppress South Carolina, but his "state would live free and die glorious." The Southerners were not opposed to the tariff because it was either unconstitutional or undesirable, but because of the way in which it affected the economic interests of the South. Hamilton met this argument with a statement that the agricultural surpluses being piled up because of foreign restrictions would be taken care of by increasing domestic markets through the increasing of industry.

We should not be confused by the laissez-faire doctrine into believing that, like church and state, the economy and government were meant to be separate. Laissez-faire as a theory has usually been in operation in economic areas as a justification for non-interference of government in private economic affairs. American commerce and industry have always sought the use of government policies in their own interests. This has been true of all interest groups everywhere, and it still is.

Industrial growth. In 1790, manufacturing in America was still largely in the domestic stage and was valued at only about $30 million annually. The British had prohibited the emigration of trained operatives and the exportation of machinery, plans, or models; these restrictions remained in effect until around 1850. In addition to this handicap, the federal government was dominated by Southern plantation owners from 1828 to 1860, who cared little about industry. For a great part of the period banking facilities were inadequate and the currency situation was in chaos. The Southerners opposed the protective tariff, a strong central bank, the transcontinental railroad in the North, free land for homesteaders, and immigration. Yet it was during this very period that the American factory system was established.

Between 1790 and the Civil War, great economic growth was in evidence in many areas. The first water-powered textile mill was established in Pawtucket, Connecticut, in 1789. By 1820 there were some 0.4 million spindles in the United States; by 1860 over 5.25 million were in operation. The Erie Canal was one of the great accomplishments of this period. When completed it was 906 miles long, built at a cost of $20,000 per mile. Completed in 1825, over 19,000 boats and rafts passed over the Erie and Champlain Canals in 1826. Industrial capital grew from $50 million in 1820 to over $1 billion in 1850. The first 13 miles of railroad were completed in 1830, and by 1860 there were over 31,000 miles.[7]

Only a very few of the industrial changes prior to the Civil War can be recorded here. The cotton gin was invented in 1793. In 1795 the annual cotton production was about 5 million pounds; by 1860 it was 1.75 billion pounds despite a decline in price from around 30 cents per pound to about 10 cents per pound.[8] Cotton mills in 1860 employed 122,000

[7] Harold Underwood Faulkner, *American Economic History* (New York, Harper, 1949), pp. 279, 285–86.
[8] *Ibid.*, p. 209.

people and produced goods valued at $116 million. At the same time woolen mills employed 48,900 people and produced goods worth over 69 million.[9] Total manufacturing in the United States in 1860 employed 1.3 million people and produced goods worth $1.9 billion.[10]

The age of steam had arrived with Fulton's steamboat in 1807 and the first steam railroad in 1830. The first Atlantic crossing by a steam-powered boat was in 1833. Improvements in iron and steel processing and in factory machinery are too numerous to relate here. The iron age had also arrived. Steam fast replaced water as the chief source of industrial power. Other innovations of the period included sulphur matches in 1836, steam ferryboat in 1830, gas lights in 1823, the typewriter in 1857, the gyroscope in 1856, the pullman car in 1859, the vulcanization process by Goodyear in 1844, the sewing machine in 1846, the steam cylinder press in 1846. In the 1850s Singer's salesmen were selling sewing machines to American housewives at a dollar down and fifty cents per week, and Gail Borden was marketing beef extract, condensed milk, and concentrated coffee. The United States Patent Office in the ten years prior to the Civil War registered more than 25,000 patents.

Problems due to rapid industrial growth. This wonderful progress, and partly because it was so rapid, brought in its wake shocking problems, many of which are still with us. In New York City in 1850 over 18,000 persons were living in damp, dark, vermin-infested cellar rooms. in Lowell, Massachusetts, a man, his wife and eight children and four adult boarders shared a one-room lodging with another family. It was inevitable that the cities should be periodically ravaged by terrible epidemics. To the attacks of yellow fever were added frequent epidemics of small-pox, typhoid fever, and other diseases. Between 1849 and 1854 plagues of cholera swept much of the country. Public water systems, beginning in Philadelphia, were eventually installed and the worst of the epidemics were checked. Other problems were those of fire and crime, thrust upon the cities with inadequate and untrained firemen and police forces.

The cities were crowded with people who were poor, uneducated, and unskilled, with large families and extremely low wages, if they were fortunate enough to have jobs. New York's population rose from 33,000 to 96,000 between 1790 and 1810, and Philadelphia from 42,000 to 91,000 for the same period. Like New York and Philadelphia, other large cities with their beautiful parks and fine streets had a majority of the population who lived in conditions of squalid poverty. Between 1847 and 1852 the number of mechanics in the country declined by 8,000 and that of farmers increased by only 12,000. Laborers, on the other hand, jumped from 36,000 to 83,000. These poverty-stricken people were forced into the

9 *Ibid.*, p. 261.
10 *Ibid.*, p. 266.

most horrible living conditions imaginable. A survey in New York in 1849 showed men, women, and children of all races and nationalities indiscriminately mixed, sometimes sleeping in filthy holes where one cent a night was charged for a "bare floor." These miserable people were not regular members of the industrial society, but the fruits of the industrial process. These conditions, revolting as they are to our sensibilities, were common in all early industrial cities, Old World as well as New.

We saw how the rise of towns with its middle-class commercial capitalism wrecked not only the feudal labor arrangement, but also the guild system. The rise of the industrial economy in the United States had a similar effect on many groups. Craftsmen of all kinds began to feel a desperate insecurity as one after another of their skilled trades were either mechanized or so simplified that their special competence was no longer necessary. Spinners and weavers saw their jobs taken by machines. Shoemakers and tailors saw their industry change and require the unskilled labor of women and children. Printers were threatened by the power-driven press. In other words, men who had once looked forward to being masters in their own shops now foresaw themselves as perpetual wage earners, and they felt keenly their loss of status. The wages, hours, and conditions under which they worked were even more degrading.

In the textile industry, women and children, some as young as nine and ten years of age, crowded men out of jobs. Hours were from daylight to dark, meaning thirteen or fourteen in summer and ten or eleven in winter. One woman writing later said she took breakfast and dinner in the mill because the time was too short to go home; she spent sixteen hours a day in the mill for eleven years, 1837–1848. Andrew Carnegie, who had come to the United States with his parents in 1848, worked in a cotton mill at $4.80 a month. In 1835, one third of the employees at a Paterson, New Jersey, factory were children under sixteen years of age. The lowest wages were represented by such cases as that of the Willard Howland family of six who, in 1828, worked seventy-two days from daylight to dark to earn $22.47, or less than 3 cents an hour.[11] Women and girls earned probably on the average from $1.50 to $2.50 per work week of as long as eighty-four hours. In Pittsburgh, tailors paid women at the rate of 12 to 15 cents a day or by the piece. Women and boys in Massachusetts shoe towns were paid 25 to 45 cents a day. Men fared better than women and children, but even they seldom received more than $25 a month. Some skilled trades received as much as $10 a week.[12] Working conditions were generally deplorable, and little or no attention was paid to the health or welfare of the workers.

Low wages and wretched working conditions were not the only

[11] James A. Barnes, *Wealth of the American People* (New York, Prentice-Hall, 1949), p. 285.

[12] *Ibid.*, pp. 288–290.

problems of the poor. The Boston Prison Discipline Society in 1829 estimated that there were 25,000 debtors a year thrown into American jails.
The poor had to compete with prison labor; debtors in prison were
generally treated worse than the criminals. Although the average sum for
which debtors were incarcerated was around $20, it was sometimes as low
as 25 cents. The militia system and the banking system both discriminated
against the poor laborer and the poor farmer. In many states every individual of military age was required to appear with arms for drill at certain times during the year, and all at his own expense. The rich escaped
this duty by being able to pay the penalty instead of doing the service.
Especially after the destruction of the second Bank of the United States,
workmen were compelled to accept at par for their labor the depreciated
bills that flooded the country. When they attempted to use them for
purchases, the merchants would take them only at the depreciated market
rate. Furthermore, during this whole period the trend in real wages of
workmen was generally downward.[13] That working men would seek some
means to improve their lot was inevitable and this they did through the
organization of labor unions.

THE BEGINNING OF THE TRANSFORMATION

Growth of specialization. Although few individuals at the time were
aware of it, American society was rapidly entering a transformation which
has not yet reached its climax. The rapid changes in transportation and
communication were making possible regional specialization. It was becoming possible for any region or locality to produce what it was best
suited to produce, sell it into the market, and buy what was needed. This
made for great efficiency, but it also made for great interdependence. The
job of the textile worker in Lowell, Massachusetts, came to depend upon
the field hands in the cotton patches of the South, and this interdependence was rapidly spreading throughout the whole economy. The more
this tendency developed, the more the society became one in which people's
income was derived from selling products or selling one's services.

But not only was regional specialization growing, a division of labor
and specialization was beginning to take place within the local community. A rural economy needed no white-collar workers. But as business
and industry developed and cities grew, the need grew for bookkeepers,
clerks, typists, telegraphers, new kinds of skilled and unskilled craftsmen
and operatives, school teachers and new programs of education. In other
words, this was the beginning of the transformation from a nation based
largely on a self-sufficient agricultural economy into an employee nation
where the average worker no longer owned the fruits of his work, where
his job and the welfare of his family depended entirely upon those over
whom he had little or no control.

13 *Ibid.*, pp. 290–291.

The transfer of functions. Another change taking place with the growing industrialization was the transfer of functions which had largely been centered in the family to profit enterprises or to government. This is a function of the division of labor. As the individual specialized, he depended on others to perform the functions which he formerly did for himself. The individual then paid, with the money he earned from his specialty, directly to business enterprises for the things he needed, and indirectly through taxation to the government for such services as police and fire protection and education. This transfer of function was far-reaching. It included education which was being transferred from the family to the school, and charity which was being transferred from the churches to organized private agencies and to the government. It cannot be so easily demonstrated, but no doubt it is true, that our value system was undergoing vast changes, too.

Summary of changes. The conditions we have described were characteristic of the large seaboard cities of New England and the Middle Atlantic states. In 1860 America was still mainly agrarian, in fact 80 percent rural. The population was only 35.6 million.

The points at which government and economic policies were intertwined were numerous, including such fundamental areas as land policies, currency control, banking, immigration, transportation, and taxation. This is not unusual because no industrial economy can prosper without governmental policies that are congenial to its development.

One of the consequences of industrialization was the rise of a class of people who were directly and solely dependent upon wages. The industrial area of American society was becoming sharply divided into the managers and the managed. The subsistence agricultural society knew no problems of unemployment or job insecurity, and no dangerous and unhealthy working conditions, all of which in the rising industrial economy were threats, not only to the worker, but to his whole family.

The conventional stabilized relations between the employee and the employer were being undermined by the changes in the economy. This led to bitter conflicts before a new equilibrium could be re-established between labor and management.

As the country became increasingly urban-industrial, the demands for money as a medium of exchange became increasingly imperative. In other words, we were becoming more and more a money economy.

The development of the industrial economy was bringing about a greater disparity of wealth among the social classes. While the business, industrial, and professional classes prospered, the wage earners shared very little of this prosperity for several generations. Of course this is the dichotomy on which Marxism was based.

One of the most significant results of the changing economy was that it gave rise to a new social class structure. Within the industrial system itself were the emerging capitalist owners and managers on the one hand, and the non-owners, non-salaried wage earners on the other. The industry needed business, banking, transportation, and the professions. The upper echelons of these groups were forming the new upper class. The bases of the class structure were shifting from the older agrarian society to an urban-industrial society. The small business, industrial, and professional groups were to become the upper middle class and the clerical and service groups, generally constituting the white-collar class, making up the lower-middle class. "Old Families" and their inherited wealth were giving way to new criteria and new channels for achieving status.

Along with industrialization and urbanization, the process described as bureaucratization was developing in all areas of social organization.

6

Cases of the changing economy

DESPITE the great expansion in agricultural production, the dominant forces in American society were becoming increasingly industrial and financial. No longer did the South dominate the policies of the federal government. Agricultural population and farm production grew smaller relative to total production. Between 1865 and 1929, the United States entered the era of mass production and mass society. Important underlying factors in the great change include (1) the rapid development of industry, (2) the division of labor and specialization, (3) the consolidation of small plants into giant industries, and (4) the growing dominance of financial capitalism.

THE NEW INDUSTRIAL NATION

We have discussed the rapid growth in industry immediately following the Civil War. Most of the industry was in the North, and the North prospered with the great impetus of war production. The demand for goods expanded after the war. In 1850 the gross value of manufactured products was a little over one billion dollars. The total annual value of manufactured products in 1860 was somewhat less than two billion dollars, only about 8 percent of which was in the South. By the end of the century it had increased to over eleven billion.[1] By 1890 the Census reported manufacturing output greater than that of farms, and by 1900 it was double the farm output. By 1910 the United States nearly doubled its nearest rival, Germany, and in 1913 it accounted for more than one third of the world's industrial production. Another illustration of the comparative growth of American industry is that, despite the fact that it was not until after the turn of the century that American manufacturers sought foreign markets, after 1875 America had a favorable balance of trade.

[1] Harold Underwood Faulkner, *American Economic History* (New York, Harper, 1949), p. 402.

THE RAILROAD INDUSTRY

Land grants and frenzied financing. One of the most frenzied areas of economic development was that of railroad building. We have noted that by 1860 some 31,000 miles of road had been constructed. Westward expansion and railroad building at this period went hand in hand. The Homestead Law passed by Congress in 1862, and the vast land grants to railroads were powerful factors in this drive. Even before the Civil War there was a demand for congressional support of a transcontinental railroad, but it was blocked by a controversy over whether it should be a southern or a northern route. With the removal of the Southerners from Congress during the Civil War, Congress passed the Pacific Railway Act in 1862, granting a charter to the Union Pacific Railroad. The construction was completed with a ceremony at Promontory Point, Utah, on May 10, 1869; the Union Pacific and the Central Pacific were united when the hammer blows that drove golden spikes were echoed by Morse's telegraph throughout the country. The signal was given by President Grant from Washington. The continent was spanned by rail, and the days of the covered wagon were over. One of the most barefaced cases of profiteering was behind this glamorous feat. The Central Pacific managed to pay its stockholders a profit of $63 million on a $121 million investment. The Union Pacific Crédit Mobilier of America was one of the most notorious scandals of the time. These cases represent the low morality that ran through other areas as well. The unsavory tactics used by many of the giants of industry and finance at this time prompted the derogatory nickname of the "Robber Barons."

Within a few years both the Southern and Northern Pacific reached from coast to coast, and a network of rails touched all settled areas of the United States and many that were not. By 1880 the United States had 93,-000 miles of rails and by 1920, as much as 254,000. The financing of these railroads is a sordid story in an era in which scandal was all too common. The United States granted to the railroads a total of about 150 million acres or 242,000 square miles—an area larger than either France or Germany—as well as bonds in the amount of $64.6 million. About 60 percent of the cost of construction was borne by the government.[2] The states played their part in the railroads. They bought stock in the railway companies, extended credit, made outright grants of land, and conducted surveys. States granted 55,000 acres to transportation companies. Besides municipal and county bonuses and state bonds, the state of Texas, which had kept its public lands on entering the Union, granted to the railroads 32.5 million acres, an area the size of Alabama.[3] The state of Michigan

[2] *Ibid.,* p. 490.

[3] Rupert Norval Richardson, *Texas: The Lone Star State* (New York, Prentice-Hall, 1943), pp. 350–351.

built three railroads. North Carolina had a majority of directors in three. Counties and cities followed the states by subscribing to stock, exchanging county and municipal bonds for railroad securities, and actually donating money.

Crisis, consolidation, and ruthless manipulation. Reckless financing by men who were mostly interested in quick fortunes and over-expansion and consequent indebtedness left most of the railroads in financial jeopardy. With their original capital gone, they watered and mortgaged their stocks to the hilt. They could hardly keep going in good times, and inevitably went bankrupt during bad times. Following the depression of 1893, some 169 roads were in the hands of receivers. A similar situation had occurred after the panics of 1857 and 1873. During the depression years of the 1870s, some 450 railroads, two-fifths of the total, were absorbed into larger systems.[4] This consolidation created great monopolies of traffic in some regions. Cut-throat competition and discriminatory practices existed where there was competition. The scandals in the construction period of the 1870s, especially the exposure of the Crédit Mobilier involving some members of Congress, the ruthless exploitation of defenseless customers, and the bribery of judges, legislators, and others in position to restrain them, brought the railroads into great disrepute. We have noted the Granger movement against the railroads. This was laissez-faire in its heyday, but the freedom was not to last. In 1887 Congress passed the Interstate Commerce Act which was designed to remedy the worst of these abuses. In practice, the law did not curtail the consolidation process, and was a weak weapon in regulating the abuses.

Financial manipulations after the railroads were built were even more reprehensible than the construction profiteering. It has been estimated that of the $7.5 billion indebtedness of the railroads in 1883, as much as $2 billion represented "water." In four years the Erie stock was watered from $17 million to $78 million in market speculation.[5] The most notorious of those parasites enriching themselves from the railroads were Daniel Drew, James Fisk, Jr., and Jay Gould of the Erie. It was a ruthless business in a ruthless age; among the most adept at stock manipulation and political bribery was Commodore Cornelius Vanderbilt. Not all were of this type: men like J. Edgar Thompson and James J. Hill ran sound and successful railroads. Among the most successful in amassing a fortune from the railroads was Edward H. Harriman who, on his death in 1909, was reputed to dominate 60,000 miles of rails, or about one quarter of the United States mileage.

We have referred to the frenzied era of railroad construction and of

---

[4] Nelson Manfred Blake, *A Short History of American Life* (New York, McGraw-Hill, 1952), p. 402.

[5] Faulkner, *op. cit.*, p. 494.

hysterical efforts of states, counties, and cities to acquire railroads. Most of them were locally financed, short, poorly constructed, and most inefficient. Some were narrow gauge, some wide gauge, some medium gauge, and the cars of one would not go over the tracks of the others. With wooden cars, wooden trestles, poor couplings and brakes, accidents and collisions were frequent. In time most of the early railroads had to be rebuilt, a situation that was also conducive to consolidation.

Railroad consolidation, which had started before the Civil War, was a process of creating continuous lines and of controlling the railroads in a given geographic area. Vanderbilt, for example, had consolidated sixteen small railroads into the New York Central by 1858. By 1906 some two-thirds of the mileage was in the hands of seven large groups. These seven groups, moreover, controlled 85 percent of the industry's earnings and were tied together by banking interests, interlocking directorates and overlapping stock ownership.

Competition and federal control. In dealing with the Granger movement we noted the efforts of the farmers, especially of the Middle West, to regulate the railroads. We also note the inevitable entry of the federal government into the field of regulation through the Interstate Commerce Act in 1887. The courts soon rendered the act totally ineffective; its chief significance was as an educational precedent in the introduction of subsequent federal regulation. Most of the abuses continued, and it remained for the Progressive Movement to provoke more effective federal control. The Elkins Act of 1903 was designed to eliminate rebates; the Expediting Act of the same year took cognizance of the welfare of the public; and the Hepburn Act of 1906 extended the Interstate Commerce Act to cover express and sleeping car companies, pipe lines, switches, spurs, tracks, and terminal facilities. The Interstate Commerce Commission was given authority to determine just and reasonable rates and to demand that carriers adhere to them; the Commission left it to the carriers to initiate court action if they desired to appeal its decision. The details of regulation continued through the Mann-Elkins Act of 1910, the Newlands Act of 1913, the Adamson Act of 1916. The Adamson Act marked a new area of regulatory activity by regulating the number of hours of labor in interstate traffic. These regulations had little to do with the consolidation movement, which was halted by the Supreme Court decision in the Northern Securities case in 1904.

The Clayton Anti-Trust Act of 1914 was intended to prevent the consolidation of corporations which would lessen the competition between them. This act was a failure. In 1920, Congress passed a Transportation Act. It granted the Interstate Commerce Commission power to permit carriers to control other carriers in any way which did not involve a single system of ownership and management. In fact, it went further and authorized the Commission to prepare plans for consolidation of the railroads into a number of competitive systems. During World War I the government had taken over the railroads and operated them as a unit—the ultimate of consolidation in management. The experience had demonstrated the folly of unrestrained competition. The advantages were obvious to all, and organized labor favored government ownership rather than a return to private ownership. Government policy was, however, dedicated to a less radical solution to the problem: competition should continue, but efficiency was also desirable, and that would be promoted by further consolidation among the many remaining railroads. Congress had placed the Commission in the difficult position of working toward consolidation while trying to maintain competition.

The Transportation Act gave the Commission new responsibilities as well as new powers. It was empowered to divide the country into rate districts and to prescribe rates for each of them; it was authorized to rule on what new securities the railroads might issue and how the money should be spent, and it permitted the consolidation of the four great express companies into one American Railway Express Company. The change in attitude toward the railroads was clear. Up to this time the job of the Commission had been to protect the public against the railroads. It was now the duty of the Commission to see that the railroads received a fair return—specifically, 6 percent—on the capital invested. The Commission produced a tentative scheme of consolidation into twenty-one systems, but the railroads found it impossible to agree on any plan and no important consolidations were ever made under the act. Consolidation did go on, however, on a less ambitious scale.

MONEY AND BANKING

The era of chaos. Money and banking had been a problem of American society since the end of the colonial period. Hamilton had secured the establishment in 1791 of a national banking system, modeled after the Bank of England, as a part of the program to promote industry and to stabilize government. This banking system had served both as a very useful agent of the government and as a restraint on the extravagant issues of paper money by state banks. When Jackson became President, he destroyed the bank, leaving the field to the state banks. Following the end of the national banking system, the number of state banks grew from 330 in 1830, to 901 in 1840, and to 1,601 in 1861. The issuance of paper money was nothing less than chaotic. The state banks had some 10,000 bank notes of different types. The value of each note depended upon the soundness of the particular bank of issue. The notes produced by counterfeit gangs added to the confusion. One private note-evaluating service listed 9,916 different notes issued from 1,365 different banks. Another service listed 5,400 counterfeit notes known to be in circulation. Coins in circulation virtually disappeared until 1853, adding to the difficulty. It is astonishing that business was transacted at all.

With the Southerners out of control of the federal government, Congress enacted the Banking Act of 1864, providing the legal framework for a national banking system. The growing national character of the economy, the increasing wealth of the country, the chaos in the currency, as well as the effects of the Civil War dramatized the need for a stable national currency. The national banking system strengthened commercial banking and made state banks more safe. More important, it replaced the heterogeneous mass of state bank notes with a uniform currency. It did not, however, relieve the problems of the farmer, whose struggle for cheap money continued. The effect of the new bank is shown by the fact that in 1861 there were 1,601 state banks and in 1867 only 272. After 1870 the number of state banks continued to grow until there were 17,500 in 1914, compared with 7,500 national banks.[6] But the problem of money was something else and continued until the turn of the century. The money problem was largely an outgrowth of business and industry; sound money was essential for its development.

Concentration of financial power. Another important aspect of the money problem was the growing concentration of financial power in a few Eastern institutions, the most important being the J.P. Morgan interests in New York. The reason for this is obvious. The great growth and consolidation in transportation and industry required tremendous amounts of capital, and banks became the middlemen between the investors and those who needed the funds. These industries were mainly on the Eastern seaboard, and when they needed to market millions of dollars in securities, they naturally availed themselves of the services of the banks. The Morgan interests reaped a $12 million reward for their part in the organization of the United States Steel Corporation. Even more important was the expanding power of financial interests over industrial management. Morgan named the officers of U.S. Steel. In 1912 the firm of J. P. Morgan and Company owned stock in the New York Central and Hudson River Railroad; the New York, New Haven, and Hartford; the Northern Pacific; the Erie; and the Atchison, Topeka, and Santa Fe. Partners in the firm were directors in other railroads. A few giants of the era such as Standard Oil, the Carnegie Company, and Ford Motor Company were built without dependence on the bankers. Such cases were, however, the exception, and more and more the power fell into the hands of Wall Street bankers. Other important firms besides J. P. Morgan were: Lee, Higginson and Company; Kidder, Peabody and Company of Boston;

[6] Ross M. Robertson, *History of the American Economy* (New York, Harcourt, Brace, 1955), pp. 150, 268.

Kuhn, Loeb and Company; the First National Bank; and the National City Bank of New York.

As we pointed out in connection with the agrarian problem, the financial power of these eastern firms also extended to banks all over the country, and this growing concentration of financial power led to great criticism of the "money trust." There was a firm conviction among many that a small group controlled the financial resources of the country and thereby held the power to manipulate the money market as they pleased. Discontent with the financial situation led to a congressional investigation by the Pujo Committee in 1912 and 1913, and its report tended to confirm the accusation. It saw the trust centered in an informal alliance among J. P. Morgan, the First National Bank of New York, and the City National Bank of New York. The power of this group was represented by 341 directorships in 112 corporations which were capitalized at $22.25 billion. While the implication of power was probably exaggerated, it could not be denied that the bankers exercised vast power in the American economy.[7]

The Federal Reserve System. Dissatisfaction with the monetary situation in the country, and the crescendo of reformism led to the Federal Reserve Act of 1913. This law established a strong national banking system—it had a strong position relative to other banks of the country and strong control over the national economy. All national banks must be members and state banks may be members of the system. It is a banker's bank, the central agency for the member banks and for the government, with twelve branches located in the chief financial and commercial centers of the United States. These branches are located in homogeneous economic areas rather than by political divisions. The theory on which the Federal Reserve System is based is that the harmful fluctuations in the economy were due to the inelasticity of the currency. The Federal Reserve System was given power to control the currency and the credit, and hence indirectly to control the functions of the economy. This means national control of the money and credit system of the United States through the centralization of authority. The idea of control of monetary problems through "elasticity" has since been considerably downgraded, but this and other essential functions have made the Federal Reserve System a tower of strength in the stability of the economy. While this era has been called the heyday of laissez-faire, it should be pointed out that "big business" of the era converted mercantilism from a government to a private policy and used it to the utmost of its ability.

THE AUTOMOBILE INDUSTRY

Development, standardization, and mass production. One of the most

---

7 Faulkner, *op. cit.,* p. 455.

fabulous stories of an era filled with fabulous stories is the rise of the automobile industry. Coming into existence at the end of the nineteenth century, it developed within the span of a single generation into the largest industry in the United States—a model of mass production, division of labor, mechanization, and scientific management. To tell the story of how this change came about is to describe the process of industrialization. As far back as the thirteenth century Roger Bacon had conceived the idea of a steam-propelled vehicle, and a Frenchman, Joseph Cugnot, actually constructed such a vehicle in 1769. By 1860 scientific experiment had gone far enough to allow inventors to use gas as a fuel. The modern car had its beginning when Dr. Nicholaus August Otto in 1876 invented a four-cycle compression internal-combustion engine. It was improved by Gottlieb Daimler and applied to automobile propulsion by Carl Benz of Germany. During the decade prior to 1900, Charles Duryea, Henry Ford, R. E. Olds, and others in the United States produced workable but unpredictable vehicles. Early attempts to use steam power were converted to electricity and by 1900 the wealthy in all cities were using the "electric buggy."

The first automobiles were produced commercially in France in 1891. By 1900 there were 10,000 in Europe, about half of them in France. R. E. Olds was the first in the United States to manufacture rather than build cars. He envisioned mass production and was the first to use division of labor. He began to build gas-driven cars in 1897, and by 1904 was producing 4,000 annually. Olds' first car, with pneumatic clutch, cushion tires, and electric starter, was not only complicated but also expensive; it sold for $1,250. In 1901 he initiated the great technological change of mass production by buying parts in quantity and assembling them on a crude assembly line. His 1901 car sold for $650. His was the first moving assembly line and the first case where materials were taken to the worker instead of the worker to the materials.[8] Henry Ford failed to raise capital for the Ford Motor Company in 1903, but by using his own profits began mass production in 1907. He produced 10,000 cars the first year. In 1908 most of the automobiles were still relatively high-priced. But in that year Ford began production of the Model-T, a completely standardized product, which eventually sold for as low as $300.[9] Mass production of cars was really on its way and by 1914 over half a million were produced annually, and by 1927 Ford alone had passed the 15 million mark in total production. In the meantime, General Motors had overtaken Ford. Installment buying, which came into vogue in the 1920s, was a great boon to the automobile industry. In 1965 the American public owed $25 billion in installment debts on cars.

[8] Herman E. Krooss, *American Economic Development* (Englewood Cliffs, N. J., Prentice-Hall, 1955), pp. 358–361.
[9] *Ibid.*, pp. 361–364.

Along with the automobile came numerous companies who mass produced all kinds of parts and accessories. At one time Ford Motor Company bought chassis from the Dodge Brothers, bodies and cushions from the C. R. Wilson Carriage Company, wheels from another company, and tires from still another company. Olds bought most of his engines in the early stages from the Leland-Faulconer Manufacturing Company, and he bought enough to afford Leland a chance to manufacture a standardized engine with interchangeable parts. Although the idea of interchangeable parts was nearly a century old, going back to Eli Whitney and the manufacture of firearms, Olds and others refused to use them. Leland entered the business for himself and produced a standardized car, the Cadillac, which also had the first steering wheel and gear shift. In 1908 Leland demonstrated the advantages of machine-made interchangeable parts by sending three unassembled Cadillacs to England, stacking all parts in one heap, and having his mechanics assemble them with only hammers, screwdrivers, pliers, and wrenches, and then driving them on a 500-mile test. The production of interchangeable parts required precision instruments and machine tools. Leland imported this precision instrument, a set of "Jo blocks" that were accurate to within four-millionths of an inch, from Sweden. In the meantime, specialized tools such as drill presses, cylinder grinding machines, and turret lathes had been developed. The essentials of mass production—the assembly line, interchangeable parts, precision instruments, machine tools, material routing, and machine layout—had been accomplished. Production in future would be limited only by the ability of the public to buy the product.

The division of labor deserves further attention. Ford found that it took one man twenty minutes to assemble a flywheel magneto, but by putting it on a conveyor and splitting the job into twenty-nine different operations, the time could be cut to thirteen minutes. By raising the height of the conveyor it could be cut to five minutes. By splitting the process into eighty-four different operations, the length of time to assemble a motor could be cut to one-third. When workers moved from unit to unit it took twelve hours and twenty-eight minutes to assemble a car. By use of the assembly line and a continuous study of time and motion, Ford reduced the time to ninety-three minutes in 1914. By low profit margins and rapid turnover he reduced the price of his car to about $300 in 1924.

Standardization spread throughout the industry and added much to mass production. The 800 different lock washers used in early cars were reduced to 16; the 1,600 types of steel tubing were reduced to 17; the stamping process simplified the making of bodies by cutting down the number of parts.[10] Some notion of the growth in complexity of the auto-

10 *Ibid.*, p. 365.

mobile can be seen from the fact that where it once had less than 100 parts, it came to have more than 8,000. Despite this, the modern assembly line moving 23 feet per minute could turn out three cars per minute.

Consolidation. Expansion of the automobile industry was not without its casualties. Over five hundred companies were formed between 1900 and 1908; most of them failed, others retired from the business altogether, and others moved into other businesses. Many people can still remember some of the cars which had their demise during the 1920s: Jackson, Metz, Halladay, Briscoe, Regal, King, Pan American, Mitchell, Saxon, Elgin, National, Crawford, Westcott, Stanley Steamer, Mercer, American, Cole, Cleveland, Apperson, Premier, Jewett, Paige, Case, Davis, Diana, Willys-Overland, Maxwell, Chalmers, Oakland, Essex. Between 1903 and 1926, some 225 companies produced cars, but by 1917, ten companies were producing three-fourths of all cars,[11] and by 1929 three companies, Ford, General Motors, and Chrysler, manufactured 90 percent of all automobiles totaling 4.8 million for that year. There were 23.1 million passenger cars registered in 1929, or one for every six people in the country. Also by 1929, the industry provided employment for 5 million persons or 10 percent of the working population, consumed 85 percent of the gasoline, 82 percent of the rubber, 68 percent of the plate glass, 50 percent or more of upholstery leather and certain types of iron and steel, over 25 percent of nickel and lead, 10 to 20 percent of aluminum, copper, and tin, 9 percent of the cotton, and 6 percent of the zinc used by the whole country.[12]

Influence of the automobile. An accurate assessment of the influence of the automobile on the American way of life is almost impossible. One of the most obvious is the vast expenditure of cash. It has been estimated that in 1929 the nation was spending 10 percent of its income on motor transportation. The car made America a mobile nation, and this brought a host of other changes such as the tourist industry, the leveling of urban and rural differences, and the migrant labor family. The tourist industry itself created a multitude of other industries and services among which were garages and service stations, parks, hotels and motels, restaurants, and amusement places and vacation spots. More basic was the part played by the automobile in the movement to the cities. In its wake the rural institutions decayed to the extent that the community spirit that once centered in them all but disappeared from American life.

THE OIL INDUSTRY: STANDARD OIL COMPANY

Early development and methods of consolidation. The development of the oil industry best illustrates the special significance of the industrial

---

11 *Ibid.*, p. 366.

12 James A. Barnes, *Wealth of the American People* (New York, Prentice-Hall, 1949), p. 584.

combination, the phases of its development, and the methods of acquiring control. The industry really began in Titusville, Pennsylvania, in 1859, and since then has spread to the ends of the earth. In 1863 John D. Rockefeller and two associates built a refining plant in Cleveland, and in 1867 five companies were united in the firm of Rockefeller, Andrews, and Flagler. A branch office had already been established in New York to handle foreign sales. During this time there were many small companies and the industry was in a state of chaos; for most it was highly unprofitable. It was said that Rockefeller was dominated by a driving passion to eliminate the waste and extravagance of the competitive practices and that he chose to absorb other companies rather than to fight them. In 1870 the Standard Oil Company of Ohio was created with Rockefeller as the unchallenged head. This company had a refining capacity of 600 barrels a day, which was about 4 percent of all United States refining at the time. Standard, however, was not the largest refinery in the country.

Up to 1879 the competition was largely in production; after that time it turned to a struggle for transportation facilities and favorable freight rates. The outcome of this bitter fight left Standard in complete control. The methods Standard used were probably no worse than those of Gould, Fisk, and others in the railroad industry. The morality of the time was the ultimate expression of the laissez-faire doctrine of "survival of the fittest," and there were few rules to go by and no laws of importance to check the predatory. Among the notorious practices of Standard and other large companies was the use of a defunct corporation, the South Improvement Company which had almost unlimited authority, to make contract agreements with the Pennsylvania, the New York Central, and the Erie Railroads whereby the first got 45 percent of the oil transport business and the other two split the remainder. In return for this privilege, the railroads agreed to give Standard rebates, in some cases up to 50 percent, to charge competitor companies full rates and to hand over to Standard a percentage of all such receipts from these companies. In addition, the railroads were to turn over to Standard all waybills of the competitor companies, which informed them of the amount of business and the people with whom it was done. This knowledge was very valuable in the game. The agreement was made in great secrecy, but it leaked out and a torrent of criticism caused the charter to be revoked. This did not end the rebates, however, nor the favorable discrimination established by the contract.

In the meantime Rockefeller in Cleveland explained to his competitors the great advantage which he had through the South Improvement Company and invited them to sell their concerns for stock or cash, on his terms. Their alternative was extinction, and at least twenty sold out. It is well to keep in mind that at this time rebates were common to all industries, and that businessmen in general were favored by this arrangement. Through the next thirty years, Standard continued to destroy its competitors. Its early success with rebates from the railroads was threatened in 1878 when the Tidewater Company started building a pipeline across the mountains to the East coast. Standard and the railroads that carried the profitable oil business fought the builders with everything at their command. Standard even bought a strip of land across the state of Pennsylvania to block the construction. The bed of an overlooked creek that had dried up provided a crossing and the pipeline was completed and pumping started. The victory was short-lived. In a short time, parallel lines had been built and the coastal refineries, outlets for the Tidewater's sales, were bought up. Most of the other pipelines were soon brought together in the United Pipe Line Company which Standard controlled. After a bitter struggle in 1883 the two rivals signed an agreement by which Standard got 88.5 percent of the business and Tidewater got the remainder.[13]

A second method used by Standard to destroy competitors was through marketing on a country-wide scale with districts and subdistricts. The organization was a most efficient one. Everywhere Standard's representatives gathered information on competitors and where necessary started competitive price wars. Standard's agents approached retailers and others dealing in competitive products and threatened a price war unless purchases from competitors ceased and the business was given to Standard. Because of Standard's control of the transportation facilities, its large sums of money available, and its great efficiency in large-scale production, it was able to drive most competitors out of business. Through these methods Standard acquired control of 90 percent of the oil refining industry of the country by 1879. Three years later, a new form of organization evolved. Under a trust agreement the stockholders surrendered their securities to nine trustees and in return received trust certificates. This was not a corporation as it had no charter and was not authorized by any legislative act.[14]

Federal regulation: the Sherman Anti-Trust Act. In the meantime, the state of New Jersey passed laws granting extremely wide powers through charters. In 1899, Standard of New Jersey was reorganized with a board of directors to take the place of the trustees. New stock was issued in exchange for the stock of the constituent concerns that refined oil, produced crude oil, owned pipelines, carried on marketing operations, and sold natural gas. The board of directors of the New Jersey company controlled these constituent companies because it held and voted their stocks. Between 1897 and 1906, the dividends of Standard were reported to range between 30 and 48 percent. As we have already seen, a wave of reformism

---

13 *Ibid.,* pp. 486–487.
14 Faulkner, *op. cit.,* pp. 440–441.

was sweeping the country, especially against the so-called "trusts." The Interstate Commerce Act was passed in 1887 in an attempt to correct the abuses of the railroads. In 1890 the courts of Ohio had dissolved the Standard Oil Company into twenty constituent companies with the intention of enforcing competition among them. In the meantime Congress had passed the Sherman Anti-Trust Act in 1890. In 1899 a second attempt was made to bring all companies under a single control through the Standard Oil Company of New Jersey, which was a holding company as well as an operating company. This effort was finally defeated in 1911 when the United States Supreme Court ordered the dissolution of Standard.

In the course of time, Standard had spread its operations into foreign fields, especially Latin America and the Middle East. The growth of the automobile industry gave great impetus to the production of oil, and new and powerful competitors entered the field. The monopolistic grip of Standard was broken, not so much by the government efforts as by these new competitors. Among the most important of the new companies were Pure Oil Company, the Texas Company, the Gulf Company, and the Shell Companies.

From industrial to financial enterprise. We have already seen how the Morgan financial interests extended themselves into the field of industry and railroads. It will be recalled that the Morgan interests actually came to control the United States Steel Corporation, upon the retirement of Carnegie. While Carnegie was the prototype of the industrial capitalist whose main interest was in the area of production, Morgan represented the financial capitalists to whom industrial production was a means to an end. Financial matters were their chief concern. The big deals of industries were made in the New York offices of the financiers, not in the offices of the industrial plants. This is the beginning of the separation of ownership and management, which has been basic to the great transformation within the economy. Another illustration of this change was the involvement of Standard Oil money in other areas as widespread as the National City Bank of New York, some half dozen railroads, the Amalgamated Copper Company, the Consolidated Gas Company, and the Edison Illuminating Company. Based on oil, this vast empire threatened to dwarf even the Morgan financial empire.

Other large consolidations: the telephone industry. We have seen the development and consolidation of railroads, money and banking, the automobile industry, and the oil industry. These amazing stories are paralleled by many others: steel, the utilities, meat packing, aviation, and dairying in the production field, and in retail outlets by department stores, variety stores, grocery chains, drug chains, mail order stores, and more recently by the radio industry, the motion picture industry, the chemical industry, the food industry, the television industry, and many others. The process of merging small businesses into larger and more efficient ones has continued to the present and, while it has created some problems, it has made the American economy the envy of the world.

The first telephone message went out over the wires in 1876, and within four years there were 148 private companies and corporations with over 3,000 employees and over 34,000 miles of wires throughout the cities of the country. The telephone industry soon became big business. In 1900 the American Telephone and Telegraph Company was organized and by 1940 it had become a huge holding company controlling the most important American systems. In 1900 there were 855,000 telephones in the country, in 1915 over 9 million.[15] In 1963 the company was the largest corporation in the United States, with assets of over $28 billion. There were also many other large corporations, such as the Bank of America and Chase Manhattan Bank with approximately $20 billion each in assets, the First National City Bank and Standard Oil of New Jersey with nearly $12 billion in assets each, and General Motors with nearly $11 billion in assets.

It has been estimated that between 1850 and 1910 each of the thirteen leading industries in the United States multiplied its capital more than thirty-nine times, its number of wage earners seven times, and the value of its products more than nineteen times. This tremendous growth was brought about in part by natural growth and by the process of merging of small businesses into giant corporations. Between 1914 and 1929, those firms doing business between $5,000 and $20,000 annually decreased from 49 percent to only 33 percent of the total while those doing over a billion dollars in business increased from 2.2 percent to 5.6 percent of the total. By 1929, businesses doing over a billion dollars constituted only 5.6 percent of the total but employed 58.3 percent of the workers, and produced 69.2 percent of the value of all products.[16]

THE LABOR MOVEMENT

Early history. The industrialization process not only brought about the middle class and the capitalist system but also the class which Marx thought would overthrow the capitalistic system, the wage-earner class. Marx was right in believing that the way people make their living has much to do with their attitudes, values, and beliefs. The processes of industrialization and urbanization offer many clues to the values, attitudes, and beliefs we hold today.

Craftsmen have always had their place in American society, and it was the middle of the nineteenth century before machines seriously interrupted their status. Early craftsmen were more than just efficient, they

---

[15] *Ibid.*, pp. 513–515; and Barnes, *op. cit.*, pp. 513–515.
[16] Faulkner, *op. cit.*, p. 433.

were also artists; and their craft or trade was more than just a job, it was a way of life. We have already seen how the machine had taken over many jobs of the skilled workers, had reduced others to semiskilled or unskilled jobs, and had become a threat to their social status. Resistance to the introduction of the machine in Europe was at times violent, and almost everywhere took on a form of sabotage, destruction of machinery. Resistance also took the form of organized political activity. The proletariat in England was influential in bringing about the Reform Bill of 1832, which actually did nothing for them, but extended suffrage to the middle classes. Disappointed at having merely changed aristocratic for bourgeois masters, the proletariat continued political agitation for two decades through the program known as "Chartism." Throughout nineteenth-century Europe, reform ideas ranged all the way from the utopianism of Robert Owen to the communism of Karl Marx. All these "isms" were efforts to solve the problems growing out of the rising industrial-capitalistic system. In any society, rapid change always brings difficult problems of readjustment. Viewed against the European background, the early American labor problem was quite mild.

Beginning of craft unionism. In the late colonial period, craftsmen had what they called benevolent and protective associations. After about 1790, the larger cities had developed unions among shoemakers, printers, carpenters, hatters, masons, and tailors. These early unions were transitory, having mostly temporary objectives. Permanency in unions was difficult to achieve because their fortunes waxed and waned with the ebb and flow of the business cycle, and because of the hostility of the employers and the courts. The courts followed the model of English common law which held workingmen's associations to be conspiracies. The people of property and the professional classes, including ministers, generally condemned labor unions. In the early 1800s, many unions were prosecuted in the courts as conspiracies, and a few judges held that any combination to raise wages was illegal under the common law. As late as 1835, in the so-called Geneva shoemakers case in which the master hired a nonunion member for below union rate, the journeymen struck and were indicted and convicted for criminal conspiracy. The United States Supreme Court upheld the conviction. Although the unions won a few concessions along the way, the courts throughout the nineteenth and the first quarter of the twentieth century were largely tools of the employers; and from the latter part of the nineteenth century the use of the injunction and of federal troops against strikers placed the government more squarely in their path.

Problems and utopian solutions. Utopian solutions to the problems growing out of industrialization were not confined to Europe. By the middle of the nineteenth century, many American middle-class reformers were offering their panaceas for the ills of industrialism. Men such as Arthur Brisbane and Horace Greeley were taken with Charles Fourier's ideas of a cooperative society. Many consumer and producer cooperatives were established, but poor planning and management brought most of them to an unhappy end. Most widely known of these cooperatives were New Harmony in Indiana, established by Robert Owen, and Brook Farm near Boston. Thomas Skidmore believed that the ills of society could be cured by a redistribution of land, and he wrote a book in an attempt to prove his case. A more practical agrarian was George Henry Evans who organized the National Reform Association to work for a change in the federal land policy. Less utopian and more intellectually challenging were the ideas of two other writers in the last quarter of the century. Henry George, obsessed with the paradox of the increasing poverty that accompanied the increasing wealth, believed the problem lay in the private ownership of land. He was convinced that land, like air and water, was a natural resource to which all should have equal access. He expounded his theory in a remarkable book entitled *Progress and Poverty*. While George's answer was too simple a solution to the gigantic problems growing out of American industrialization, it was a powerful outcry against the social injustices that accompanied it. Even more popular was Edward Bellamy's *Looking Backward,* which has since become a classic. It pictured a society in the year 2000, free from poverty and crime, achieved through peaceful social evolution. The utopians, however, had little influence on the practical solutions of the problems. Bellamy's ideas especially appealed to those who felt that some solution to the problems of the day must be found, but who would have been repelled by the idea of a class struggle, violent revolution, and other ideas of Karl Marx.

Knights of Labor. Trade or craft unions were organizations of skilled craftsmen. Some craft unions became organized at the national level, but many thought that an effective labor movement required a broader base from which to operate. The most romantic of the early American labor organizations was the Knights of Labor, organized in 1869. It differed from trade unions in that its membership was open to both skilled and unskilled, male and female. It was very popular from the beginning and its membership reached 750,000 by 1886. After disastrous strike failures it lost the confidence of workers and its prestige declined rapidly. The Knights had a far-reaching program, including the promotion of education, greater equality of income and opportunity, the maintenance of good government, the prohibition of child labor, equal pay for women, and the eight-hour day. This was a kind of utopian labor dream, and its failure ended labor's great experiment of the nineteenth century of "one big union."

As industry grew and prospered, union members were not content with the more long-term objectives of the Knights of Labor, and demanded shorter hours and higher wages. Neither the organization nor the heterogeneous membership of the Knights was suited to the pursuit of these more limited objectives. Thus, when the American Federation of Labor promised to fight for better wages, shorter hours, and better working conditions, the broadly based utopian movement collapsed. The American Federation of Labor drew from the Knights the elite of labor, the craftsmen; it took not only the main organizational strength but also the main source of funds. The failure of the Knights had convinced labor organizations that their gains would be made by fights for concrete objectives, not for broad reform programs.

Industrial unionism. Samuel Gompers, the guiding force of the AFL for four decades, had no sympathy with the visionary projects of the leaders of the Knights of Labor. Born in London and brought up in the tradition of unionism, he believed in "pure and simple unionism." He was opposed to an independent labor party or to aligning the AFL with either existing party; he believed that it was in the best interest of labor to be free to vote for its friends and against its enemies regardless of party. This policy was rather strictly adhered to until 1916, and has been more or less adhered to since then.

The AFL had a modest beginning in Pittsburgh in 1881, when six of the strongest craft unions organized the Federation of Organized Trades and Labor Unions. It grew slowly until the strong national unions of the Knights of Labor united with it in 1886 under the name of the American Federation of Labor. With the improvement of economic conditions about a decade later, it began a period of rapid growth, reaching over 1.5 million members by 1904. By 1920 the AFL had over 5 million or some four-fifths of all union members. The AFL was an organization of self-governing craft unions. It unified the struggle for better job opportunities and job conditions by eliminating competition among its members. The idea of a single union to a trade created a number of problems, one of which was "jurisdictional" disputes. This problem is still unsettled and the public is beginning to demand that labor put its own house in order. The creation of "industrial unions" was partly a response to the problems of craft unionism. An industrial union was one organized among the workers within a single industry, and included both the skilled and semiskilled. The first such union was the Union of Mine Workers, organized in 1902. The craft unions, however, continued to dominate the AFL. As late as 1920, twenty-four different unions claimed jurisdiction over some segment of the steel workers, and the majority of unskilled workers were still unaffiliated with any union.

The industrial unions within the AFL became dissatisfied with its failure to organize the rapidly growing mass production industries. In

1935, eight of the most powerful industrial unions organized the Congress of Industrial Organization with John L. Lewis as President. The New Deal legislation gave labor a great boost and union membership increased from less than 3 million in 1933 to over 8 million in 1940. By 1953, 17 million workers were organized, some 28 percent of the labor force. Of the 17 million, about half belonged to the AFL, some 30 percent to the CIO.

The National Labor Relations Act of 1935. Labor was on the short end of the bargaining until the National Labor Relations Act was passed in 1935. This act, generally called the Wagner Act, was the Magna Carta of labor. It required management to recognize and deal with labor organizations in good faith, and it made collective bargaining the basis for industrial relations. With general public acceptance, favorable government policy, and a great increase in membership, labor became one of the big forces in modern American society, taking its place with "big business" and "big government." By 1947, a reaction had asserted itself with the passage of the Taft-Hartley Act.

Labor's struggle for well-being and status. To the early American capitalist, labor was just another cost of production, like the cost of materials or equipment. The industrialization process created an employer-employee relationship which was completely impersonal: neither party had any responsibility beyond the terms of the contract. The popular concept of property rights—the owner has the right to do with his property what he pleases—left the propertyless laborer in an indefensible position. To fight his way out of this situation, and to fight the laws that discriminated against him were the problems the laborer faced.

Another obstacle in the path of American labor was the immigrant. Most of the immigrants, especially in the period of the mid-1880s to 1914, were poor peasants from Central and Southern Europe. These "uprooted," who had expected to find a warm welcome in the land of opportunity, instead found themselves cheated and swindled on every side. They were exploited by employers who took advantage of their ignorance and inability to communicate, herded into the clutches of corrupt city bosses, and heartily disliked by native American labor. Labor's demand for restrictions on immigration is understandable. The tremendous supply of immigrant labor kept wages low and placed native labor in competition with immigrant labor. What was wretchedly low wages by American standards seemed adequate to the immigrant. Employers also used immigrant laborers, especially French-Canadian and Chinese, as strike-breakers. A look at the statistics will give some idea of the significance of the immigration problem. The numbers arriving by decades were for the 1860s 2,304,000; for the 1870s, 2,812,000, in spite of the severe depression; for the 1880s, 5,246,000; the increase continued until it reached a million in the year of 1905; and it fluctuated from that until 1914. Most of the so-called anarchy and other radicalism that entered the labor movement in this era was brought over by the more skilled immigrants, mostly from Western Europe, who had knowledge of and experience in the labor movements of Europe. The labor movement in America, however, was not essentially radical. It sought, basically, to improve the position of labor under the status quo; the older craft unions were thoroughly capitalistic.

The use of state militia and federal troops, ostensibly to keep order, was common. Some companies hired their own private police force, mostly Pinkerton guards. The result was frequent clashes between police and strikers. When the railroad strikers, for example, seized control of the terminal at Cumberland, the governor of Maryland ordered two regiments of Baltimore militiamen to Cumberland. When a Baltimore crowd attempted to halt the troops, the troops opened fire, killing twelve and wounding eighteen. In Pittsburgh, strikers took control of the switches and refused to allow freight trains to move. The governor sent 650 militiamen to the spot. Upon the first display of hostility, the troops fired on a crowd, killing twenty-five persons and wounding as many more. This act aroused not only the railroad men but the factory workers, miners and others. They secured arms and an all-night battle ensued. The militiamen were repulsed and devastation followed: two thousand cars, twenty-five locomotives, the roundhouse, machine shops, grain elevators, and other property were destroyed. Warehouses and shops were indiscriminately looted by hoodlums.[17] These are but examples of the violence of the "desperate seventies."

In the Haymarket Square incident in 1886, a bomb was thrown into a company of 180 policemen, killing seven. Many arrests were made and eight anarchists—a term loosely applied to all extremists—were tried for murder. Seven were condemned to death and one to fifteen years imprisonment even though there was no evidence that they had actually thrown the bomb. It was charged that by their revolutionary propaganda they had incited the workers and were, therefore, accessories before the fact. In the same year, Gould's Southern Railroad System was struck. In desperation the strikers sabotaged engines, wrecked trains, and threatened engineers and conductors who ran them. But Gould's lieutenants were prepared for trouble, and through vigorous use of strike-breakers, Pinkerton guards, and state militiamen, the strike was broken. In the Homestead strike in 1892, the Carnegie Steel Company hired a private army of three hundred Pinkerton guards equipped with rifles in preparation for use in strike-breaking. The strikers resisted the attempts to use these guards and an all-day battle followed in which three guards and seven strikers were killed and many others wounded. The militia moved

17 Barnes, *op. cit.*, pp. 422–423.

in, strike-breakers took the jobs of unionists, the strike was lost, and only a portion of the union men got their jobs back.[18] Neither the violence, nor the battles between the employers and the employees ended here. As late of 1919 in a strike against the United States Steel Company, the Pennsylvania Constabulary rode their horses into groups of strikers, clubbed them, and made arbitrary arrests; and in Gary, Indiana, federal troops entered the scene to keep order, strike-breakers were used, and the strike was lost. Twenty people had been killed, eighteen of them strikers.

The federal government continued to stand in the way of labor success. Between 1917 and 1923, the Supreme Court upheld "yellow dog" contracts—contracts that bound workers to a promise not to join a labor union—upheld the right of courts to restrict picketing, invalidated state laws limiting courts in the use of the injunction, denied the power of Congress to pass a minimum wage law for women and children in the District of Columbia, and ruled that secondary boycotts were not protected by the Clayton Act. The federal injunction was still a tool which worked in the interest of the employer. Up to this time labor had made only modest gains and this was due more to times of prosperity than to their success in the struggle with the employers. The disastrous failures of labor following World War I sent labor unions into a decline in membership from which it did not recover even in the prosperous twenties. In 1933 they had less than 3 million members compared with over 5 million in 1920.

We have made little attempt to assess the responsibility for this tragic era of management-labor relations, and any generalization is bound to be dangerously oversimplified. It is generally accepted that labor was tragically underpaid, especially unskilled labor, and that working hours were notoriously long. In the case of United States Steel, as late as 1919, half the employees worked twelve hours a day, one quarter worked seven days a week, and the average for the industry was sixty-nine hours a week. The twelve-hour day was not eliminated until 1923. Employers as a rule, especially late in the nineteenth century, used every tool at their command to destroy the unions, and the unions in desperation frequently turned to violence to gain their ends. In what has been termed "welfare capitalism," employers began to turn to company unions. Although they continued to combat union organization through the use of labor spies, arbitrary discharge, blacklisting, and company police, their most effective approach was to convince their employees that it was in the latter's interest to cooperate with management. This approach brought great improvement to labor and represented the beginning of a rather complete transformation in the ideology of labor-management relations. Many companies improved working conditions, established cafeterias, and recreation halls, initiated employee-group life and disability insurance poli-

18 *Ibid.*, pp. 426–427.

cies, and developed old-age pension plans. Between 1914 and 1928, real wages increased by about 32 percent, still partly wrested from unwilling management by union effort. Also part of the improved standard of living of labor rested on the misfortune of the farmer whose crop prices lagged far behind the wages of labor.

It took a long and tragically disastrous industrial warfare before it was recognized that the interests of management and labor were not mutually exclusive, and that cooperation rather than competition was to their mutual advantage. It was even longer before it became recognized that the consuming public had a claim to be represented in the activities on which not only its welfare but its very life depended. This is understandable in the light of nineteenth-century ideology under which the new industrial society emerged—the doctrine of self-interest as expressed in laissez-faire theory. The idea that the economy was self-regulating through the medium of the market, and that the interest of the society was best served through the best interest of the individual created an atmosphere which was conducive to the highly competitive struggle which we have observed in all of the areas we have studied. But even before the end of the nineteenth century, it was becoming evident to advanced thinkers that social disorder unparalleled in American history was being produced, and that a modification in both ideas and practices would have to be made in seeking a solution to these problems.

BIBLIOGRAPHY

Barnes, James A., *Wealth of the American People: A History of Their Economic Life*. New York, Prentice-Hall, 1949.

Edwards, Edgar O., *The Nation's Economic Objectives*. Chicago, University of Chicago Press, 1964.

Faulkner, Harold U., *American Economic History*, 6th ed. New York, Harper, 1949.

Faulkner, Harold U., *The Decline of Laissez Faire, 1897–1917*. New York, Rinehart, 1951.

Fox, Karl A., Verner W. Ruttan, and Lawrence W. Witt, *Farming, Farmers, and Markets for Farm Goods*, No. 15. New York, Committee for Economic Development, 1962.

Hansen, Alvin H., *The American Economy*. New York, McGraw-Hill, 1957.

Hathaway, Dale E., *Government and Agriculture*. New York, Macmillan, 1963.

Higbee, Edward, *Farms and Farmers in an Urban Age*. New York, Twentieth Century Fund, 1963.

Kirkland, Edward C., *A History of American Economic Life*. New York, Appleton-Century-Crofts, 1951.

Krooss, Herman E., *American Economic Development*. Englewood Cliffs, N. J., Prentice-Hall, 1955.

Marx, Herbert L., *American Labor Today*. New York, W. H. Wilson, 1965.

Morris, Bruce R. *Problems of American Economic Growth*. New York, Oxford, 1961.

Nevins, Allan, *Ford: The Times, the Man, the Company*. New York, Scribner, 1954.

Olson, Philip, *America as a Mass Society*. New York, Free Press, 1963.

Paarlberg, Don, *American Farm Policy*. New York, Wiley, 1964.

Rasmussen, Wayne D., *Readings in the History of American Agriculture*. Urbana, University of Illinois Press, 1960.

Robertson, Ross M., *History of the American Economy*. New York, Harcourt, Brace, 1955.

Russell, Robert R., *A History of the American Economic System*. New York, Appleton-Century-Crofts, 1964.

Shepherd, Geoffrey S., *Farm Policy: New Directions*. Ames, Iowa State University Press, 1964.

SUMMARY OF PART I

The need for understanding society in modern times becomes increasingly imperative. In simple societies change was slow and adjustment was no problem. Individuals learned largely by rote to perform the tasks that had to be done and there was little variation from generation to generation. Today change is so rapid that the skills of the individual become greatly changed, or sometimes obsolete, within his own lifetime. We obviously need to understand the rapid changes which have taken place and are taking place and, as far as possible, to know what to expect of the future. In specific cases we can at least know the direction which we are going by knowing the historical development up to the present. For example, the population growth, the rate of divorce, the crime rate, the amount of insurance sold, and the national income within the next year can be reasonably predicted on the basis of the annual statistics of each one of these over the past several years. That is to say that the understanding of any problem lies in the adequate knowledge of the immediate and remote past. This is the problem to which we have addressed ourselves up to this point.

To talk about the transition in American society in general terms makes little sense. We must answer the question, What is it that changes? To answer this question we began with patterns of behavior as the bases of social organization and developed the concepts of groups, associations, institutions, and society. We saw that the transformation in society is mainly the transformation within its institutions. While individuals are involved in some ways with institutions at the societal level, the direct concern of most individuals is at the community level.

Our thesis is the change or transformation in American society, and our attention was directed to the most observable factor in that change—urbanization.

The roots of institutional change in the United States and Western

Europe lie deeply embedded in the breakup of the medieval feudal system, the Renaissance and Reformation, the rise of commercial capitalism and the middle classes, mercantilism and colonialism, the industrial revolution and the doctrine of laissez-faire. These are only the bold outlines of forces in the background of industrialized Western society. More immediately, the great transformation in American society rests upon its own agricultural and industrial development. The increase in productivity was essential before any great departure from a strictly agrarian society could take place.

For people who were born after World War II, it is difficult to understand either the extent or the rapidity of the changes which have taken place in recent American society: the urban-industrial society, universal education, and highly centralized government are commonplace. The agrarian society, with its high degree of self-sufficiency, political provincialism, and evangelical religion, has given way to the mass society, with its giant and complex economic, social, and political organizations. Social power is largely dominated by those who have access to the mass media for purposes of manipulation of public opinion. The recent high degree of mobility has largely eliminated local loyalties, and the traditional family has been rent asunder. This transition has followed the development of interdependence within the various areas of American society, especially in the economic areas.

Modern American society is integrated to a degree and in ways that were impossible for an agrarian way of life. The individual today, whether he sells his services or products, is distributing them in a nation-wide market dominated by large corporations. Almost every aspect of his business is touched by some form of government regulation. Modern communication and transportation have broken down former isolation so that today all Americans buy the same standardized products, advertised and sold on a nation-wide basis; listen to standardized programs on television and radio on nation-wide broadcasting systems; and read newspaper columns, magazines, and books distributed on a nation-wide scale. Because of these things, Americans have developed more or less nation-wide tastes and values, but competition and conflict have hardly been thereby eliminated. The existing inequalities and the desire for both status and power probably make for a more wide-spread and driving competition than at any time in the past.

Competition is both individual and corporate. The violence of the conflict between labor and management of earlier times has been eliminated, not because competition has been eliminated, but because regulations and procedures for dealing with their problems have been largely institutionalized. Government has often come in to referee, or, increasingly, to prevail upon both unions and management to act in the public interest.

PART II

American institutions

in the mass society

7

From laissez-faire to welfare capitalism

I N Chapter 4 we discussed the rise of the middle class, capitalism, and the doctrine of economic liberalism. Early American economic theory was profoundly influenced by these developments. In Europe the old landed aristocracy had been the upper or ruling class. The rise to control of the state by the middle class brought an end to their dominance. The upper classes in early American history constituted what we have referred to as the "middle class" in discussing European social changes.

BACKGROUNDS OF AMERICAN ECONOMIC THEORY

The chief tenets of British economic liberalism were freedom from arbitrary use of power by the king, the right of the middle class to participate in government, freedom from arbitrary imposition of taxes, freedom of worship, and the abolition of restrictions on economic activities imposed by the government. The last of these, the doctrine of laissez-faire, was the most distinctive idea of nineteenth-century liberalism, and although it became the cornerstone of American economic theory, it proved to be the most vulnerable element in the ideology of middle-class liberalism.

As liberalism achieved its goals, both in Europe and America, it became the status quo and its defenders became what we now generally call conservatives. In America they were represented by Alexander Hamilton and the Federalists. While economic theory is an explanation of the working of the economy, it may or may not closely represent the real economy. What is probably more important is that these theoretical assumptions became the accepted justification for the course of action whether the theory was applicable to the case or not.

Some assumptions of laissez-faire doctrine. The basic assumption of the laissez-faire theory of economics is the idea that the economy functions best as an automatic, self-regulating system, which operates through the market-price mechanism to allocate capital, labor, and natural resources to the best advantage. Among other assumptions, either stated or implied, were the following:

1. That need, or demand, is unlimited;
2. That goods are in limited supply;
3. That man weighs his alternatives rationally, and that his choices effectively determine demand, what and how much of a particular thing would be produced;
4. That in the market-price system, there would be substantial equality of bargaining power because producing, buying and selling units would be small and their number so great that the behavior of one could not appreciably affect the market;
5. That the factors of production—labor, capital, resources, and management —may be shifted freely from less to more productive lines;
6. That free competition or rivalry among buyers and sellers in the market leaves the individual without any control over either the price or the character of his product;
7. That under pure or perfect competition non-price competition would not exist;
8. That, working within the framework of competition, the individual would unwittingly promote the welfare of society despite his exclusive concern with his own interests;
9. That economic ends are assumed to be quantitative and measurable in terms of money;
10. That the marketplace, the activity of buyers and sellers, is the dynamic mechanism operating the economy;
11. That progress comes through the competitive struggle of individuals—this was justified first by the Protestant ethic and the doctrine of natural rights, and later by social Darwinism, whose most powerful American advocate was William Graham Sumner.

The term "laissez-faire" is generally used to represent the whole range of ideas mentioned above. In a more accurate sense, it is only one phase of the classical theory of economics. As such it represented the demand that the government not interfere in private economic affairs; it originated in opposition to mercantilist restrictions. In the beginning it was a radical phrase used by the opponents of mercantilism against the status quo; when this group, the middle-class liberals, came to power in the Western world, it became a conservative phrase used to support their powerful private interests.

Importance of assumptions. We have tried to make clear the implications of laissez-faire theory in its "ideal" form. The economy of no society has ever, or ever could, operate in complete accordance with these ideas. The United States in the last half of the nineteenth century made the closest approach. This is not to say that the doctrine had no validity. As a set of abstractions, laissez-faire serves as a methodological device in the analysis of economic behavior. Whether or not the theories exactly fit the realities of economic behavior is immaterial under the circumstances. The problem in regard to theory and practice comes when these theoretical abstractions become so embedded in the culture that they become accepted as facts rather than as assumptions. If the idea that the government under no condition is justified in interfering in private enterprise is completely accepted, then no matter how much suffering a depression may bring to people, the government should do nothing about it. It is important to distinguish between laissez-faire as an explanation of the operation of the economy when Adam Smith presented it in 1776 and as a justification for the United States government's refusal to prohibit child labor in the middle of the nineteenth century. Adam Smith was a liberal whose doctrine was designed to bring about social justice, in the second case, the doctrine was used as a legal justification for the exploitation of one class by another.

Business enterprise in the United States opposed government regulation from the beginning. It did not follow from the beginning, however, Adam Smith's most cogent argument that all government aid to business should be abolished because it created special privileges and monopolies. In fact, it believed that the government should aid economic expansion—a kind of reverse mercantilism—and this was the heart of Hamilton's policy. The evidence of federal government aid is clear: the passage of the protective tariff, the establishment of the Bank of the United States, the assumption of debts incurred during the Revolution and the assumption of state debts, and the efforts to promote manufacturing. With some deviation, business enterprise followed this bifurcated policy well into the twentieth century.

Evaluation of laissez-faire assumptions. Some specific points on which the assumptions of the classical theory of economics listed above are untrue or only partly true in present-day society should be noted. First, economists no longer assume that the individual "economic man" will act rationally in choosing what he buys and sells. The "pleasure-pain calculus" has ceased to have much pain for the extremely rich and little pleasure for the extremely poor—the rich man buys what he fancies and the poor man buys what he has to. In fact, this assumes that demand could exist only for those things already in existence. Today, thousands of new things are produced for which there could conceivably be no prior demand. Furthermore, improvement and new uses of things already in existence have made advertising one of the biggest industries in the country. In the theory of laissez-faire, it is assumed that the individual has sufficient knowledge of all of his alternatives. At present the best the individual can do is to make "educated" guesses. Nor are prices determined in the marketplace by the bargaining of buyers and sellers. In the United States there is a one-price system and the buyer takes or leaves it. Furthermore, this price is usually an "administered price," a price determined before the article is up for sale, and it is the supply which is adjusted rather than the price. The automobile manufacturer does not make all of the cars he can and then sell them for what he can get for them. He knows in advance what he must get for his cars and the number that he must sell to stay in business and make a profit. In fact, any enterprise which does not operate in this way is not likely to stay in business very long. The situation today is a far cry from the classical assumption of many small producers and many small buyers competing in the market and thus automatically regulating the economy.

Economists no longer believe that individual wants are unlimited and that the supply of goods is limited. Our productive capacity has reached the point that we have to spend billions of dollars annually to acquaint the public with new and improved products before there can be any demand for them. It is not demand that brings about the production of goods but the existence of the goods along with advertising which creates the demand. All kinds of gadgets, new machines, and tools are invented and produced for which there could conceivably have been no prior demand. The postulate of "scarcity" does not fit our affluent society. The assumption that the operation of supply and demand in the market would leave the individual without control over either the price or character of his product—this would be necessary for supply and demand to regulate the economy—is obviously not the case. The mobility of factors of production is certainly not perfect. Capital may be shifted from place to place rather readily, but resources and labor are hardly free to be shifted from place to place, and everybody knows that the government interferes with the free play of supply and demand in dozens of ways. One of the most unsound of all of laissez-faire assumptions is that price is the only valid factor in competition. This is patently not the case in American society of today. The non-price competition in quality, styling, packaging, servicing, and advertising is obviously more important than price competition in many areas of our market.

Another assumption of laissez-faire, that the individual seeking to promote his own selfish interests would thereby promote the welfare of society, is far from the whole truth. There are hundreds of federal and state laws, in the interest of the general welfare which place restrictions on the individual's economic pursuits. This assumption in its ultimate form represents the rankest kind of individualism—one which places property rights above human rights and the welfare of the individual above that of the society to which he belongs. No society ever existed, nor could long exist, which tried to follow this dictum. Unbridled competition in the early period of small enterprises may have been an adequate modus operandi, but it should not be overlooked that the purpose of unfettered competition is to gain as much of the market as possible, and the ultimate of this is monopoly. Complete freedom of competition is freedom to gain a monopoly. This is the history of monopoly and the best example is that of the Standard Oil Company, mentioned previously.

Finally, the idea that progress comes through the natural competitive struggle of individuals is at best only partly true. It could be said with equal truth that progress comes through the cooperation of individuals. William Graham Sumner, the outstanding American apostle of laissez-faire, contended that the progress of civilization depended upon the selection process, which in turn depended upon unrestricted competition; and that competition was a law of nature which could no more be done away with than gravitation. The truth, however, is that the American capitalistic system is an artificial, man-made creation planned on the European model. It was the creation of the bourgeoisie. Sumner's extreme assumption that the forces in history were based on the process of unfettered competition led him to the logical and fatalistic conclusion that reform or any attempt to plan a society would be not only useless but foolish. The only solution to poverty and other social evils lay in the more energetic pursuit of the struggle. A look at the progress of the planned communist societies of the present day, as well as the enormous amount of both private and public planning in capitalistic societies today indicates the degree to which this tenet of laissez-faire missed the mark.

There are other barriers to the operation of laissez-faire. Some cultures frown on competition. In our present stage of development, the cost of entering business is a great barrier to competition. Then there are exclusive dealers, price guarantees, labor contracts, price controls, limiting franchises, licenses, and patents. More recently, military demands have come to exercise a powerful control over the allocation of capital, labor, and resources. In fact, the laissez-faire idea which operated so freely in America in the last half of last century is hedged in on every side, and competition in the old sense has largely been replaced by financial and organizational control by giant corporations, government, and organized labor, exercising power over nearly all aspects of the economy. This kind of change—if not a change in theory, at least a change in modus operandi —represents not change by a physical, purposeless evolution in society, but one of human evolution which can be definitely modified by purposive human action. It runs counter to the assumptions of social Darwinism, natural law, and laissez-faire individualism. These changes are obvious enough. Yet average middle-class Americans, if they think about it at all, still largely subscribe to the nineteenth-century ideology of laissez-faire. The transformation of most Americans from independent small property owners into dependent employees has not brought about a corresponding change in their way of thinking. Because the assumptions of laissez-faire were considered to be natural, they were, and still are, considered to be good. The objective truth is that men's efforts are mostly directed at creating an artificial environment which they must believe to be good.

Even though much in the basic ideology of laissez-faire has been repudiated, it does not mean that the operations in the marketplace have no effect on the economy; it does mean that they do not operate in strict accordance with the theory which purports to explain them. This would be relatively unimportant except for the fact that economic policies are shaped in accordance with them. The adherence to the classical or orthodox theory of economics is understandable in the light of its relationship to all formal economic theory. Adam Smith's *The Wealth of Nations* is the first, and still most significant attempt, to formulate a universal theory of how an economy operates. Much theory has been developed since then, but it has largely been modifications of his ideas or additions based on them.

In modified form the classical theory of economics still holds the stage in American society. It passed first into the "neoclassical" period in which mathematical formulations were used to represent the operation of supply and demand. These hypothetical formulations became so intricate and detached that they seemed to ordinary students more like exercises in plane geometry. Despite the increased widening of the gap between theory and reality, this mathematical framework gave economic theory a formidable appearance, and the emerging of what has been called the "economics of the firm" found extensive use for the mathematical formulations, and while it tended to make the theory still more unrealistic, it did make economics more operational.[1]

Keynes and the decline of laissez-faire. No discussion of economic theory is complete without some reference to John Maynard Keynes. Second only to Marx, Keynes has been more discussed and more criticized than any man dealing with economic theory. His ideas challenged contemporary economic theory as well as public policy. In brief, Keynes challenged the basic assumption that the economy could be depended upon to function automatically to ensure the optimum use of productive resources—full employment, proper distribution, and so on. He believed that men could control the course of history. This is in direct opposition to the laissez-faire position, whose defendants were many and important. The reason is clear. Freedom of the economic system from politics was the tenet most dear to the hearts of classical economists as well as to business. But Keynes was no radical reformer; he demanded no new institutions and made no attacks on private enterprise. He believed, in fact, that it was necessary to bring the government into the partnership in order to save private enterprise.

[1] A good resume of Keynesian theory can be found in Alvin H. Hansen, *The American Economy* (New York, McGraw-Hill, 1957), pp. 152–175.

Several other reasons were responsible in part for the decline of laissez-faire. Among the most important of these was the degree of social injustice in our economic life. The freedom of the individual was too often freedom of the strong to oppress the weak; freedom of contract was a snare and delusion to children of tender years working sixteen to eighteen hours a day in the factories; and the interest of each was not always the interest of all. The growth of giant corporations and the rude awakening to the realization that, in many areas, unrestrained competition did not exist brought discredit to the idea of effective competition as an adequate regulator of the economy. This was particularly true in regard to the field of public utilities. With the growth of specialization and economic interdependence, it was finally understood that the effective and uninterrupted functioning of the economy could not be left to the free dictates of laissez-faire individualists.

The depression of the 1930s brought to light better than anything else the failure of a self-regulating economy. Those who hang on to the classical conception of a self-regulating economy take refuge in the idea that it will work "in the long run." American society, however, is committed to the welfare state. The evidence is objectively verifiable. Both in Europe and America, governments in recent decades have taken more and more control over the economy. Especially beginning with the New Deal, the government has increasingly established itself as the dominant partner in a public-private economy. The evidences of this are found in the abandonment of the gold standard, the control over currency and credit, social security, the Employment Act of 1946, the extensive control over agriculture, the stock exchange, railroads, airlines, communications of all kinds, the Taft-Hartley Act, and dozens of other laws concerning every aspect of our economy. On the whole, if Americans oppose the government's intervention in these matters at all, it is largely a question of degree rather than opposition to the principle.

DOMINANCE OF THE CORPORATION

Today the most significant single factor in the lives of most of us is the corporation; and this is because the values in American life today are largely those of the corporation: we are dependent upon corporations for most everything we need. The social and political authority that was formerly centered in the individual or local unit is now largely transferred to corporate organizations—economic, political, religious, educational, philanthropic. This power has moved increasingly away from local control.

Development of the corporation. The corporation is not an end in itself, but a useful mechanism or device which has been developed to meet important needs in the industrial society. Its roots go back at least to the medieval guilds and boroughs, but its use in business goes back to the English overseas trading ventures of the sixteenth and seventeenth centuries. Colonial Americans exhibited considerable hostility toward business in general and toward chartered companies in particular. Even so, as the eighteenth century advanced, the number of business, educational, religious, and political incorporations continued to increase. Independence forced Americans to depend on their own organizations for the operation of business and the collection of capital. In fact, they were forced into business and industry despite their agrarian and commercial biases, and the states soon assumed the power to grant charters to corporations.

At this early time, the legal concept of the corporation, adopted from the British, was that a charter was a privilege, not a right. It was granted by a special act of the state legislature, and was considered to be an agent of the state, a matter of public welfare, rather than a private enterprise whose sole purpose was profit. Most charters of this time were for turnpikes, canals, docks, water, firefighting, and so on. In the course of time, business groups pressured state legislatures to make incorporation easier, and available to all legitimate businesses. The incorporation process by special act of the legislature frequently required the submission of elaborate petitions and long hearings, as well as political bargaining which was time-consuming and uncertain. In the end the businessmen won, and legislatures passed general acts for incorporation which permitted an officer of the state to issue a charter. Eventually incorporation was permitted for any purpose which was legitimate. During the decade prior to 1800, some three hundred business corporations were chartered.

Nature and advantages of the corporation. The corporation is one of the great social inventions of all times, and its development was essential to the industrialization process. We need to point to only three of its features to make clear why the corporation has become the accepted universal form for large businesses. First, incorporation is the chief avenue of collecting vast quantities of capital, the first requirement in setting up a business. The new corporation's stock is divided into transferrable shares which may be purchased in small and large quantities. A second point is the principle of limited liability. This makes it possible for an individual to invest in the stock of a corporation with his liability limited only to his investment. If this were not the case, a man might, in case of bankruptcy, lose everything he owned. A third reason for the importance of the corporation is that it is an artificial person "in the contemplation of law" which may sue and be sued, make contracts, own property, and generally do business. Only the corporation can raise the tremendous sums of capital which modern industry and business require, and also take the risks. The advantages in respect to "bigness" lie in the efficiency of large-scale operation, and the greater possibilities for research and development.

Degree of concentration. A few statistics reveal the great growth of corporations of all kinds and sizes. In 1964 there were 1,367,000 corporation income-tax returns filed. In 1962 there were 2,832 corporations with assets of over $50 million each; 69,596 with assets between $1 million and $50 million each; and 708,113 with assets of less than $100,000 each. Corporations were distributed as follows:

Agriculture	22,130	gas, sanitary	52,701
Mining	13,539	Wholesale and retail	388,852
Construction	90,604	Finance, insurance,	
Manufacturing	183,149	and real estate	359,229
Transportation, com-		Service	150,082
munication, electric,		Miscellaneous	7,756

Source: Table constructed from *Statistics of Income, 1962, Corporation Income Tax Returns* (Washington, U. S. Treasury Department, Internal Revenue Service, 1963), pp. 48–54.

The average person is affected one way or another by a hundred or more different corporations. The rise of corporation law as a specialized field of law illustrates the importance of the corporation in our society.

A few corporations have grown to be giants. In 1967 American Telephone and Telegraph Company had assets of $37.6 billion; Metropolitan Life Insurance Company had $24.6 billion; the Bank of America had $21.3 billion; General Motors had $13.3 billion; and in sales Great Atlantic and Pacific Tea company had $5.5 billion; Sears, Roebuck and Company had $7.3 billion; and J. C. Penney Company $2.7 billion.[2]

Although there are more than a million corporations in the United States, a relatively small number are extremely large. They do, however, produce most of the goods. It was estimated a few years ago that 150 corporations held 50 percent of all assets of manufacturing, and that two-thirds of all productive assets were owned by not more than 500 corporations.[3] In 1954 the 100 largest manufacturing corporations produced 30 percent of all manufacturing production. In 1958, manufacturing establishments employing four or less people constituted 35.4 percent of all establishments but employed only 1.4 percent of all employed in that industry. At the same time establishments employing over 100 people constituted only 9.1 percent of all establishments but employed 73 percent

[2] *Information Please Almanac for 1969* (New York, Dan Golenpaul Associates, 1968), p. 705.

[3] Gardner C. Means, *The Corporate Revolution in America* (New York, Crowell-Collier, 1962), p. 101.

of all employed in manufacturing; and establishments employing over 2,500 were only 0.2 percent, but employed 17.2 percent of all workers.[4] The concentration in manufacturing varies widely. The four largest corporations making telephone and telegraphic equipment have 92 percent of all employees in that industry. The four largest in motor vehicles and parts have 70 percent of all employees in that industry. Of 1,492 life insurance companies in 1963 with total assets of a little less than $150 billion,[5] the five largest had approximately $67 billion or 44 percent of the total assets. The lowest concentration is in the manufacturing of women's apparel where the four largest firms make only about 2 percent of the total.[6]

Despite the importance of the large corporations in America, most employees work in industries with a low degree of concentration. There has been little concentration in such areas as textiles and apparel, wood processing, and printing. In the service industries especially, the small unit predominates. Over 500,000 service establishments, more than half, are operated by persons who are self-employed. In this area of the economy there are many opportunities for those who want to run their own businesses. In 1968 there were nearly 14 million people engaged in wholesale and retail trade and about 10.5 million in services. This was approximately one third of the labor force.[7]

Ownership and control. The ownership in corporations is widely dispersed. The 1962 census of shareholders showed some 17 million in the United States. This represented all publicly owned issues of common and preferred stocks. In recent years probably a million are added annually. Many more people own interests indirectly through their investments in life insurance and pension funds. Most of the holdings are relatively small, but this does not make the corporations more democratic. In fact, the trend in the large corporations is increasingly toward management autonomy, self-perpetuating oligarchy. A well-known university professor of economics said in a public address recently that he was well paid as an adviser to a large corporation, that the directors and other officers were well paid, and that nobody gave a damn about the stockholder. This may be an exaggeration, but it does illustrate the point. Management control is based largely on the power to use the proxy machinery, and this can be done in most cases with a relatively small percent of the stock ownership. Some of the corporations usually cited to illustrate this are American Telephone and Telegraph, General Electric, and United States Steel.

[4] *The U. S. Book of Facts, Statistics and Information for 1966* (New York, Herald Tribune, 1965), p. 775.

[5] *Ibid.*, p. 477.

[6] *Ibid.*, p. 786.

[7] *Information Please* . . . , p. 701.

Most of the stock is bought and sold in the public market and is owned by investors whose main interest is in the dividends.

While there are laws to protect stockholders who do not participate in management, there is considerable doubt as to whether they adequately do the job. It is generally accepted that the corporate system has separated ownership from control in the same way that the factory system has separated labor from ownership. It is obvious that members of control groups get themselves elected to the boards of directors, appointed to the important offices at exorbitant salaries, sometimes voted stock options at much below the market price, and often award contracts on very favorable terms to companies in which they have great financial interests. Records of the Securities Exchange Commission and the courts indicate numerous efforts to milk the stockholders for the benefit of the control group. That the majority of the shareholders should be blamed for these abuses because of lack of interest is not justifiable. Americans are generally favorable to large-scale enterprise which requires tremendous capital, much of which is raised from small investors. These investors are interested in income from the investment, and usually have neither time nor inclination to study the operation of the corporation in which they own a small equity. The investor should be adequately protected. Loss of confidence of the investors in corporate industry wherever it happens is unfortunate, both for the investment-seeking public and for the capital-seeking corporation.

One of the amazing developments within the past few decades has to do with the participation of pension and life insurance funds in corporate affairs. Because of their more fixed obligations, insurance funds are invested mostly in other than common stock; whereas pension funds, whose long-term obligations are more indefinite, have invested about one-third of their assets in common-stock equities. This, of course, runs well into billions of dollars; that of the American Telephone and Telegraph Company alone is over $2 billion. About half of the pension funds is in the hands of insurance companies, most of the remainder is in the hands of New York banks. This raises the question of who controls the corporations. Pension funds are invested in the best corporation equities, and these are voting stocks. With the tremendous expansion in welfare and pension funds, one wonders whether the trustees of these funds may not be able to take over the control of corporations in which they have the investments. Sears, Roebuck is an example. The successful culmination of this trend would leave the traditional stockholder a mere pensioner, and management would find itself in the unusual position of being responsible to the trustees of its own employees' pension fund.

Whether we like it or not, the big corporation has become a dominant feature of American society, and history is not likely to reverse itself. Bureaucracy is a necessary condition of the large-scale operation whether it is in business, government, education, or religion. In fact, over 80 percent of all people employed, other than farmers, are in corporations of one kind or another. But Americans no longer oppose bigness either as individuals or as government policy, and they take the efficiency of the large-scale operation for granted. In fact, the destinies of most of us are bound up in corporations as factory workers, bureaucrats, managers, and so on, and we could not escape them if we wanted to.

The growth and complexity of corporate enterprise has not yet reached its maximum. According to the Federal Trade Commission, between 1950 and 1962, the share of manufacturing assets held by the 200 largest corporations increased from 46.7 percent to 54.6 percent of the total; the share held by the 100 largest increased from 36.6 to 45 percent. Also, during 1964, some 1,797 mergers occurred, and in manufacturing and mining alone, between 1959 and 1964, there were slightly less than 900. In 1964 alone, 207 such mergers involved companies with assets of at least $100 million. The number in this same category in 1955 was only 109. Corporations producing electrical machinery and chemicals accounted for 20 percent of all consolidations in the decade ending 1964.[8] The food industry is also an area of heavy concentration of mergers.

The largest corporations, however, are not only growing in size at the expense of smaller businesses, they are also increasing their ratio of sales and profits. The top 500 industrial corporations in the United States increased their share of all industrial sales from 62 percent in 1967 to 64 percent in 1968 and their profits from 72.8 to 74.4 percent. In 1968, the top 50 corporations had 48.4 percent of all sales for the group of 500, 30.9 percent of sales for all industrial corporations in the United States, 53.4 percent of earnings of the group, and 39.8 percent of earnings of all industrial corporations in the United States. The top 10, with 21 percent of the assets and 23 percent of the sales for the 500, increased their earnings by 21 percent, more than doubling the rate for the other 490, and employed 2.6 million or 19 percent of the 14 million employees for the group.[9]

The corporation and the individual. Two of the larger problems of corporate life involve its relationships to the individual and to the democratic process. Mass production long ago separated most people from the end products of their labor. The file clerk, the machine operator, and the technician can hardly take pride in the product they help to make. Or is it necessary that the individual find in his work something which is worth

---

[8] from reports by the U. S. Federal Trade Commission, quoted by Beaumont Enterprise in bulletins of April 20, 1965, and May 7, 1965 (Beaumont, Tex., Beaumont Enterprise, 1965).

[9] "The Fortune Directory of the 500 Largest Industrial Corporations," *Fortune* (May 15, 1969), pp. 166–202.

doing for its own sake? Most of us today are tied to our jobs. Promotion plans, pension plans, and other fringe benefits make changing jobs, especially to another company or business, more difficult. Employees who seek a greater part in the management of their enterprise, especially if they become stockholders, will find themselves still more tied to their jobs.

The complexity of the world today makes this the era of the little man in the big world. Today the individual counts for little in his labor union, his political party, or the corporation which employs him. The general idea seems to prevail "that you can't buck the system," you can only adjust to it. There is some justification for this because the large organizations are pretty well controlled by a small elite. But if the youth of today think the road to success is hard, they should read the stories of Galileo and Pasteur and all of the others who had to buck the system in the past. In fact, the possibility for rising in the world has probably never been better than it is today, and the avenues open to the individual are a thousand times more numerous than they have ever been before. Because they are so numerous and change so rapidly, the problem of finding these avenues is more difficult. Increasing automation and the use of computers may change all of this in two or three decades. No matter what the area, the most important channel to upward mobility is a sound education.

The complexity of the organization of all institutions today is discouraging to the individual who wants to participate in it. Political parties have difficulty in getting workers; in fact, they even have difficulty in getting people to vote. The churches and schools also have the same difficulty. Most people seem willing to let a small group run the policy-making machinery, whether political, religious, or educational. Corporations generally discourage political activity on the part of their employees. They encourage civic work instead. The close ties between government and business corporations is such that one's economic interests are generally a pretty good clue to his political attitudes. Democracy has always placed a premium on participation in the process of self-government, and this was predicated on the dispersion of power among many interacting groups of individuals joined together voluntarily to further their common interests. When the large corporations enter the scene, the picture is different. It makes no difference that there are laws against corporations contributing to political campaigns. There are no laws against individuals contributing in any amounts from funds they derive from corporations. This goes for labor organizations, too. That the influence of money adversely affects the democratic process seems a justifiable conclusion.

Given the present type of economic organization, large businesses of one kind or another and the powerful labor unions with huge funds at their disposal, it is doubtful that any other arrangement is possible. Because of the cost of campaigning, many state offices, and sometimes congressional seats, go unchallenged in the primaries. This is unfortunate. Certainly candidates who do not have vast financial support are at a serious disadvantage. To make an all-out state-wide campaign in California, New York, or Texas could cost as much as $5 million. The argument may be true that those who run for office with such backing do not commit themselves because they already believe what their supporters want them to. This only means that they are already committed to certain interest groups, and the situation is still the same. The democratic process presumes that those who represent the people are free agents. The Founding Fathers were concerned with political democracy, and we have never given much thought to democracy in other institutions—the family, the church, the corporation. It is probably time that the society consider how long political democracy can survive without a strong democratic underpinning in these other institutions.

The apathy of those who believe that it makes no difference cannot be justified in a democratic society. The democratic process is based on participation of the people. That the problems are difficult and that the individual is an insignificant unit in our vast system is not a valid argument for indifference. Unless a society is satisfied to be run by an elite oligarchy, the individual must participate.

CHANGING TECHNOLOGY AND ITS IMPLICATIONS

Marx's statement that changes in technology caused changes in the whole relationships of society and Veblen's idea that changes in technology were the chief causes of institutional change no longer seem radical. With the rise of capitalism came changes in the class structure. With the advent of farm machinery, the urban-industrial era was made possible. Capitalism has brought fundamental changes not only in the economic processes, but also in the scheme of values, in the educational aims and processes, and in the family. Changes in methods of production necessarily bring changes in the structure of society.

Our present industrial system rests solidly on the evolution of technology. Today we think of technology as science applied to industrial processes. But it is much more than this: it represents the shift of work from the hands of man to power-driven machines. In the areas where technology brought about an industrial society, it largely destroyed the power of the old landed aristocracy, brought into power the middle class, and created a powerful industrial labor class, the proletariat.

Changes or innovations in technology are much more likely to be accepted than are changes in values or beliefs. This is because changes in technology are directed toward satisfying specific scientific or industrial problems. This is not the case with values and beliefs. Technological innovations, especially those of serious magnitude, should not be uncritically accepted. The results are not always good. Technology as organized knowledge and techniques is of course neutral. It is the planned, or the unplanned, uses to which it is directed, or not directed, that can make a present-day society a paradise or a slave camp.

Development: hand tools to automation. Technological development includes all of the various technical ways in which man has increased his ability to produce the necessary things to sustain life—starting with learning how to start a fire and chip stone. Technology, as the accumulation of organized knowledge and techniques, has exerted a powerful influence upon the evolutionary progress of society.

When we speak of our technological society we think particularly of the changes which began in the eighteenth century—work done by hand is now done by power machines; equipment and specialization of tasks are standardized; articles are produced in a "continuous flow" from the assembly line; the stages of production are connected by automatic transfer machines run by remote control. These are only the latest changes resulting from automation.

The era of computers. Scientific developments along with the drive to industrialization in the United States in the three or four decades prior to World War I gave great emphasis to technological improvement, and after the war great strides were made in many industries. The first completely automatic hydroelectric station was built in 1917, and it continued to operate year after year with no permanent attendants. As early as 1915, General Electric had built a crude computer, by 1932 MIT had an analog computer, and many other companies were working in the field. With the vast scientific and technical knowledge gained in World War II, automation became practical on a large scale, and it has since made great inroads in the office, in industry, and in communications.

The period since World War II may be called the era of computers. The rapidity of development has made the first crude models antiques. The electronic computer performs "mental labor." It not only saves on labor costs but makes it possible to do some things which could not otherwise be done. It is said that a computer can work out weather predictions in three hours that would take one man with an adding machine three centuries. In fact, some of the machines can multiply 500,000 ten-digit numbers in one second. IBM's STRETCH can take two million instructions per second and perform seventy-five million computations in twenty-four hours.

UNIVAC, the first large-scale electronic computer, was delivered to the U. S. Bureau of the Census in April 1951; as late as 1955 there were only a few dozen electronic computers in the whole country. Up to this time computers were mostly experimental and custom designed. It was not until 1958 when transistors came into use that the computer production hit its stride. By 1960 it was estimated that there were around 11,000 in use, by the beginning of 1965 there were 22,000, and the production rate was 8,000 per year.[10] It appears that computers can be produced that can be used by almost anybody for almost any purpose. Offices use them for payroll preparation, customer billing, revenue accounting, and inventory control. Factories use computers to operate production machines, control machines, and material-handling equipment. The development in the field of communications is one of the marvels of the era, the most illustrious example of which is Telstar. In addition to the uses indicated above, a plant may be completely integrated by linking computers together in such a way that all of the functions from beginning to end can be performed with a single set of programmed instructions.

The prospects are that most large-scale office, industry, and communications businesses will become highly automated and that many medium and small businesses will also. The transistorized computer requires little or no air conditioning, is reasonably priced, and can be smaller than a desk. *Time* magazine reported that Philco had developed a computer for medical diagnosis that could read a patient's pulse, check his respiration, and produce an electrocardiogram within twenty seconds after he was seated. They also reported that in 1964 there were 21 computer companies employing 650,000 people and with sales of $5 billion. These computers ranged in price from $8,800 to $4.3 million and in weight from 59 pounds to 180,000 pounds.[11] A problem arises with the replacement of workers by machines. The expanding population requires over a million new jobs a year—the reduction in the number of jobs becomes a moral as well as an economic problem.

The effects of automation on employment are vigorously debated. Most labor leaders say that it eliminates jobs. Most business leaders contend that it does not, at least in the long run. Many statistics are quoted to show the number of job displacements when firms have introduced automated machines. There is no doubt that jobs are eliminated. In fact, in 1962, there were 700,000 fewer factory production and maintenance jobs than at the close of the Korean War. Employment in coal mining fell by 46 percent between 1947 and 1954. The poverty in Appalachia is evidence of our failure to cope with the problem. The unanswered question is whether in the long run new jobs in equal or greater numbers will result from the change. Even if they do, it will still be true that doing the same work within a given firm will require less workers. While there are some things that cannot be done except by automation, most of the use of automation is "labor saving." In the past, the greatest production cost were wages paid to labor. Thomas J. Watson, Jr., president of

10 *Time Magazine* (April 2, 1965), p. 86.
11 *Ibid.*

IBM, says that technological changes and automation are labor-saving processes, that they do displace people, and that this is one of their purposes. To the 600,000 railroad employees, the 300,000 miners, and the thousands in the automobile and meat-packing industries who have lost their jobs, any argument over whether they are unemployed or only displaced is purely academic. It is unfortunate, especially with the efforts being made to slow down the economy, that President Nixon's welfare proposals to Congress provide no plans for the creation of new jobs.

Automation and the use of computers is an extremely significant factor in the problem of having enough jobs for our future labor force, which is expanding at the rate of over a million a year. The author remembers some twenty-five years ago when Henry Wallace said that we should start thinking in terms of a labor force of 60 million. He was castigated on every side, and the mildest thing he was called was a dreamer. In June 1968, the civilian labor force was 79 million. In 1945 it was about 54 million. The specter that haunts people is the fear that we may come to the point where we will have millions entering the labor market for whom there are no jobs at all. To most Americans, there is nothing more dismal than the prospect of mass unemployment or the relief rolls. How devastating unemployment can be is attested to by those who witnessed the 1930s or by those who have seen some of the depressed areas of the present. An at-home example of displacement is the American farm. Improved farm technology drove millions from the country to the city. The farm tractor not only replaced the mule, it also displaced most of the farm employees. Fifty years ago 54 percent of the population were farmers. In 1967 it was less than 6 percent and that was still too many. Many poor whites and more poor Negroes were pushed out of the rural areas and drifted to the cities in search of a means of livelihood. Unfortunately, they were mostly uneducated and unskilled, and they arrived at a time when technology was taking over the only kind of work they could do. They still constitute a great part of our serious unemployment.

Automation and employment. Technology is not the only factor involved in the employment equation. The fact that in recent years we have had a reduction in unemployment can be misleading unless we are aware of certain facts. We have mentioned the military as an important part of the present power structure. In 1963, defense-related employment amounted to 6.7 million people. Of these about 3.8 million or 54.8 percent were federal; 1 million, civilian; and 3 million or 44.2 percent, in private industry. Another factor in the growth in the American economy is military expenditures. In 1964, the net value of military procurement was $28.8 billion and of this sum $26.2 billion was spent with business firms. At the same time the military had available for obligation $65.2 billion, and available for expenditure $81.1 billion. Such tremendous expenditures obviously affect the growth of the economy as well as the employment. Is this to become a permanent part of our economy? If it does not, what will happen?

Another factor which disguises the effects of change due to increased technology has been the recent rapid growth of the economy. In 1940 the GNP was $100 billion; in 1950 it was $284 billion; in 1960 it was $502 billion[12]; and by mid-1968 it was over $850 billion.[13] This rapid growth, especially since 1960, means that new jobs were created faster than jobs were lost by improved technology. This situation points up the tremendous significance of rapid economic growth, and at the same time raises the specter of unemployment in case we cannot maintain this growth. A few ratios may help to clarify this growth rate. Between 1950 and 1960 the GNP increased by 176 percent while the population increased only 12 percent. Between 1960 and 1964 the GNP increased by 24 percent while the population increased by only 7 percent. For the period 1940 to 1964 the GNP increased over 500 percent while the population increased by 69 percent. During most of this time we had serious unemployment. With the growth of population requiring more jobs and the increasing automation eliminating jobs, the question arises as to how far the economy can be expanded to take care of the employment problem.

Probably most misleading is the claim of those who automate that they have not replaced any employees. The problem is not so much how many have been fired as how many have not been hired. Through the policy of encouraging early retirement and making no replacements for those who retire, reductions are made without replacing many, sometimes none. This policy obviously reduces the number of people employed. As a large firm improves its technology over the years, it may continue to reduce its work force while it increases its output. It is this long-run attrition of jobs which is the serious problem.

That automation will continue at an increasing rate there is little doubt, but what the consequences of such drastic change will be are less certain. There is no question that big businesses will become almost completely automated, and it appears that medium and small businesses will be to a much greater extent than was formerly believed. Like all other important innovations automation will, no doubt, be extended to more and more areas until it becomes as common as other technological innovations. In 1962 in *A Report to the Center for the Study of Democratic Institutions,* Donald N. Michael made some dire predictions from what he called "cybernation." The term was used to refer to both automation and computer technology. Looking forward twenty years he envisioned a society in which machines will have taken over, a new class which he

---

[12] *The U. S. Book of Facts . . . ,* pp. 324–325.
[13] *Information Please . . . ,* p. 695.

called "cyberneticians," a large portion of the people engaged in endless public tasks of the welfare state, the masses troubled by the problems of leisure and searching for something in which to believe and to which to aspire. He envisioned greatly changed attitudes toward work, play, and social responsibility, the centralization of authority and a governing elite; and a blandly accepting, even indifferent, public. He concluded that we must develop a new "logic" for this new society. If we do not, we face frustration and pointlessness that may drive us to a war of desperation, subconsciously intended to destroy our sophisticated technology.[14] While Michael's report created something of a sensation, it contained little that could not be found in the literature of the preceding fifteen years. Norbert Wiener, author of *Cybernetics*[15] and one of the early authorities on automation, writing in *Science* in the issue of May 6, 1960, said that the problem being faced was a moral one and very close to one of the great problems of slavery. By the beginning of 1968 some of the earlier fears of automation had subsided because of the low level of unemployment. But whether this was due to an abnormal demand for labor because of the war in Vietnam remains to be seen.

Advantages and problems of automation. The advantages of automation are well known. A second industrial revolution is taking place and its results may affect our lives even more than the first. Our productive capacity is the most astonishing feat in the annals of economic history. The problem is one of attempting to reap the advantages of improved technology while avoiding the problems it creates. Technology, however, does nothing except what people make it do. This means that the problems are those of planning, or lack of planning. Employers have tried to ease the transition to automation through the policy of "not firing but not hiring." But automation is still in its adolescence and the problem of unemployment has been, basically, disguised.

Some of the results of automation are more obvious. There are the "depressed areas" with which the Area Redevelopment Act of 1961 is designed to deal. One of the purposes of this act is to retrain those who are unemployed. It is clear that automation hits hardest the unskilled and the semi-skilled. The retraining of this group is at best difficult, and the prospects for success are limited because of the generally low level of education. For the entire country the proportion of the manual workers declined 4 percent in the decade prior to 1960 despite a population gain of 28 million. In recent years membership in labor unions has decreased even while one million people per year were added to the labor force.

[14] Donald N. Michael, *Cybernation: The Silent Conquest* (Santa Barbara, Cal., Center for the Study of Democratic Institutions, 1962), pp. 44–46.

[15] *Cybernetics, or Control and Communication in the Animal and Machine* (New York, Wiley, 1948).

Automation is also invading white-collar work, and one can easily predict that all types of jobs that can be made routine will become automated. This will change many types of work, but what it will do in regard to the number of employees is still uncertain.

Automation will also have its impact on management. As automation takes over more and more of the work done by unskilled and white-collar groups, the group Donald N. Michael called "cyberneticians"—programmers, research analysts, coordinators—are finding their place within the ranks of top management.[16] There are those who believe that this could break the traditional promotional scheme of the rising class of middle management and leave them stranded as a white-collar proletariat. The new class of specialists, called by Vance Packard "the diploma elite," would enter the organization at the middle or upper levels because they have the necessary expensive and adequate formal education. Expressed in different terms, there are those who believe that a professional, technical, managerial class composed of a young, highly educated, affluent group will become the center of the power structure in the United States. This point of view has been expressed by Peter F. Drucker, eminent authority in the field, J. C. Warner, president emeritus of Carnegie Institute of Technology, and others. This new group would displace labor, the farm bloc, and big business as the power center. As far as management is concerned, it appears that greater authority in planning and policy making will be centered in the top-level specialist-manager group, and that this will separate this group more sharply from middle management.

The industrial revolution brought in its wake dire conditions of poverty, misery, and human degradation to some segments of society. The current technological revolution has done the same thing in the "depressed areas." What the future holds in store in this respect depends upon the degree of planning which precedes the change to automation. Nobody in this country, not even the unions, the organizations that feel the adverse consequences of automation most, oppose automation. Decisions today tend to be based on information supplied by departments of research and development, marketing, computer programming, accounting, legal, engineering, and on outside specialist-consultants. Labor organizations have developed to the point that their leadership depends on specialists in the same areas as management. Unions are trying to attract people employed in jobs created by automation, and management is trying to maintain its initiative in all aspects of preparing for the transition to automation. The hope for smooth adjustment as automation continues rests on the cooperation and statesmanship of these groups in planning and preparing for the change. No major union opposed automation per se and many welcomed it. Studies indicate that the most successful transi-

16 Michael, *op. cit.,* pp. 18–20.

tions to automation result when workers have played a major role. Among the things about which workers want to be informed are the approximate date of change, the nature of new assignments, the expected pay scale, and what provisions will be made for employees affected by the transition. Lack of knowledge of what is going on has led to exaggerated fear and resentment; prior consultation has minimized both unemployment and employee dissatisfaction.

With the most cooperative efforts in the process of changing over to automation, however, there will still be the problem of worker displacement. To those displaced it is unemployment. Many different plans have been devised to meet this problem. Among these have been early retirement benefits, retraining programs, and numerous means of raising funds to aid their programs. Among the fund-raising schemes are Kaiser Steel's profit-sharing plan, U. S. Industries' "Dues" plan based on sales of machines, the United Mine Workers' Welfare Fund derived from a royalty of forty cents a ton on coal, and the American Federation of Musicians' royalty payment on "canned" music. The problem of all of these is that the funds are inadequate to do all of the things that are needed to be done. They do, however, help in the adjustment of what would otherwise be a much worse problem, and they express an attitude of responsibility of both management and labor which is essential to the survival of the free enterprise system. The giant corporations and labor unions of today can no longer ignore the public welfare.

Government involvement. Government has always been involved in the economy in one way or another. It has promoted innovation and change in technology through such devices as copyrights and patents, state agricultural colleges, and vocational education. With the New Deal, the federal government began to accept responsibility for those individuals who could not make their own way in our disrupted economy. It also began programs to prevent others from falling into the indigent class. By the Employment Act of 1946, the government attempted to ensure a high level of employment, and by the Area Redevelopment Act of 1961, it accepted responsibility for problem areas. These and dozens of other acts of Congress have established the responsibility of the government in dealing with problems within the economy, problems of a general as well as more specific nature. Government intervention in the economy is a fait accompli. The extent to which government intervention in the economy is desirable is still debatable, but the fact of its intervention is not. That it will continue and increase seems inevitable. Much planning at the national level is done in a haphazard and uncoordinated way. Much is done in regard to general conservation of our natural resources, agriculture, the railroads, airways, television and radio, stock exchanges, money and banking, the oil industry, water conservation and dozens of other areas. But there are so many programs that they cause a tremendous amount of confusion and duplication of effort and too few improvements.

The possibility of complete and sudden economic collapse such as we had in the 1930s with 25 percent of the work force unemployed, many others on reduced employment and nearly everybody with greatly reduced income has been greatly reduced by many built-in stabilizers. The unemployment problem today is different. It is not just concern for the 3 or 4 percent unemployed and their dependents, but also one of the increasingly large numbers of permanently unemployed. There are thousands of families who have hardly known any way of life except on relief. These people, through no fault of their own, are the main burden of the relief rolls, and they add very little to the economic value of society. Furthermore, their children furnish a disproportionate number of those who will be a future burden on society. Some already are. It is neither morally justifiable nor economically expedient for an affluent society to permit such pockets of poverty and degradation to exist. Our society can well afford to take whatever action is necessary to eliminate this situation. Most of the nations of Western Europe with much less wealth and resources have not permitted such situations to develop. Although the government has taken some steps to remedy the situation, the steps are so far inadequate.

Many outstanding scholars are disturbed and fearful of the outcome of the present transformation through which American society is going. As we have already indicated, many believe we are subject to the control of some kind of "power elite," and most all are concerned about the American democratic way of life because of the growing bureaucratic structures of government and industry.

The solution to the problem of the economic security of the individual is difficult and can be accomplished only by the efforts of labor, management, and government. The alternative to cooperation is for government to take over completely.

In 1964 Congress authorized the National Commission on Technology, Automation, and Economic Progress to study economic trends of the next decade. Their report, made in February 1966, shows a surprising cooperation and consensus of business leaders such as Thomas J. Watson, Jr., Patrick E. Haggerty, and Philip Sporn, and such labor leaders as Walter P. Reuther, Joseph A. Beirne, and Albert J. Hayes. The commission included other business, education, and professional members, and a competent staff. They estimated that within the next decade farm employment would decline by around a million and that other employment would increase by over 19 million leaving a net employment gain of 18.3 million. The "goods producing" industries would have a moderate increase of 17 percent while the "service producing" sector including trade, finance, government, transportation, and public utilities would increase by 38 percent. Looked at as a whole the "goods" sector would decline from 41 to 36 percent and the "service" sector would increase from 59 to 64 percent by 1975. The greatest growth would be in the following: professional, technical, and kindred, 54 percent; clerical and kindred, 37 percent, service workers, 35 percent; and sales workers, 30 percent. If nonwhites continue to hold the same proportion of jobs in each occupation as in 1964, the nonwhite unemployment rate in 1975 will be five times that for the labor force as a whole. If present opportunities for younger workers continue on the same basis, there will be fewer jobs than workers seeking work.

The report places the responsibility for facilitating adjustment to change squarely on the shoulders of labor and management, designating government's role as that of providing a favorable environment and co-operating when needed. An adequate adjustment program should require (1) that displaced workers should be offered equivalent alternative jobs or the training or education requisite to obtain such jobs; (2) that they should be guaranteed adequate financial security while searching for a job or while in training; (3) that they should be given financial assistance to permit them to relocate their families if this becomes necessary; and (4) that they should be protected against forfeiture of earned security rights such as retirement and insurance.

After placing major responsibility on management and labor in matters of adjusting to change in the economy, the report recommended government involvement to a much greater extent than at present. It recommended the use of tax reduction and increased federal spending when the economy needs stimulation. It also recommended that the Neighborhood Youth Corps be expanded and made applicable to public-service areas, where important social needs are inadequately met. This would include such areas as medical and health services, educational institutions, national beautification, welfare, home care, public protection, urban renewal, and sanitation. It was estimated that this would create 5.3 million new jobs. The finances for such projects would be largely from the federal government but the administration would be by state and local agencies. This program would be directed at the permanent or "hard core" unemployment. It further recommended (1) a federal guarantee of security to every American family by setting a minimum family income, (2) a guarantee of two years of college to every qualified young person, (3) that the Federal Reserve bank in each district provide leadership for economic development activities in its region. The Commission placed its greatest emphasis on education, and on the development of the individual as a responsible citizen.

This report may not be the blueprint for national planning, but it is significant because:

1. It represents the thinking of a new generation of leaders in business and labor. This generation accepts the point of view that the welfare of society is also their own welfare and that, as centers of the power structure, they cannot ignore their responsibility.

2. It represents a change in philosophy. The recognition of the interdependence of all important economic areas gives them the status of quasi-public utilities. Hopefully, the spirit of cooperation will replace the "law of the jungle" approach of the past.

3. The report is the kind of blueprint on which a national planning program could be based. There are in existence programs of the kind recommended, but government programs are uncoordinated, they have no overall goals or administration. In a society which subscribes to the principle of free private enterprise but where government is inevitably involved in every aspect of the economy, it would seem to make sense that an overall program placing responsibility largely on management and labor with the aid of government in making explicit the goals, relationships, and processes involved would be desirable.

4. Many of those who oppose national planning think of it as authoritarian. But there is no reason why a national plan could not be adopted and run by democratic processes. To the experts in administration and management, planning is essential to success. Planning for the individual, the city, the corporation, and the state is commendable. Planning for the national economy is just as essential. In fact, in a world in which planned totalitarian states predominate, national planning in the democracies may be essential to survival.

THE OPERATIONAL ECONOMY

From a policy of laissez-faire, characteristic of the American policies at least until the turn of the century, we have come to a welfare policy. From the position of denial of governmental responsibility for the economy, we have moved to the opposite pole where the public expects, at least in emergencies, that the government will take most of the responsibility. The importance of the New Deal was not in its specific welfare programs, most of which were temporary, but in the acceptance of the idea of permanent government intervention in the economy. This became a bi-partisan policy when former President Eisenhower announced his support of full employment as envisioned in the Employment Act of 1946. Today everybody expects the President and Congress, regardless of party affiliation, to do the same.

The welfare state. The welfare state is not socialism. Socialism is government ownership and operation of the instruments of production and economic services; it is essentially an economic concept rather than a political one. Public enterprise has had no significant growth in the United States. The welfare state is concerned with the use of the monetary and fiscal policies to control the fluctuations in the economy and to promote the welfare of the less fortunate. At present the government spends tremendous sums of money, but private enterprise does most of the work. Through farm subsidies, veterans programs, highway funds, education funds, social security, and dozens of other programs, the government makes a major contribution to the economy and to production. Through monetary operations, especially the Federal Reserve System, the government attempts to manipulate money and credit so as to level out business fluctuations. It regulates the stock markets for the same reason. More recently, a policy of reducing or raising taxes for the same purpose has been accepted. The fiscal policy, which has to do with the budget and annual expenditures, is also important to the economy. The higher the budget, the greater the amount of money flushed into the economy. The fiscal policy has not, however, been used directly to any large extent to regulate the fluctuations in the economy. In case of a serious depression, no doubt the President would ask and Congress would grant large sums of money to relieve suffering and stimulate business. Not too long ago there was a continuous and vociferous clamor to pay off the huge national debt, and to stop deficit spending by balancing the budget. Apparently we have decided that these are not so important as long as we can keep the economy in high gear. The emphasis is on economic growth as the means to full employment and a generally higher standard of living, and for this we expect the government to take the major responsibility.

While Americans generally disavow Keynesian economic theory, they demand it operationally from the federal administration and from Congress. The chief significance of Keynes' work was his attack on the belief that the economy tends to operate automatically to the best advantage of society. It was an attack on the freedom of the economic system from politics. The objective facts indicate that the government and the economy cannot operate separately and that government is increasingly in the seat of power. The real question is the extent to which control will be carried. The strong opposition of business to the welfare state is understandable. An economy that is self-governing is one in which businessmen have no rivals except among themselves. They feared that their authority might be challenged, and they were right. As we have already pointed out, we have a regulated or public-private economy. In fact, we have accepted, mostly without being conscious of it, the idea that economic stability is the major function of government.

Since World War II, the American economy has demonstrated what can be achieved under the pressure of adequate demand. This has been, in part, due to welfare and military spending. The welfare idea is the basis of a great many of the built-in stabilizers such as the progressive income tax, farm subsidies, social security, and government lending and guaranteeing. The great depression demonstrated visibly the inability of the self-governing economy to meet such emergencies. The facts were sufficient to justify abandoning the ideas as a practical operating policy, but not enough to change the belief in the theory. Americans go on believing in the shibboleths of laissez-faire while they participate in the welfare state.

Let us look at the extent to which the United States government is involved in the economy through expenditures alone. In 1964 the government was involved in welfare expenditure programs as indicated below:

	Federal	State & Local	Total
Social insurance	$20,523,000,000	$6,323,000,000	$26,846,000,000
Public aid	3,161,000,000	2,404,800,000	5,565,800,000
Health and medical	2,742,300,000	3,335,600,000	6,078,900,000
Other welfare services	608,300,000	1,326,500,000	1,934,800,000
Veterans' programs	5,647,200,000	20,000,000	5,667,200,000
Education	2,207,000,000	22,440,000,000	24,647,000,000
Public housing	207,400,000	64,500,000	271,900,000
Totals	35,096,200,000	35,914,400,000	71,010,600,000

Note: Federal and state and local equaled 5.8 percent and 6.0 percent respectively or a total of 11.8 percent of the gross national product, and 29.2 percent for the federal and 58 percent for state and local expenditures for all purposes.
Source: Social Security Bulletin, Vol. 27 (Oct. 1964), pp. 6–7.

In 1960, about 25 million persons—veterans and members of the armed forces and the Coast Guard, Indians, and federal prisoners—received federal medical care. This, of course, pre-dates Medicare by six years. Also, in 1960, over 20 million people were recipients of social welfare benefits from the federal government: 15 million were retired workers and their dependents; 2.4 million were elderly persons on relief; 1.1 million were disabled persons; 1.9 million were veterans or their families; 0.6 million were retired civil servants; 100,000 were students who were financing their college education with federal loans. This does not include 13.5 million school children who participated in the federal lunch program, nor 2.5 million unemployed receiving benefits from state programs partly financed by federal aid. Neither does it include any state programs not partly financed by federal aid. Despite the great increase in expenditure, the total cost of federal, state, and local welfare including education fell from over 50 percent of all government expenditures in 1935 to about 35 percent in 1960. State and local expenditures accounted for about 55 percent of the total in both 1935 and 1960.

In the decade 1955–1965 government expenditures, excluding education, jumped from about $20 billion to $46 billion. The most rapid rise was in social insurance, due to the maturing of the social security program. During this decade the GNP increased by 62 percent. Most of the programs listed above climbed faster than the GNP. Even with these impressive amounts for welfare, we were outranked by all Western European countries, most of whom spent two or three times as great a percentage of their GNP on welfare as we did. For 1963 and 1964, the United States committed 6 percent of its GNP to welfare. In 1963, the Organization for European Economic Cooperation reported that only Portugal had a poorer welfare record than the United States. The International Labour Office, reporting data on social security expenditures including health insurance and health service programs in 1963, rated all Western European countries above the United States. The addition of private welfare expenditures, in which the United States leads, would not appreciably change the picture. We outranked only the poorer countries in Asia and Africa. We are indeed a "reluctant welfare state."

It might be thought that our affluent society has little need for welfare support. Such is not the case. The Conference on Economic Progress in 1962 reported that there were, in 1960, some 10.5 million families with 34 million people whose income was less than $4,000 annually. There were an additional 10.5 million families of some 37 million people with incomes between $4,000 and $6,000 annually. Classified with the first group were some 4 million unattached individuals, and with the latter, 2 million. The first group was classified as living in poverty and the latter in deprivation.[17] *Time* magazine for May 13, 1966, taking the Conference on Economic Progress's poverty line of $3,130 per family annually, stated the number in poverty at 32 million, people who were living in the rural backwaters and urban ghettos. Of these, 30 percent were nonwhite. This 30 percent represented more than half the total nonwhite population, mostly Negroes. Of the 32 million poor people, slightly less than 14 million were children under fifteen years of age. This figure also represented one-fourth of the aged and half of all families headed by women. Furthermore, 7.5 million of these Americans lived in rat-infested tenements; 6 million subsisted on free government surpluses; 1,500 died annually from malnutrition; and almost all of the nation's 11 million functional illiterates are relegated for life to the precarious ranks of the poor.

The change in the attitude of Americans within the past few years on the subject of government and the economy has been nothing short of fantastic. In the 1960 presidential campaign when the Peace Corps idea was first presented, it was regarded generally as a political gimmick, an unrealistic and impractical dream. Although it is a foreign welfare program, it captured the imagination not only of American youth, but of the whole country. Those who had accused the younger generation of being excessively selfish, materialistic, and security-minded were forced to re-

[17] *Poverty and Deprivation in the United States* (Washington, Conference of Economic Progress, 1962), pp. 22, 29.

vise their evaluation. The same idealistic spirit pervaded the "domestic peace corps," VISTA. The passage of the federal aid to education bill and Medicare were recent great extentions into the welfare area. Most significant, as a program for relieving a great deal of the present need for welfare programs, was the "war on poverty."

The antipoverty program or OEO (Office of Economic Opportunity) was designed to strike at the roots of poverty rather than to treat its symptoms. It was aimed at the young who are more trainable and who would benefit more in the long run. Most of the welfare programs have not reached those who most needed them. Farm subsidies have mostly enriched the prosperous, public housing has not been much help to the very poor, and the majority of the poor reap no benefits from social security and unemployment insurance. Critics of all categories have made the most of its mistakes, and some have offered substitutes. One substitute which has at least some support is a guaranteed minimum annual income. But this type of program like many others would leave untouched the most basic roots of the problem. It is not a program to make individuals self-sustaining. The self-respect and dignity of the individual demand that he be able to support himself and his family. The guaranteed minimum annual income for the permanently disabled and other such unfortunates might not be objectionable provided the major welfare emphasis is always on programs for making every individual who is capable of it self-supporting.

President Nixon's welfare proposals to Congress in August 1969 intended to reshuffle OEO agencies, not to overhaul them to make them a really effective force in the attack on poverty. If enacted, they would shift operating authority to already existing agencies, leaving OEO the responsibility for research and development of new programs only. Thus the one program designed to strike at the roots of poverty seems on the way out. The concentration of all federal agencies dealing with poverty into one with authority and commitment to the task seems as far away as ever. Instead, it appears that the bitter power struggle between the competing agencies will be permitted to go on at the expense of the poor in our society.

One of the justifiable criticisms of the antipoverty programs is the lack of adequate administration. OEO has direct administration over three of eight major antipoverty programs and supervision over the others at the federal, state, and local levels. The welfare program, if it can be called a program, is scattered throughout the administrative branch of government. According to *Time,* some 200 federal projects are administered by 21 different federal agencies. Despite the criticism, however, most of the antipoverty programs, especially the Neighborhood Youth Corps and Head Start, have been received well enough by the public for Congress to continue to appropriate money for their operation. If we are serious about abolishing poverty in American society, it is prudent to concentrate on the young. For the illiterate adults as well as those of low level education, the prospects of successful training are poor. It is obvious that the United States is a welfare state and that there is little serious objection to it. Most of the objection is to particular programs which affect certain groups adversely, and not to the policy as a whole.

The ideal of the welfare state is a decent standard of living for every individual. Full employment has top priority of the social goals to be supported by public policy. The expenditure of public funds for this purpose implies a redistribution of income and an equal opportunity for all. Of course this promise is nowhere fulfilled, and any argument that welfare programs redistribute wealth have to be made specific. Such federal programs as public housing, public assistance, and medical aid, which are not based on social security, are the most egalitarian. Those programs based on social insurance are least egalitarian. Social insurance takes a larger proportion of the income of the poor than of the well-to-do. Since this type of program is increasingly a greater part of the total, the effect on the redistribution of income is insignificant. Social security and unemployment insurance, however, do not depend on this for their justification. They are justifiable on the grounds of humanitarianism and individual and family security.

Problems of growth and stability. Changes in technology have always been a major source of change in government, the family, and other institutions, as well as the economy. With only 6 percent of the labor force employed on the farm, the vast majority of Americans are completely divorced from any possible way of sustaining life should they be thrown completely on their own resources. This makes job security the number one concern of everyone.

A study of the business cycle shows that, when left to its own automatic operation, the American economy has fluctuated from wild expansion to deep depression. The worst of the depression of the 1930s left some one-fourth of the labor force unemployed. This is only part of the picture. There were millions who were under-employed, and many women, students, and others who were not considered unemployed but who would have worked had jobs been available. Those in our affluent society who have never faced having a family without food and being without a job, money, or credit, and with little prospect for any kind of work, cannot place a realistic value on the importance of a job. The haunting fear of unemployment such as we had in the 1930s forces those in responsible positions in our government to be on the alert to keep the economy growing in order to provide as many jobs as possible. Because of this push toward economic growth, we have had continuously rising prices, or creeping inflation, which creates another serious problem.

For over a century and a half prior to 1960, the American economy

had grown at a rate of over 3 percent a year; the rate of increase had declined from about 4 percent to about 3 percent, while the population
increase had declined from over 2.5 percent to a little over 1.5 percent.
From 1946 to 1962, the average annual growth rate was 3.3 percent, or
a more significant figure, an annual rate of 1.54 percent in proportion to
our population. At the same time, the per capita production doubled.
This long-run picture of the growth rate of the American economy shows
why the per capita income of Americans is the highest in the world.

Between 1960 and 1965, the GNP increased from about $500 billion
to $675 billion, while between 1961 and March 1966, the unemployment
rate was reduced from 7 percent to 3.7 percent, with labor shortages in
some areas. In the past, unemployment has fluctuated widely. It was approximately 1 percent in 1905; 9 percent in 1907; 1.5 percent in 1916;
12 percent in 1922; 2 percent in 1926; 25 percent in 1933; 2 percent in
1944. Over a long period of time there has been a hard core of unemployed; they are probably mostly unemployable because of lack of education or skills or because of physical handicap. This so-called "acceptable"
unemployment ranges between 2.5 and 3 percent.

Stabilization is a slippery concept because there is no widely accepted
definition and because it is a dynamic process—an unstable equilibrium.
It means that the variable factors will fluctuate within certain recognized
guidelines. A stable economy is one in which the relationships between
production, unemployment, and prices are not so drastically changed as
to create serious problems of overproduction, unemployment, or inflation. By making a gradual rather than an abrupt and complete change
to automation without regard to consequences, private enterprise has
created a much smaller labor displacement problem than would otherwise have resulted; and of course the government has many programs to
promote the growth of business and industry to insure employment and
greater economic well-being.

Because of the rapid growth in American population and the loss of
jobs due to automation, the problem of the rate of growth of the economy
is crucial. The results of the recent rapid growth are revealing. In 1965
the GNP reached $675 billion; the rate of increase for the year was 7.5
percent as compared with an average of 3.8 percent for the period 1946–
1957. Private spending in 1965 for new plant and equipment rose 15.5
percent from a previous year record. Despite the loss of thousands of jobs
to automation and a residue of those least employable, the rate of unemployment dropped to 3.7 percent with labor shortages in some areas.

Efforts to control the business cycle. Fluctuations in the business cycle are
nothing new to American history. Recessions have occurred with considerable regularity every few years, as have depressions or panics. This
was as true when America was a rural society as it is today. Serious de-

pressions in an industrial society, however, are much more devastating because so few people have any means of sustaining life when thrown completely on their own resources. Serious panics or depressions have occurred in 1785, 1819, 1837, 1857, 1873, 1893, 1907, and 1929. Several smaller fluctuations in the business cycle have occurred between these more severe fluctuations. Depressions have always closed factories and businesses, brought unemployment and human deprivation, bankruptcies and general loss in all kinds of wealth. But never had America experienced anything like the results of the stock market crash of October 1929. It shocked the whole country and its repercussions were felt throughout the whole world. Property values of all kinds melted away; businesses were destroyed; one-sixth of the population was dependent upon public support; between one-fourth and one-third of the labor force was unemployed; and the GNP fell from $104 billion to $55 billion. The human suffering and personal indignity forced on a proud people were not only humiliating but morally and spiritually degrading. If this was the way a self-regulating economy worked, Americans would have no more of it.

The depression of the 1930s was severe and recovery was slow. Before it was completed, another one hit, raising the unemployment rate from 14.3 percent in 1937 to 19 percent in 1938. In fact the unemployment rate for the whole decade prior to 1941 was never under 14.3 percent. Because of the unsatisfactory operation of the economy, it was natural that people turned to the government to correct it. Although a great many of the New Deal relief measures were temporary, some permanent built-in stabilizers were enacted. Their purpose was to sustain the spendable income. Among these are the social security programs, farm programs, guaranteed bank deposits, collective bargaining, a great number of lending and insuring operations of the government, and housing programs. The graduated income tax is also in this category. But a stabilization policy cannot be built solely on these. The government must be prepared to act in order to prevent a serious drop in economic activities from developing into a serious depression. For this purpose "discretionary" stabilizers have also become a matter of government policy. The best known is the Federal Reserve System which in the past fifteen years has returned to its traditional purpose of attempting to moderate both expansions and contractions in the economy in an effort to maintain price stability. Because economic expansion normally leads to greater production and greater profits as well as increased employment, efforts of the Federal Reserve System to check expansion are sometimes criticized by businessmen, politicians, and labor organizations.

The results of World War II in relieving the unemployment and economic stagnation which had dominated our economy for a dozen years were proof enough for most Americans that the government could raise the level of the national income by its own expenditures. In other words, they came to accept Keynesian economics in practice. Having accepted the idea that the government could do something to regulate the fluctuations—recessions, depressions, inflation—in the business cycle, regulation has become a matter of public policy. Even though the timing and methods may be debated, the principle of manipulating the monetary and fiscal policies to maintain a stable economy is generally accepted. In addition to these, a Public Works Planning Unit has been established within the federal government. This agency has the responsibility of preparing projects to be used in case they are needed. More recently the government has resorted to the use of tax measures for the same purpose. This policy of attempting to sustain purchasing power is a change of approach from emphasizing production to emphasizing consumption as a means of sustaining stability. It is the "pump priming" idea which was so much criticized during the 1930s. It failed then because the application was not on a massive scale. The size of the government's spending commitments today makes the possibility of success of such a program much more feasible.

The problem of full employment. One particular aspect of the economic stabilization policy deserves special attention. This is the Employment Act of 1946. The purpose of this act is to maintain the maximum of production, employment, and purchasing power. The act has also been an important source of economic education of the American public. A Council of Economic Advisers with an adequate professional staff was added to the executive office. The President, with the aid of the Council of Economic Advisers, was directed to report to Congress annually on the current economic situation and to recommend necessary legislation. The act also provided for a standing Joint Committee of the House and the Senate on the Economic Report to study the President's report, hold hearings, and in turn make a report to Congress. These two reports, plus the minority report of the Joint Committee, have become a great source of economic information which is used widely by journalists, editorial writers, and scholars. The hearings before the Joint Committee provide an unusual opportunity for the dissemination of economic information. Those who appear before it are mostly economists from universities, labor organizations, farm organizations, and business. The new availability of sound economic knowledge is beginning to make inroads on our vast economic illiteracy.

The Employment Act of 1946 has been called the Magna Carta of government planning for full employment. The Council of Economic Advisers is an agency staffed by technical experts. Their job is to study the economic situation; to advise the President and to work out the technical aspects of his policy. While members of the Council are political appointees, their job is not that of policy spokesmen. The decision on what action is to be taken rightly belongs in the field of politics, that is, to the President and Congress.

This act was not an intended intrusion on private enterprise, but an effort to make the capitalistic economy function more smoothly and with greater social justice. Achieving the goals of the act has thus far depended more upon the "stabilizers" previously mentioned than upon specific legislation. Because of this act, the policy makers of today are better informed than ever before in regard to production, sales, plans, orders, inventories, employment, prices, credit, income and all other aspects of the economy. The government has avoided monetary and fiscal actions that might have caused an economic crisis. It is generally conceded that government stabilization policy since World War II has served to prevent severe depressions and to ameliorate the recessions. In this respect, the Employment Act has, no doubt, served to strengthen the confidence in the economy and to promote the rapid growth of this period.

The confidence in the stability of the economy as expressed through the recent rapid expansion has, no doubt, given force to an inflationary tendency. As long as the public believes that the government can and will prevent excessive instability at the proper time, this confidence will tend to encourage expansion. The real test as to the ability to stabilize the economy is yet to come. Powerful inflationary forces are at work and any serious effort to stem the rise in prices involves unpalatable choices. Some of the things which might be done include directly controlling wages, prices, and credit; cutting back on spending for national defense; cutting back on education, and welfare programs; raising the rediscount rate; and raising taxes to cut down on available funds for expenditure. Any of these would certainly meet with opposition from many sources. In a democratic society economic policies have to be hammered out by compromise. With our many group interests it could hardly be any other way. The Federal Reserve Bank on December 5, 1965, raised the rediscount rate, which caused considerable debate. Although the interest rate rose sharply and loans became harder to get than at any time in recent years, the 1966 GNP rose to an all-time high of $739 billion, or an 8.5 percent increase over 1965, the number of jobs increased over two million, and family income rose by about 5 percent. The stock market fell abruptly and housing construction fell to the lowest level since World War II; but consumer prices rose by about 3.6 percent. Because of the increased spending on the war in Vietnam and recently enacted domestic programs, and the rise in the standard of living, the attempt to stabilize the economy through manipulation of the monetary policy—tight money—failed, and inflation continued. During the 1957–1958 recession, production and employment in manufacturing fell by 14 percent, but prices rose by 2 percent. This indicates that even if the economy were slowed down, because of rising costs and the power of large producers to pass them on to the consumer, prices might still rise instead of fall. This was the case in 1967 when the economy was substantially slowed down but consumer prices continued to rise. Furthermore, the 10 percent surtax which became effective April 1, 1968, did not appreciably slow down the economy, and by the end of the year the GNP had reached approximately $900 billion and prices had increased more rapidly than in preceding years. It still remains to be seen whether the government can, through monetary and fiscal policies, slow down the economy enough to prevent undesirable inflation and at the same time not create a high degree of unemployment.

THE CHANGING STRUCTURE OF THE ECONOMY

More than half of all enterprises are still locally owned and operated, but more and more businesses and industries come under control of those who do not live in the community. It is particularly significant that those who dominate the various areas of the power structure are more frequently at the regional or national level. This is true for goods which are produced and sold, for services, for finances, and for labor unions. The growth and consolidation of transportation and communication facilities which transcend local and regional areas has made for economic interdependence on a national level. Ours has become a national economy, although not organized as a single overall unit. One of the most important aspects is the extensive national government control over the economy. Communities, like people, live by selling their goods and services, and their widespread interdependence tends to obliterate local boundaries and to minimize those of states and regions. Two of the areas of most significant change in the structure of the economy have been the growth to dominance of the corporation and of the large-scale bureaucracy.

Change in occupations and employment. The "professions" have undergone great change in their organization. Specialization has gone to great lengths. In the field of medicine, laboratory and other equipment hardly known a hundred years ago play an increasing role both in diagnosis and treatment. The physicians, nurses, and other helpers are concentrated into great medical centers and hospitals in which specialized work is more easily accomplished. That this specialization has its advantages is obvious. But it also has its disadvantages. In the first place it is extremely expensive. The large hospital is a bureaucracy in a real sense. Modern hospitals with up-to-date equipment and trained personnel are so costly and hospital charges so high that it is almost mandatory for everybody to have hospital insurance. Doctor's fees and medical expenses are equally costly. Doctors in America are the aristocrats of the professions—they have by far the highest incomes. All medical personnel other than doctors tend to become salaried employees of one sort or another. The relationships between the doctor and the patient are drastically changed. Formerly the doctor not only prescribed medicine, he was a friend of the family and a counsellor in time of need. He came to the patient's home at any time, day or night, and stayed as long as was necessary. He was something more than just a doctor. Today the doctor's relationships with patients may be classified as "business-like." The increased tempo of industrial society no longer leaves the doctor the time for leisurely visits with his patients. He does not call on them; they go to him and even then usually find him under pressure with people waiting to see him. The physician's relationship with his patients makes it necessary for him to deal not only with his colleagues as consultants, but also with many new kinds of medical workers. The whole system of these relationships has become institutionalized.

The client of the today's lawyer is likely to be a company, a government agency, or an association rather than an individual. For purposes of serving the large corporations, lawyers are more frequently organized into firms so that specialization can better be carried out. The conception of the lawyer as one who studied the law and pleaded cases is completely out-dated. Today the law profession is specialized, and the young lawyer more and more often goes to work for a law firm which pays him a salary and where he works for an employer rather than for his own clients.

Lawyers services are for hire and they tend to serve those who can afford their services. Handling cases for the propertyless, consumers, and unorganized small investors is not the road to success in law. The "successful" lawyer is created in the image of the corporation which he increasingly serves. Here he is not only a consultant and legal counsellor but also the servant and apologist for the corporation.

These two brief illustrations indicate what is happening to the professions in general. Many newer occupations are striving for professional status. Among them are psychiatrists, librarians, social workers, and nurses. Most of the new professions or would-be professions are built up around certain institutions.

One of the major changes is the rising employment in service industries from about 3 million in 1929 to approximately three times that number in 1964. The most important change is the number of people employed in government service. Between 1947 and 1962, the number increased from 10 to 15 percent of all employed. The fact that will surprise most people is that the greater part of this gain is at the state and local levels. During this period the federal government increased by about 25 percent, state and local governments rose by 65 percent. Increase in educational personnel accounted for slightly less than half the gains at state and local levels.

In the field of business the larger firms continue to grow at the expense of the smaller ones, and the larger they are the greater their growth. The number of acquisitions by merger by the 500 largest American industrial firms between 1951 and 1961 showed that the 50 largest acquired 471 firms while the lowest 50 acquired only 194; the 100 largest acquired 884 while the lowest 100 acquired 431. In the field of merchandising the same trend holds true. Of the 332 mergers, acquiring firms in the upper 40 percent acquired 281, while the lowest 60 percent acquired only 51. Of manufacturing and mining concerns acquired between 1948 and 1961, firms with assets of less than $1 million acquired less than one percent of the total, while firms with more than $10 million acquired 64 percent.[18] During 1968 there were ten times as many mergers as in 1960, and conglomerate mergers represented the overwhelming majority of all mergers.

There are important reasons why the large corporations continue to grow. They have a distinct advantage in the ability to raise huge amounts of capital. The matter of repairs is also important. Small concerns that make and sell products are in no position to furnish the parts and services that many large retail outlets do. Nor do they have the advantage of national advertising. But perhaps the most important factor of all is the superior efficiency of bureaucratic organization, the effective use of technology and skills. The efforts of government to make small businesses more competitive have failed because they cannot overcome this advantage. There are certain types of businesses, however, which do not lend themselves to large-scale operation. Among these are barbershops, television repair shops, and bakeries.

Labor and the changing economy. Organized labor has never organized more than one-fourth of all employed workers. It reached its peak in 1953 with 25.2 percent of the labor force. Its membership was 17.5 million in 1956, but in 1962 its membership declined to 16.6 million, and its percent of the total to 22.2. By 1967 it had increased to over 19 million, to about the same ratio as in 1953. The results of NLRB elections show that its election successes have slipped considerably since 1952.[19] After two decades of tremendous growth, this record is somewhat surprising. The question is frequently raised as to whether organized labor has not passed the peak of its power. Some writers think it has.

This does not mean that organized labor has been unsuccessful. The criticism today is that it has been too successful in raising wages, and hence causing increased prices. In the 1964 contract with the automobile industry, the labor cost was estimated to rise 4.5 percent despite the government's appeal to keep it within the 3.2 percent guideline established

---

[18] *The U. S. Book of Facts . . . ,* p. 504.
[19] Herbert L. Marx, ed., *American Labor Today* (New York, H. W. Wilson, 1965), pp. 17–18.

by the Council of Economic Advisers. These successes indicate the power of labor in bargaining. In national legislation, labor has not been so successful. This is shown by the passage of the Taft-Hartley Act, which it bitterly opposed, and by the failure to repeal that act, or even to repeal Section 14B, the "right-to-work" provision. On the other hand, much legislation favored by labor, such as changes in social security, the minimum wage law, housing for depressed areas, has been enacted.

A number of factors enter into organized labor's failure to continue its phenomenal growth—from 4.5 million in 1935 to 17.5 million in 1956. Automation, already discussed, has not only eliminated jobs but has made it possible for supervisory and other personnel outside the bargaining unit to maintain production or services in some industries in spite of strikes by union members. Another factor is the decreasing number of blue-collar workers and the increasing number of white-collar workers. White-collar workers outnumber blue-collar workers, who constitute most of the union membership. Out of some 20 million white-collar workers only about 2.5 million are union members. Because of the lack of prestige attached to blue-collar work, it is unlikely that white-collar workers will join the unions in any large numbers in the near future. In other words, the strength of labor is centered in the declining areas of the economy. The number of women, now about one-third of the labor force, and federal restrictions on picketing and boycotting are also adverse factors in unionization.

Labor also has some internal handicaps. One of these has been the vast proliferation of small unions with their jurisdictional disputes. These make little sense in a complex and interdependent society in which the economy is increasingly integrated. The public image of unionism, as acquired from the mass media, is that of corruption and dictatorial practices, especially among its leaders. This has led to federal regulation through the Landrum-Griffin Act of 1959. This image has certainly not been helped by the exorbitant salaries paid many labor leaders. The union leader's position is a precarious one at best whether he is a Dave Beck, Jimmy Hoffa, James B. Carey, or David McDonald. Until labor is able to install better trained leaders in an orderly way, it is probably stuck with its image. Also some of the illusions about "the worker" have been dispelled. Because labor had been so cruelly exploited in the past, it was easy to overestimate the extent of its magnanimity when it acquired power. It has proved to be much like all other power groups and, because it wields such great power, it is greatly feared. Its power to paralyze society and to ruin certain industries through strikes is very real, as has been evidenced by strikes in New York and other places in recent years.

The typical labor leader, at least in image, is one who has scratched and clawed his way to the top in a ruthless power struggle; when he has reached the top, he has to continue the struggle to stay there. He is a practical manipulator rather than a labor "statesman." There are some notable exceptions to this picture, but they are not the ones whose image is reflected to the public. In its rise to power, labor was greatly aided by American intellectuals whose objectivity and ideals of social justice made them favorable to labor. In this respect one is reminded of such men as Professor John R. Commons of the University of Wisconsin. Because of their lack of respect for the idealists and intellectuals, labor leaders have largely forfeited their support. The relationships between the corporation, labor, and the government are complex, and require a high degree of statesmanship in making adjustments to the revolutionary changes that are at present taking place. The kind of insight required derives from a broad theoretical concept of the forces operating not only in the economy but also in the society.

In recent years, labor's emphasis has justifiably shifted to achievement of the greatest possible job security. In this respect a ludicrous situation has developed within the larger labor organizations. The staffs have organized themselves to bargain with their own union leaders. It is ironical that in these cases the union leaders act like typical industrial employers who use all devices at their command to subvert these efforts. They have been unsuccessful. This and other dissatisfactions indicate that within the labor organization, as in the corporation, middle management has lost most of its power—the union member is increasingly removed from the seat of power. The operation of bureaucracy is no more a stranger to "big labor" than it is to "big business." Furthermore, the decentralizing process which has been in evidence in recent years in the corporation is not the case with labor management. There is considerable evidence of alienation and dissatisfaction at the grass-roots level of labor.

Several labor and industry practices are inimical to the growth of the economy and hence to the welfare of society as a whole. The single rate of pay practice is a deadening and leveling process in which there is no penalty for shoddy work and no reward for excellent work. This principle runs counter to the basic American ideals of individual differences, opportunities to rise, and incentives based on accomplishment. What kind of philosophy is it that fails to reward merit or to penalize sloth? By breaking tasks into minute operations and the standardization procedures, management has contributed to this fallacious idea. Studies by Peter Drucker indicate that, in certain cases at least, enlargement of jobs increased workers' initiative, satisfaction, and output. Job enlargement programs have been tried by Sears, Roebuck, IBM, Detroit Edison, and General Motors.

Along with the single rate of pay went the slogan "a fair day's wage for a fair day's work." This was the appeal of early union organizers in their attempt to raise inadequate wages. Now it means that the maximum effort should not exceed the standard quantity established by the union;

if he exceeds that amount, the worker will suffer the disapproval of the union. In practice this means, "a fair day's work for a fair day's pay." The simple economic facts are that increased labor efficiency is essential to increase production, the only source from which increase in wages, profits, and the number of jobs can come. The seniority rule is another practice that handicaps efficiency and places a barrier before the competent and ambitious worker. What incentive is there when the more competent worker cannot be rewarded by pay increases because of the single-rate system nor by promotion because of the seniority rule? Seniority is an easy standard for promotion and pay raises, but surely American ingenuity can find a better one.

Much has been written lately about the responsibility, or lack of it, of the corporation. This must be extended to include organized labor. The economic realities of today's world are such that America can no longer afford the more or less callous disregard for the general welfare. The right of labor to strike the New York newspapers or to stop the city's transportation is one thing. The right of 15 million innocent bystanders, in a controversy between labor and management, to have newspapers and transportation is something else. The only feasible labor-management relationship in today's world is that of partnership. If they cannot settle their controversies and at the same time promote the highest degree of public welfare, the answer is obvious. State regulation, which they both fear, will justifiably be upon them by default.

BIBLIOGRAPHY

Beaumont, Richard A., and Roy B. Helfgott, *Management, Automation, and People*. New York, Industrial Press, 1964.

Bendix, Reinhard, *Work and Authority in Industry*. New York, Harper & Row, 1963.

Berle, Adolph A., Jr., and Gardner C. Means, *The Modern Corporation and Private Property*. New York, Macmillan, 1948.

Blauner, Robert, *Alienation and Freedom: The Factory Worker and His Industry*. Chicago, University of Chicago Press, 1964.

Buckingham, Walter, *Automation: Its Impact on Business and People*. New York, New American Library, 1963.

Demczyski, S., *Automation and the Future of Man*. London, G. Allen, 1964.

Drucker, Peter F., *Concept of the Corporation*. New York, John Day, 1946.

Edwards, Edgar O., ed., *The Nation's Economic Objectives*. Chicago, University of Chicago Press, 1964.

Eells, Richard, *The Meaning of Modern Business*. New York, Columbia, 1960.

Fitch, John A., *Social Responsibilities of Organized Labor*. New York, Harper, 1957.

Friedmann, Georges, *The Anatomy of Work*. New York, Free Press, 1964.

Hacker, Andrew, *The Corporation Take-Over*. New York, Harper & Row, 1964.

Hansen, Alvin H., *The American Economy*. New York, McGraw-Hill, 1957.

Hickman, Bert G., *Growth and Stabilization of the Postwar Economy*. Washington, Brookings, 1960.

Laird, Donald A., and Eleanor C. Laird, *How to Get Along with Automation*. New York, McGraw-Hill, 1964.

Lindahl, Martin L., and William C. Carter, *Corporate Concentration and Public Policy*. Englewood Cliffs, N. J., Prentice-Hall, 1959.

Marx, Hubert L., Jr., *American Labor Today*. New York, H. W. Wilson, 1965.

Means, Gardner C., *The Corporate Revolution in America*. New York, Crowell-Collier, 1962.

Myrdal, Gunnar, *Beyond the Welfare State*. New Haven, Conn., Yale, 1960.

Philipson, Morris, *Automation: Implications for the Future*. New York, Random House, 1962.

Robinson, Joan, *Economic Philosophy*. Chicago, Aldine, 1963.

Samuelson, Paul A., *Economics: An Introductory Analysis*, 6th ed. New York, McGraw-Hill, 1964.

Schlicter, Sumner H., *Economic Growth in the United States*. Baltimore, J. H. Furst, 1961.

Silberman, Charles E., and the Editors of *Fortune, The Myth of Automation*. New York, Harper & Row, 1966.

Warner, W. Lloyd, *The Corporation in the Emergent American Society*. New York, Harper & Row, 1962.

Wiener, Norbert, *Cybernation, or Control and Communication in the Animal and Machine*. New York, Wiley, 1948.

Wilensky, Harold L., and Charles N. Lebeaux, *Industrial Society and Social Welfare*. New York, Free Press, 1965.

Williams, Robin A., Jr., *American Society: A Sociological Interpretation*. New York, Knopf, 1960.

8

From individualism to the welfare state

SOCIAL order is the one universal and indispensable condition of social organization without which there could be no society. A society must have peace, internal cohesion, and effective operation. The public in general gives little heed to the forces that maintain an orderly society, that hold a society together. The maintenance of order has always been the basic function of social control. Men are not by nature peaceable; the ideas of the utopians who believed in a stateless society have been much less appropriate in the modern world than those of Machiavelli who was a realist. All societies have means of controlling predatory or threatening actions. There are many means whereby a society secures order—conformity to its usages and values—but we shall be concerned especially with law, which, of course, operates through the agency of government.

The purpose of any group, large or small, in regulating the behavior of its members is to preserve and continue its existence. It is also believed that this is best for the individual members. One cannot imagine a society, especially a large one, where there was no restraint or likelihood of restraint on the behavior of the individual. The unorganized frontier in American history is an illustration of a society without such restraints. The divergent interests, values, and beliefs of individuals and groups make it necessary for a society to have norms of required behavior and means to enforce them. Different societies have different means of enforcing control. In a homogeneous agrarian community, approval or disapproval is a powerful factor. In such a society, the question of reputation is of tremendous importance, it is a matter of personal and family welfare because one cannot easily survive alone. Urban societies, composed of many heterogeneous culture groups, function largely through the legal norms. As the divergent culture groups become assimilated, as they acquire the same ideas, values, and beliefs, this will be less true. Complex industrial societies always require control through the legal norms to a greater extent than do simple rural societies.

Some of the means whereby a society secures conformity to its norms are consciously promoted others are not. The most significant means to

149

conformity is socialization. Socialization is the process by which a child, as he grows up, acquires a personality and the culture of the society, including its norms. The family is the most important determinant of personality. The individual who is socialized in Mongolia, for example, will have the language, ideas, religion, values, tastes, beliefs—the culture—of the Mongolians. The individual does not feel that he is forced to conform. He feels that this is just the way things are done, and he accepts them as right even though they are sometimes known to be different in other cultures. Socialization is never perfect. One never assimilates all of the culture norms of his parents and their generation, and he acquires some that they do not have. This is one of the generally unconscious, but important sources of social change. The institutions of the family, the school, and the church as well as the state are important agencies in the process of socialization and hence of social control.

The function of control, generally called government, is universal among people in groups. Government is the mechanism through which regulations or legal norms—laws, ordinances, orders, judicial decisions—are made and enforced. A family living in isolation would have no need for government beyond that which regulated the relationships within the family. Several families might live in an isolated community and still require only family control. In fact, rural societies have always been largely controlled through the family and very little through legal norms. As the population of the community grows and their interests and ideas become diversified, the need for community-wide government evolves. The need for keeping order and meting justice, as well as for providing roads, schools, utilities, soon requires regularized norms—provisions by government—for meeting these needs. But legal norms are not self-enforcing. They require the designation of certain individuals with power to require the other members of the group to comply with them. The power they exercise is called *authority*. Authority which officials exercise over an individual, even against his will, is legitimate authority. It is sanctioned by society and is always limited. As communities expand, individual and group relationships likewise expand, and government at the higher levels—state and eventually national—becomes essential. The greater the number of individuals and groups and the more complex the relationships become, the greater will be the need for legal norms to ensure orderly and efficient operation of the activities of the society. This extends even to the international level.

Society does not require legal norms for all areas of conformity. Through socialization the individual acquires ideas of what is right and proper, and the desire to do what he considers to be right. The desire for group approval is sufficient to cause conformity in most of his daily activities. Probably the greatest force requiring legal restraint arises from competition of one kind or another—for the acquisition of property and property rights, social status, and social power. It has always been true that possessors of wealth and status have held the power. The first written code, that of Hammurabi about 2000 B.C., distinguished between laws dealing with persons and laws dealing with things. Babylonia was a class society. It had no equality of rights under the Code; slaves, women, farmers, husbands were recognized as possessors of rights and were guaranteed the exercise of these rights. What is especially significant about this is that four thousand years ago, private justice had given way to public protection—social control or the rule of law.

DEVELOPMENT OF THE AMERICAN POLITICAL ORDER

The British Empire and the Colonies. The colonial enterprises of the European states were essential aspects of the struggle for national power as well as a part of the international rivalry of the period. It was the British mercantile policy, reflected in the Navigation Acts, which was the center of most of the controversy between the mother country and the American colonies, and which finally after 1760, led to the American Revolution. As we have stated before, American society has always been middle class, as opposed to the prevailing aristocracies in Western Europe, and its ideology developed accordingly. The isolated position and economic condition of the colonies were also important factors in shaping American political ideas.

The British Empire existed as a reality, but at no time did it have an imperial constitution. It was the effort of George III, after 1760, to establish an imperial commercial policy which brought the American colonies to revolt. In fact, the legal relationship between the mother country and the colonies was a continuous matter of debate. The government of each colony was determined in general by its charter with the mother country. But there was no agreement that the British common law and the laws passed by Parliament applied equally to the colonies. It seems that the colonies exercised a wide discretion in adopting the common law and that they largely excluded statute law. Each colony developed its own local government and colonial assembly.

By the end of the colonial period, the colonies had developed practical models for the later state governments. They each had an assembly or lower house and a chief executive in the person of a governor or proprietor. What later came to be known as the state senate developed from the colonial council appointed by the crown. Both the local and colonial governments were permitted to govern as they saw fit except when their laws were counter to British policy or interest. These colonial governments served as excellent training schools for those who were to later take over the government of the states and eventually of the federal government. They afforded practical experience in developing ideas and forms that were suitable to the American scene.

The nation in the making. During the period of the Revolution and the Articles of Confederation, the states exercised almost complete autonomy and the doctrine of "states rights" became deeply rooted. This period was also filled with serious controversies between the states and with problems related to foreign affairs. In addition, the economic situation was chaotic. In view of these problems, it became obvious that a central government with power to deal with these problems was a necessity. The strong state loyalties determined that the central government should have limited powers. The idea that prevailed was that the federal government should exercise only those functions which the states could not perform or which the federal government could perform better. This is a subtle generalization with which it is easy to agree, but when it comes to determining which functions are appropriate for federal administration, and whether they can in reality be performed better at the federal level, all kinds of problems and controversies arise. This is inevitable in a federal system and the problem of "states rights" versus federal power still persists. If society remained static, we could eventually allocate the various functions or services to be performed at the federal, state, and local levels and settle the issue of power allocation. The fact, of course, is that an increasingly urban-industrial society brings new demands for services of various kinds at all levels. It causes the shifting of some of these from one level to another, and it causes some duplication of function. The problem of the allocation of functions becomes increasingly more complex. This is especially true of taxation, welfare, and education.

Government as an institution. Government is a special kind of association; it is only one of the ways of regulating human behavior. It is a form of social control which has acquired institutional organization and operates through legal mandates enforced by specific penalties. Unlike economic institutions, which are very diffuse, the various systems and subsystems of government institutions are specific, and their relationships and functions are fairly well defined. The political structure of American society consists of all aspects of the executive, legislative, and judicial branches of federal, state, and local governments as well as certain aspects of the less formally organized political parties, political customs, and traditions. It is the national or societal level with which we are mostly concerned.

The *state* is the political organization of society; the *government* is the organization through which the state functions. We shall, however, use the term *government* in the generic sense, for as Laski says, "the State is, for the purposes of practical administration, the government."[1] It is generally stated that government has final authority over all other institutions and the individuals who constitute them. This is true, however,

---

[1] Harold J. Laski, *A Grammar of Politics,* 5th ed. (London, G. Allen, 1948), p. 131.

only in those matters for which government is assigned responsibility. There is, theoretically, no limit to the functions which might be assigned to the political agencies of a society. In other words, theoretically, the American people can organize society and regulate their collective relationships in any way they see fit.

Functions of government. The question of the proper function of the federal government is not a unique problem. The last half century or so has seen tremendous changes in the functions of the national state the world over. The most dramatic changes have been in the communist and fascist states. The changes are not only in structure and functions of government but also in the ruling-class structure. Elsewhere in the world the same changes have taken place to a lesser degree, and this of course includes our own. No large nation today could survive, at least as a world power, without a strong national government. The vast economic and technological changes have created profound and still largely unsettled political problems. Different states have attempted to meet these problems in different ways: in Russia by communism; in Italy by fascism; in Sweden by democratic socialism; in the United States by government-regulated capitalism. This does not mean that, because the American federal government becomes increasingly more pervasive in the functions or services it performs, state and local governments are becoming obsolete. On the contrary, both state and local governments are being called upon to render more and more services. As we have pointed out, since World War II the increases in percentages of both expenditure and number of employees has been much greater at the state and local levels than at the federal level. As the federal government assumes new functions and some of those previously performed at the state level, so the states assume new functions and some previously performed at the local level. The local governments also are called upon for more services and for greater expenditures on those they already perform.

The makers of the American Constitution stated the functions and procedures of government in more general terms. Their wisdom has been amply demonstrated. The American government under the Constitution is one of the oldest, most stable, and least altered in existence today. Article VI, Section 2, which made the federal government's mandates the supreme law of the land, and the flexibility of the Constitution have made it possible for the American government to change to meet the needs of the rapid changes in society. While the Supreme Court has at times by its conservatism stood as a bulwark against change, it has, especially under Chief Justice John Marshall and in the past several decades, been a powerful force for change. The American constitutional system today is approaching the British idea that almost any act of Parliament that seems necessary or desirable is permitted to stand. No longer does the Supreme

Court outlaw general welfare legislation on a constricted view of the functions of government under the Constitution.

The growing power of the federal government can best be understood by trying to answer the question, What is it that the government is called upon to do? The policy of isolation which our government followed until World War I, for example, is totally inappropriate at the present time. American involvement in two world wars, two undeclared wars, the United Nations, and foreign aid require different political concepts and different political machinery from that which existed before 1900. Our present position in world affairs demands government machinery and power that would have been completely inappropriate and unacceptable to Americans before the turn of the century. At that time both compulsory military training and strong military power were obnoxious ideas to most Americans. Both are considered necessary today and this has made the military one of the important centers of power. That most Americans may not really like the part the United States is called upon to play as a great world power has little influence on what we actually do.

There is something naive about those, some in high places, who prate about our departure from the concepts of the Founding Fathers and who wish to restore the government to its original purposes and spheres of activity. This is a cry for a return to the stagecoach and the peaceful countryside. From the time of Hammurabi to the present, order and justice have been universal functions of government. But the maintenance of order in the ghettos of New York, Cleveland, or Los Angeles is something different from maintaining order in rural America of the past, or any other agrarian society. One can imagine that should Patrick Henry return to earth he would be so horrified at present regulations that he would be speechless. But he would soon find out that these regulations— speed laws, laws against crime, laws to regulate labor and corporations, sanitation, safety, and thousands of other things—and the many agencies for their enforcement were absolutely necessary to guarantee his personal safety and the security of his property rights. Furthermore, he would find that in many ways they are still inadequate.

The attainment of justice in a mass society is an even more difficult and more controversial function than the attainment of order, although they must go together. Theoretical principles such as equality before the law or freedom of contract have no meaning unless they underlie enforceable legal norms. As Justice Frankfurter stated, "The tasks of government have meaning only as they are set in the perspective of the forces outside government."[2] Neither individual nor property rights are guaranteed by nature. These rights must be determined by authority and enforced by

[2] Felix Frankfurter, *The Public and Its Government* (Boston, Beacon Press, 1930), p. 24.

law. The problem of justice is a complex one. In important cases there is always a question of whether justice has been satisfied. For example, is a sales tax a just tax for all individuals affected? Or, does the individual without money get justice in the courtroom? Because we do not have explicit statements of what justice requires in so many areas of our activities, justice remains one of the perplexing functions of government. Even so, it is only through the functioning of order and justice among men that a society can exist.

The makers of the United States Constitution were men of wide experience in government and in business. Of the fifty-five who attended the Constitutional Convention, twenty-five were college men and thirty-three were lawyers. If they were not "an assembly of demi-gods" as Jefferson called them, they were the intellectual elite of America. Constitutions are not self-enforcing. We are aware that the Russian Constitution of 1937 and the constitutions of the Latin American states all provide for democratic governments, but the operation of some of the governments under these constitutions have fallen far short of their promises.

Madison played a leading role in the adoption of the Constitution; Jefferson finally recommended its adoption with amendments. Later, however, they became the leading opponents of the centralized power provided by the Constitution. Both the Jeffersonians and the Hamiltonians knew that the actual government would depend upon the interpretations of those selected to run the government. Early in Washington's first term, Jefferson as Secretary of State and Hamilton as Secretary of Treasury held different interpretations. In the political struggle which followed, Jefferson and the Democrats (called Republicans at that time) won the battle in the election of 1800, but they lost the cause to the increasing demands for a government that would render more service to the ruling classes. From this time on, the government has become increasingly responsive to the demands of the people, sometimes reluctantly. Neither the Constitution nor the government is sovereign. Sovereignty resides in the people, and the Constitution and the government are devices which the people use to govern themselves. Because government has been and still is responsive to the needs growing out of our increasingly complex society, we are continuously increasing the number of services and regulations which we expect of government.

AMERICAN POLITICAL PHILOSOPHY

America and European liberalism. Early American political philosophy is tied closely to the English doctrine of liberalism. The immediate purpose of the bourgeoisie in their effort to control the government was to abolish the restrictions on economic activities. The rise of industrialism also brought about demands for the removal of restraints based on social class and on the old guilds.

The security of the individual against the arbitrary use of power by the king and his officials in America, became the theory that ours was a "government of laws and not of men." This is, of course, less true than it appears on the surface because men both make and interpret the laws which are supposed to do the restricting. In England, this resulted in the supremacy of Parliament, and the King exercising very little political power. This successful claim of the rights of the individual became the foundation of our "civil rights" as expressed in both our federal and state constitutions. The aspirations of the middle classes for improved status and power to which they felt entitled, demanded the right of participation in government as a means to these ends.

The tax controversy of the American colonies with the mother country after 1760 was essentially a challenge to the right of the King and of Parliament to levy taxes on the colonies. Patrick Henry in his famous speech to the House of Burgesses on the Stamp Act declared that only the General Assembly of Virginia had the power to tax the people of the colony. This sentiment was widespread throughout the colonies. It was as much an expression of growing American nationalism as it was a protest against unjust taxation.

Another important aspect of the liberals' movement had to do with religion. The British middle classes were often nonconformists who feared discrimination and persecution by both church and state. This led to the demand for freedom of worship, and eventually to the demand for freedom of thought and political opinion. All of these ideas were a part of the growing belief in the dignity of the individual which found expression in the American Bill of Rights.

The early liberals were men of property and education who did not wish to extend suffrage to the uneducated and propertyless masses. The fusion of liberalism and democracy was a later development. The rise of industrialism had created a new class of industrial workers, who later generally aligned themselves, at least in Europe, with socialistic movements. By the end of the nineteenth century, the bourgeoisie had largely achieved its goals, and it competed strongly with the old European aristocracies as powers in politics. A new class alignment, so dramatically proclaimed by Marx, had been taking place. In the United States, the industrial working classes remained largely middle class in their ideas; what they wanted was a greater share in both the government and the capitalist system. The American farmers remained supporters of the capitalistic system and, like the industrial workers, wanted a greater share of what it produced.

The middle classes, especially the upper strata, having been successful in business, industry, banking, commerce and the professions, came largely to dominate the industrial societies in Europe and America and to shift politically toward conservatism. They favored the use of tariffs and other forms of state support for themselves, but they continued to hang on doggedly to laissez-faire as far as any restrictions on themselves were concerned. Both labor and the farmers in America found themselves exploited by this group, and their unhappiness found expression in industrial and political strife toward the end of the last century. The political attitudes of people are in a large measure the result of the way they live and make their living. It is this development that explains the change in the Democratic Party from being the party in opposition to federal control and regulation under Jefferson to being the party which has gone further in this direction, and which is willing to go still further. Of course the party of Hamilton, the present Republican Party, which was historically liberal has become the conservative party. This is not as inconsistent as it may appear. Both parties have remained consistently loyal to the interests of the social classes they have represented. Only the nature of the issues has changed.

Government and the individual. It is ironical that in America today, and probably in all highly industrialized societies, the freedom and security of the individual depend upon strong government and greater and greater restrictions on the behavior of individuals. This was not so in 1789. The Constitution and especially the Bill of Rights was designed to protect the individual from government. Guaranteed order and justice, the individual had little to fear except from government. But today with giant labor unions and corporations, a huge military establishment and an economy that is integrated and interdependent on a nation-wide scale, the freedom and security of the individual is increasingly dependent upon government regulation and other involvements. Laski has stated that in the modern world the contours of the life of every citizen are set by the norms that the state imposes.[3]

The American principles of justice and equality before the law had been gained in England by long centuries of political struggle. Perhaps America's greatest political debt to the mother country is the democratic concept of law and order which made easy the acceptance of our basic articles of faith: rule by consent of the governed, majority rule, the right of trial by jury, freedom of speech, press, assembly, and religion. Broadly speaking, the American democratic profession of faith is expressed in the American Creed which is centered around the belief in equality and in the rights of liberty. As expressed by Jefferson in the Declaration of Independence, equality was of first importance and from it the rights of liberty were derived. Among these rights, religion was of special importance. The idea that nearly all of the colonists came to America for religious freedom became a widely accepted myth. Although greatly exag-

[3] Harold J. Laski, *An Introduction to Politics,* rev. ed. (London, G. Allen, 1951), p. 11.

gerated, the acceptance of the myth made it an important part of the American Creed.

Although the American Creed cannot be precisely stated, it is more than the liberalism which we have already discussed. It developed a humanistic quality which gives the average American a feeling of world mission. It is true that the ideas of the Creed have fallen far short of realization in many respects; even so, their rightness has never been seriously questioned. The Creed has been a vital force in the development of American democracy. It became the embodiment of the spirit of the frontier, of Wilson's Fourteen Points, and of Roosevelt's Four Freedoms. It has grown and adapted to the needs of American nationalism. John Dewey said, "Call it a dream or call it a vision, it has been interwoven in a tradition that has had an immense effect on American life."[4]

THE AMERICAN POLITICAL SYSTEM

Every American high school student has learned that the American government under the Constitution is a federal system with certain powers delegated to the federal government and all others reserved to the states; that it is a "government of laws and not of men," and that great emphasis is placed on the Constitution; that there is a separation of powers among the three branches with a complicated system of checks and balances; that it is a representative constitutional democracy with universal adult suffrage; that the President and Vice President and Congress are elected and that all other federal officials and employees are appointed; that Congress makes the laws and the executive branch enforces them and administers the government and that the Supreme Court is the guardian of the Constitution; that the Bill of Rights and other provisions of the Constitution provide an elaborate system of civil rights for individuals; that there is an increasing number of regulatory commissions and other agencies which, although a part of the executive branch, are little governments within themselves largely making, interpreting, and enforcing their own rules; that neither the Cabinet nor political parties are provided for in the Constitution but that they are just as important as if they were. But one may know all of these things and much more and still have little conception of how the government actually works. It may be well at this point to emphasize that the complex system of government in the United States is more the result of unplanned growth than of political vision and planning.

Some underlying assumptions. It may help us to see what has happened to government if we look at some of the early basic assumptions on which democratic government in the United States was predicated. If we con-

4 John Dewey, *Freedom and Culture* (New York, Putnam, 1939), p. 55.

sider the rural community, we find the area was small, the groups more homogeneous and integrated, and the political issues relatively simple. The stand of candidates on issues could become well known and through discussion the electorate was able to vote on issues intelligently. There were differences, of course, but they were differences on policies and did not involve the misunderstanding of facts or of conditions on which issues were based which generally characterize most of today's issues. Through this process the candidates best suited to carry out the general interests were elected. Furthermore, the elected officials being much closer to the electorate were subject to close scrutiny. This was the kind of society on which Jefferson based his philosophy of government. It was this agrarian or pre-industrial society in which the government of the United States had its origin.

As urbanization and industrialization spread, the assumptions and conditions discussed above became less and less applicable. The increase in size of economic and political units along with the great increase in population made it impossible for the issues to be local, clear-cut, and easily understood, or for candidates to become well known. In Texas today a member of the lower house of the legislature represents some 70,000 people, a senator some 400,000, and a United States Congressman approximately 500,000. In today's complex industrial society there are hundreds of different groups whose interests are variously affected by every government act or policy. These many interests make it difficult for the voter to sort out the issues and match them with the candidates. They also create conditions that are open invitations to shrewd politicians and demagogues. Furthermore, the candidate who has access to unlimited campaign funds has a distinct advantage. At the national and state levels the elected officials are so far removed from the average citizen that his influence is non-existent.

Democratization of the government. There has been a definite change in the area of participation in government. All of the presidents down to Andrew Jackson were men of learning, representative of the elite ruling class who elected them. While Jefferson's election in 1800 gave impulse to greater democratization, this was not realized until the states generally removed the restrictions on adult male voting immediately before and during the Jacksonian era. This democratization process was extended in theory by the Civil War amendments. Of course it is common knowledge that extension of the franchise to the Negro was widely evaded down to the middle of this century. Finally, after World War I suffrage was extended to women. Important as participation is in a democratic society, it is probably more significant that our norms of political behavior have become increasingly more consistent with our values placed on the democratic process. Before the Jacksonian era it was generally the belief of the politically elite that the people would be satisfied to fill the offices with their "betters." The "revolution of 1828" meant that the common people should choose their officials from among themselves. A new concept of democracy had arrived and with it came elected officials whom Hamilton, and most of the elite, had feared would deprive them of their property rights. Jackson's inauguration was accompanied by crude, noisy, and vulgar demonstrators who had come to celebrate the rescue of government from the "aristocrats." Another result of the democratization process has been to make just about all state and local offices elective. This has made the main qualification for office the ability to get elected. With the high cost of present-day campaigning, the field is pretty well limited to those who have money. What this does to the basic assumptions with which we started this discussion is not difficult to see.

Change in structure: amendments. There have been twenty-four amendments to the Constitution; most of them are of great importance. The first ten, known as the Bill of Rights, specifically protect the individual. While the Constitution was being ratified, seven of the original states proposed 124 amendments, and the minorities of several other states asked for amendments. While it had been generally assumed that some of these amendments would become part of the Constitution, the resolution proposing them was one of the most hard-fought political battles of the early history of Congress. Twelve were finally passed and presented to the states, and ten of them were ratified and became effective December 15, 1791. The southern states with the exception of Georgia ratified all of them; Massachusetts and Connecticut ratified none of them. It seems rather astonishing that such astute men as John Quincy Adams, Fisher Ames, most of the leaders from New England, and many from the middle states opposed the Bill of Rights. The aristocracy who had favored a strong central government opposed the amendments, and the more democratic who opposed strong central government favored them. The eleventh amendment limited judicial power. The twelfth, ratified after the election of 1800 had been thrown into the House of Representatives, separated the election of the President and Vice President. From 1804 to 1865 no amendments were made. The Civil War amendments limited the powers of the states in dealing with the freed Negroes. The Civil War amendments, especially the fourteenth, have been used for many other purposes than settling the slavery issue.

The amendments came more or less in clusters. No new amendments were added until the culmination of the Progressive Movement in 1913. The sixteenth permitted the government to levy an income tax, now the chief source of federal revenue. The seventeenth carried the democratization process to a more consistent conclusion by making senators subject to popular election rather than to the election of state legislatures. The nineteenth extended the right to vote to women. The eighteenth, the prohibition amendment, was passed in 1920, and repealed by the twenty-first amendment in 1933. The twentieth and twenty-second made fundamental changes in the political structure. The twentieth amendment, adopted in 1933, changed the time of meeting of Congress from December to January, and eliminated the short or lame-duck session of Congress. The twenty-second, adopted in 1951, limited the President to two terms. The twenty-third, adopted in 1961, gave the District of Columbia representation in the Electoral College. The twenty-fourth, adopted in 1964, abolished the poll tax in national elections.

Change in the power structure. There has been in the twentieth century a dramatic increase in federal power at the expense of the states. Laski thinks that the states are obsolete and that regions would be a more rational political arrangement. No matter how much more politically and economically efficient a regional system might be, and certainly economic and cultural boundaries make a lot more sense than do political boundaries, one can imagine the anguished outbursts such a proposal would provoke. State governors have made great gains in power because the Founding Fathers pretty well stripped governors of all important powers. State legislatures and judiciaries have not gained like power and respect. In fact, their status is pretty low. At the federal level, the office of the President has become the outstanding repository of power. It is probably inevitable that a large urban-industrial society should have a strong executive. John Jay, the first Chief Justice of the Supreme Court, resigned because he did not consider the position important. Today justices of the Supreme Court are given status above all other positions in the United States except the office of the President. The federal court system is highly respected. Congress has granted the President more power. It can still, however, give the President a setback when it wants to, especially through the means of appropriations. The Senate has maintained greater prestige than the House of Representatives, partly because the House committee system obscures the important work it does. The Senate gets most of the publicity.

One other structural aspect of government, because of its recent growth and relevance to present-day complex industrial society, must be mentioned. This is the tremendous growth in the number of government civilian employees. In 1929 the total number, including state and local, of such employees was slightly over 3 million. In 1968 it was approximately 12 million, of which approximately three-fourths were state and local.[5] While the population increased about 65 percent between 1929 and 1965, the number of government employees increased nearly 300 percent.

[5] *Information Please Almanac for 1969* (New York, Dan Golenpaul Associates, 1968), pp. 701–702.

At the state and local levels this great increase was in large part due to the services demanded. Those employed in education accounted for about half of the 8.5 million. Other services with great numbers of employees are: hospitals, highways, police and fire departments, and welfare.[6] At the federal level in 1965, there were some 2.5 million civilian employees of which all but about 31,000 were attached in one way or another to the executive branch. Of these federal employees, about 84 percent were under civil service. Of the approximately 2.5 million civilian employees, over 1 million are assigned to the military, and 600,000 to the Post Office. Four departments, Agriculture, Treasury, Health, Education, and Welfare, and Interior account for some 332,000 more. Other departments have smaller numbers, some running as high as 30,000 or 40,000. Some of the independent agencies have huge numbers of employees: Veterans Administration, 171,000; Federal Aviation Agency, 44,700; General Services Administration, 34,800; National Aeronautics and Space Administration, 33,000. These services account for 2.2 million of the 2.5 million civilian employees in the administrative branch of the government.[7] Most of these employees do not live in Washington; they are employed in the regional and local offices throughout the United States.

The administrative branch of the federal government is composed of some twenty corporations, and fifty or more independent agencies, together embracing over 2,000 bureaus and other subunits. These are in addition to such agencies as the Bureau of the Budget and the National Security Council. The very size of these units makes necessary a huge bureaucratic organization. Members of Congress and Presidents come and go. The smooth functioning of government from day to day depends upon the effectiveness of these permanent organizations. The stability of their permanent personnel, representative of the whole American people, is one of our greatest political assets. When Congress creates one of these agencies, it determines the functions and appropriates the money for its operation, and the President, like the corporation head, is expected to see that the agency operates accordingly. These agencies have been established to serve certain useful purposes and, if they do not do so, Congress can abolish them.

Democratic society in operation: political parties. The essential function of a political party is to select candidates, get them elected to office, and keep them there. In our large and heterogeneous society, parties are an absolute necessity. Although they are not provided for in the Constitution, they are a thoroughly institutionalized part of our governing process. Political party organization requires some sort of differential groupings,

---

[6] *Ibid.*, p. 702.

[7] *The U. S. Book of Facts, Statistics and Information for 1966* (New York, Herald Tribune, 1965), pp. 410–412.

otherwise there would be no basis for more than one party. In the history of American political parties, the group differentiations have been reasonably clear-cut, especially in the earliest period. As supporters of strong central government, Hamilton and the federalists were the spokesmen for the commercial, financial, manufacturing, and trading interests—the rising bourgeoisie, or middle classes. Jefferson's motley support included small farmers, laborers, mechanics, debtors, frontiersmen, small proprietors, and plantation slaveowners. It was essentially an agrarian grouping.

One of the distinguishing features of American politics is its two-party system. Why this is true is still an open question. Whatever the reasons, the two largest parties are the only ones with much chance to win elections. Third parties seldom ever win. Since American society is extremely heterogeneous, both parties must be coalitions of many groups. Whoever said that "politics makes strange bedfellows" understated the facts. Both parties do, in fact, include individuals and groups whose political ideas range from liberal to conservative. With only two parties, groups do not have much choice: they settle for the one which they believe offers them the most and do not expect to get everything they want. The party becomes something of a mediator among many groups with conflicting interests. It is the organization within which these groups combine their efforts to reach some of their goals. Party leaders try to state the areas of agreement in acceptable generalizations. Thus, their essential aim is to achieve a consensus.

The extension of suffrage and the rise of political parties were developments which the makers of the Constitution either did not foresee or whose influence they misjudged. The Constitution provided for the President to be chosen by the Electoral College whose members were to be chosen by state legislatures, and senators to be chosen directly by the legislatures. Members of the House of Representatives were the only federal officials to be chosen by direct popular election. The election of representatives and state officials required some kind of organization; as this organization developed into political parties, it was considered "private"—not a part of the governmental process. In the course of time, parties came to be considered public and their activities were regulated by law. This, however, was a long, drawn-out process. The so-called "white primary" in the South was based on the idea that political parties are private associations and their primaries (nominating elections) were likewise private and not subject to the regulations for general elections. The United States Supreme Court in 1935 upheld this position, but in 1944 it reversed the previous decision and the general and primary elections were united into a single electoral process.

We have already seen how the extension of the democratic process led to the popular election of senators. No amendment has been passed to do the same for the election of the President and Vice President. Concerning the Electoral College, the Constitution says, "they shall make a List of all persons voted for, and of the Number of Votes for each," indicating that the electors were expected to vote as individuals and not as a group. By the election of 1800, however, party unity had caused a constitutional problem. The Constitution provided that electors should vote only for President and that the candidate receiving the next largest vote should be Vice President. It was well understood, in 1800, that Jefferson was the Democratic candidate for President and that Burr was the candidate for Vice President; the Democratic electors voted unanimously for both Jefferson and Burr, causing a tie vote for President. This threw the election into the House of Representatives. A great political crisis took place before partisanship gave way and Jefferson was elected, as the voters intended. Now, because we know that the electors will vote for the party which elects them, we know immediately after the general election who the next President will be. Constitutionally, the vote of the Electoral College is taken over a month after the general election.

The two major parties are frequently criticized because they stand for so nearly the same things. Since 1900 the two major parties have differed very little on major policy or ideology. This does, indeed, make it difficult for the voters, who are as likely to vote on the basis of personality as on issues. Until radio and television came along, campaigns were frequently vicious and abusive personal attacks on the opposing candidate. The two major parties vie in their allegiance to the established political and economic system. Because of this, the issues are pretty well narrowed down to who can best promote the major goals on which both in general agree.

American political parties are not based on social classes in either the Marxian or the traditional sense. In a society where parties are based on classes, party control means class control, and the demanded changes are frequently in the institutional areas. Our parties are composed of groups from all classes and mainly compete for control of our institutions as they are. This requires that both major parties remain reasonably moderate. The Republican defeat in 1964 amply illustrates that extreme party positions are unpopular in the United States. If this means that "there is not enough difference to make a difference," it also means that changes come more slowly and are less socially disorganizing. The extension of suffrage which brought many and varied interest groups into the major parties may have tended to focus interest on issues rather than classes. It is also argued that this organization is only a façade which obscures the basic class interests of the various groups. There is probably some truth in both of these positions.

Although the formal organization of the major political parties is extremely complex, they are rather amorphous beings to which Americans pledge their allegiance rather lightly. Of those entitled to vote, at best only 60 or 70 percent do so in national elections. In some state and local elections it runs as low as 10 or 15 percent. Those who actually work in the party organization constitute only a very small group at any level. Most Americans seem unconcerned about party machinery and, in fact, look upon it with a jaundiced eye. The demagoguery, abuse, and unscrupulous scheming, even corruption, in which some politicians have participated have left their stains on the parties. As the legal procedures through which we select our governing officials and the policies of our governments at all levels, parties, like Caesar's wife, ought to be above reproach. Our political parties provide us with the legal procedures for selecting both the officials who will govern us and the policies they will carry out.

Public opinion. If democracy is rule by the people, then there must be some way to determine what the public wants. In simple, stable societies most issues that arise can be settled by custom or tradition. In modern industrial societies rapid changes continuously create new conditions out of which new issues arise which somehow must be resolved; the need for ascertaining public opinion has greatly increased. From the time of the American and French Revolutions, the idea that government should be by the consent of the governed took deep root. More recently, however, there has been considerable disillusionment with the democratic process. Not only has it failed in many parts of the world, but propaganda and advertising have given the impression that with enough money anything can be sold. Public relations firms even attempt to sell political candidates. C. Wright Mills, among many others, sees behind the façade of democratic trappings a "power elite" who actually control the individuals who represent the public.

Pressure groups and lobbyists must be a part of any consideration of public opinion. There are thousands of these groups of all kinds and sizes. Many of them try to influence public opinion to turn government representatives toward policies in keeping with their interests. Others attempt to influence the government representatives more directly. One recent example of a clear attempt to influence public opinion has been the activities of the American Medical Association in its efforts to defeat the compulsory national health insurance bill, generally known as Medicare. In the first nine months of 1950 it distributed 43 million pieces of literature, placed advertisements in 1,100 newspapers and 30 magazines, and broadcast over 1,200 radio stations. This was by no means all of its activities during this period. It secured the support of insurance and real estate groups and attempted to put direct pressure on members of Congress. This is not an unusual case, only more out in the open because of its supreme effort to influence public opinion. Not all efforts are directed at keeping certain laws from being passed, or policies from being initiated. Groups are also interested in the type of persons selected to carry out the laws or policies after they are made. Some of these organizations are very large. The National Association of Manufacturers represents the broad category of industries. Each large industry is likely to have its own lobbyist. Business interests are also represented by the United States Chamber of Commerce. Labor is represented by the AFL-CIO. Farmers' and veterans' groups are also among the most influential in Washington. Some reach beyond the boundaries of the United States. There are lobbyists for Spain's Generalisimo Franco, Chiang Kai-shek, German industrialists, and so on.

The question arises as to what it requires to make democracy work. Two things, at least, will help: education and freedom of communication, in their broadest implications. With regard to the first, we can do no better than to go back to the concept of the Founding Fathers that a democratic society must be based on an enlightened electorate. This is, in fact, more significant now than it was then because the American electorate today includes all adults, not just "the rich and well born."

The freedom of communication is a much more complex problem. Its spirit is expressed in the First Amendment which guarantees freedom of religion, speech, the press, assembly, and petition. This, however, is only a barrier against the government and not against other forces that might do the same things. There is a surprising amount of anti-freedom of speech, anti-freedom of the press, anti-freedom of assembly throughout this country, and we sometimes surprisingly find it in ourselves. All over the country there are vigilante committees who wish to censor the bookstores and libraries and to remove certain books for no other reason than that they contain things with which the individual or group disagrees. There are those who try to force school boards not to adopt certain textbooks for the same reason. It is all too common for groups to try to remove college and public-school teachers because they hold views with which they disagree. Practically nowhere in this country could a citizen who is a known Nazi or Communist make a speech, regardless of his subject, in a public facility without a bitter protest, but a Democrat or Republican would not be questioned. It is easy for all of us to agree to freedom of speech, freedom of assembly, and freedom of the press as abstract sentiments; it is something different with many, if not most, of us, when a known Nazi or Communist agitator wants to use the high school auditorium for a public speech. This is another "great dilemma" with which Americans must come to terms.

Plight of the states. States are more than cogs in the federal system. They have the major responsibilities in the areas of education, law enforcement, health and welfare, highways and safety, the administration of justice, the regulation of public utilities, elections and suffrage, and many others. The states have not kept pace with the rapidly growing needs of an urban-industrial society. Many people have been concerned with the growing complexity of federal intragovernmental relationships and the relationship between the states and the federal government. In the latter case, it was Eisenhower who was most persistent in attempting to find some solution to the increasing usurpation of state functions by the federal government. It was apparent to him that many functions of the states had been gradually assumed by the federal government through the neglect or acquiescence of the states. In 1957 he said, "Opposed though I am to needless federal expansion, since 1953 I have found it necessary to urge action in some areas traditionally reserved to the states. In each instance state inaction, or inadequate action, coupled with undeniable national need, has forced emergency federal intervention."[8]

One of the most serious impediments to better state government is their antiquated constitutions. Many of them are detailed, long, and inflexible, and require frequent amendment. The Texas constitution runs 55,000 words and has had over 175 amendments, with 16 voted on in November 1966; California's runs 85,000 words and has been amended about 400 times; Louisiana's is 184,000 words or the equivalent of a 350-page book. In 1954 the Louisiana voters were presented 31 proposed amendments of which it would have taken five hours to read the texts, and it is doubtful that even then the voters could have understood most of them. A great deal of the content of these constitutions is out-dated and trivial. Some prohibit dueling, limit the time of wrestling matches, and demand the flash test for kerosene. Such trivia are harmless, but the strenuous limitations on activities of state officials is a serious problem, as is indicated by the flood of amendments presented to the voters at each election. These amendments are intended to remove restrictions so that the legislatures can perform their functions, but many of them are so written that the vicious cycle continues. Many amendments are about problems that concern only a small area of the state or a small group of individuals so that most people hardly know what they are voting on. One such amendment was to permit a certain area of a certain county in Texas to create a hospital district; another would permit a county to provide retirement for a specific group of its employees. These constitutions remain in effect despite their flaws. Groups who are favored by the present situation, and politicians who know how to manipulate the cumbersome machinery have vested interests in keeping them as they are. Furthermore, there is no great demand among the people of the states for a revision. A recent vote on calling a constitutional convention to revise the constitution of Texas was decisively defeated.

The state legislatures deserve some blame for the low esteem in

---

[8] *Annals of the Academy of Political and Social Science,* Vol. 359 (May 1965), pp. 109–110.

which state government and they themselves are held. Their machinery is both antiquated and inadequate. Most legislatures meet only once every two years and for terms of 60, 90, or 120 days, they lack adequate permanent research and technical staffs, they have too many committee assignments, they lack adequate facilities for checking on expenditures of funds which they have appropriated. Many legislatures are still dominated by rural representatives. The move to the cities has resulted in a great over-representation of rural areas and a great under-representation of cities. Many of the legislatures could not bring themselves to reapportion the states in over forty years, thus forcing federal action through the Supreme Court in an area in which their own state constitutions specifically required them to take action. Another such example of failure of the states to fulfill their responsibility is that of civil rights. Too many cases of so-called "federal encroachment" have been the results of failure of the states to do their jobs adequately. In December 1963, former Governor Leroy Collins of Florida stated, "The sad truth is that the states have allowed their own prominence to be lowered, their own effectiveness to be impaired, their own stature to be tarnished, by their failure to serve that fundamental purpose of meeting the clear needs of their citizens."[9]

The contention of states'-righters, that the federal government is rapidly taking over functions of state and local governments against their interests and wills, is patently false. They had many of these functions, and if they had performed them better, there would have been no demand for the federal government to assume them. Furthermore, the states do not really want these functions back. This was adequately shown by a study made by a joint federal-state commission created by President Eisenhower in cooperation with the Council of State Governments. The commission set out to identify the functions which should be returned to state jurisdiction. According to Governor Leroy Collins who was a member of the commission, "It turned out to be an exercise in futility. We found that, notwithstanding all the return-to-states'-rights talk, there was no substantial federal function that the states really wanted back."[10] The reasons became obvious: in some the functions were national in scope and in others the states were either unable or unwilling to try to provide such services. Furthermore, the states were already hard-pressed for revenues. Such functions as aid for the construction of hospitals, college dormitories, and grants for improved health and education services were considered. Every state already had the legal authority to perform these functions. Despite President Nixon's proposal to share the cost and to shift some functions and authority back to the states, the sixty-first annual conference of governors in September 1969 proposed a total federali-

9 *The Maze of Modern Government* (Santa Barbara, Cal., The Center for the Study of Democratic Institutions, 1964), p. 4.
10 *Ibid.*

zation of public welfare. The governors would shift to Washington not only the cost but also the problems and responsibilities of public welfare.[11]

The states'-rights issue has always been a political weapon used by anyone whose interests would be served by it, especially by those who feared government regulation. Most of those who use the argument are not really opposed to federal encroachment on state functions, or to state encroachment on local functions, but to the enactment of the specific law or regulation over which the issue of authority arose. The argument has recently been applied to the federal urban-renewal program. What is deplorable is the use of a spurious, emotional issue to prevent the settling of important problems of human rights and needs on the basis of their own merits.

The rapid urbanization of the United States has made not only state governments outmoded, but county governments even more so. Texas has 254 counties all of which maintain full staffs of county officials. Of these 254 counties, the 1960 census showed that one had a population of 226; two had less than 1,000 people; 99 had less than 10,000; and 68 had between 10,000 and 20,000. These 254 sets of county officials, of course, are supported by taxes.[12] Towns within the counties also have their sets of officials. In some of the large metropolitan areas the cities virtually cover the entire land area of the county. Not only are these duplications expensive luxuries for which the tax money could be better spent, they are also a great source of confusion and conflict the result of which is poorer services. The reasons for the low esteem of the state and local governments is obvious: they do not render the quality of services which command respect.

Summary: bureaucracy and the welfare state. We have discussed the great growth of government administration and personnel at all levels. This has created a great demand for skilled technicians and scientists in government. Until recently there was never any question but that government policy was made by the civilians who had been elected to do the job. It is undoubtedly true that in such complex governments as ours the policy makers must rely more and more on experts. Since World War II, military advisors are called upon more often concerning matters of policy. Political bureaucrats work under conditions and face problems unlike any others. The range of authority, the specialization and compartmentalization of functions, and the political considerations in selection and promotion all tend to develop an exaggerated attitude of shunning experimentation and responsibility by slavishly following rules of the department. Both seniority and "correct" procedures are more important than

[11] From the *Wall Street Journal,* quoted in Beaumont, Texas, Beaumont Enterprise (September 13, 1969).

[12] *Texas Almanac, 1964–65* (Dallas, The Dallas Morning News, 1963), pp. 117–121.

efficiency. "Red tape" and the "run-around" are in too many cases justifiable descriptions of procedure. It is a system for which the individual civil servant should not be held responsible. These shortcomings are not, however, irremediable, nor are they in themselves justifiable arguments against government assumption of functions which are in the public interest.

We have previously discussed the expansion of government functions in connection with the welfare state and with the regulation of economic activities; we have assumed that a democratic society has the right to assign any functions it wishes to any level of government. But we should not assume that government is a free and responsive agent in adjusting its functions to the needs of the situation. All democratic governments are caught up in the crosscurrents of the struggle of special interest groups. Every political party and candidate is pledged to certain platform policies that help or hinder certain groups, and when in office the party and the candidate are expected to honor these pledges. Every government is, then, at the mercy of many groups which it cannot afford to alienate. In this light, the increased functions or services which a government assumes are in response to the demands of public opinion.

Governments in the past were mostly instruments of power; their functions were largely limited to keeping order, rendering justice, enforcing contracts and so on. In modern times they are increasingly service institutions. Six of our federal departments—Post Office, Interior, Agriculture, Labor, Commerce, and Health, Education, and Welfare—are essentially designed as service agencies to the American people. With the exception of the Post Office, none of these six existed before about 1850. This is also true of the Veterans Administration, the Federal Aviation Commission, the Atomic Energy Commission. The public may plead ignorance, but it cannot plead innocence for this development. Apparently the vociferous howls against "big government" are not really directed against big government, but only against certain policies or actions which affect the complainants adversely.

There are certainly many areas in which the functions can be better performed by government. It is generally accepted that government cannot permit excessive unemployment, strikes that threaten the welfare of the public, the deprivation of the individual of his rights, excessive fluctuations in the economy. A great deal of government planning is necessary to carry out these and the many other functions which the public demands and on which the welfare of society depends. As American society grows more and more complex, government—federal, state, and local—will be called upon to render an increasing number of services and to increasingly regulate the rights of individuals in the interest of society. This is perhaps inevitable. It is not so much the number of services which government renders that is the problem as it is the acceptance of the idea that they can be performed only by the government. Within the family, church, and school, the functions of government should be limited to the more general aspects of order, security, and justice. In these institutions are located the values, morals, beliefs, and customs of the individual. Here exist all of those areas of life which ought to be beyond the reach of government. There is a great temptation for government to invade the private lives of people. Behavior which is clearly detrimental to the greater society cannot be tolerated; but a scrupulous regard for the rights of the individual is an imperative. Freedom of the individual must be protected from within as well as from without.

One other important consideration is the question of the compatibility of the welfare or service state and the democratic process. Sweden, Denmark, and England have developed the welfare or service state to a much higher degree than has the United States and have at the same time maintained democracies. Change has come slowly; and the purpose has always been to make the existing institutions more effective instruments in serving the needs of the people.

BIBLIOGRAPHY

Barker, Ernest, *Principles of Social and Political Theory.* Oxford, The Clarendon Press, 1951.

Center for the Study of Democratic Institutions, *The Maze of Modern Government.* Santa Barbara, Cal., The Center, 1964.

Christensen, Reo M., and Robert O. McWilliams, *Voice of the People: Readings in Public Opinion and Propaganda.* New York, McGraw-Hill, 1962.

Fabricant, Solomon, *The Trend of Government Activity in the United States Since 1900.* New York, National Bureau of Economic Research, 1952.

Key, V. O., Jr., *Politics and Pressure Groups.* New York, Crowell, 1953.

Key, V. O., Jr., *Public Opinion and American Democracy.* New York, Knopf, 1964.

Laski, Harold J., *American Democracy.* New York, Viking, 1948.

Lipson, Leslie, *The Great Issues in Politics.* Englewood Cliffs, N. J., Prentice-Hall, 1965.

MacIver, Robert M., *The Web of Government.* New York, Macmillan, 1947.

Michaels, Robert, *Political Parties: A Sociological Study of the Oligarchical Tendencies in Modern Democracy,* trans. by Eden and Cedar Paul. New York, Collier, 1962.

Mitchell, William C., *The American Polity.* New York, Free Press, 1962.

Monsen, R. Joseph, Jr., and Mark W. Cannon, *The Makers of Public Policy: American Power Groups and Their Ideologies.* New York, McGraw-Hill, 1965.

Roucek, Joseph S., *Social Control.* New York, Van Nostrand, 1947.

Runciman, W. G., *Social Science and Political Theory*. Cambridge, England, University Press, 1963.

Schettler, Clarence, *Public Opinion in American Society*. New York, Harper, 1960.

Snyder, Richard Carlton and H. Herbert Wilson, eds. *Roots of Political Behavior: Introduction to Government and Politics*. New York, American Book, 1949.

Williams, Robin M., Jr., *American Society: A Sociological Interpretation*. New York, Knopf, 1960.

9

The American family

THE change from an agricultural to an urban-industrial society has been accompanied by changes in the American family. This transition in the family is best understood in terms of a change from the institutional or old type of family to the present or companionship type of family. It should be understood that this is an "ideal type," a construct used only for purposes of clarity. The American family system is, in fact, probably the most varied of any society in the world. American families differ widely by sections of the country, by economic and social classes, ethnic and religious groups, sections of the cities in which they live, and the kinds of work which they do. They also differ in respect to being authoritarian or egalitarian, and the degree to which either spouse exercises authority over the family. The traditional "mountaineer" family is largely a kinship group; the old Amish are patriarchial; modern urban families are largely democratic or egalitarian.

A comparison of types. Although the American family has never been highly institutionalized in comparison with the old Chinese or Japanese families, it was much more so in the past than it is at present. The true institutional family is the extended or large family; in societies where it is highly developed, its influence and power are very great. In old China, the family dominated all other institutions. In the highly institutionalized family system, the family selects the marriage partners for their children, and they do it on a rather strictly utilitarian basis. Everything is done in the interest of the family as a unit; the wishes of the individual are important only as they relate to the family. In contrast, American parents permit their children to make their own choice of spouses regardless of how immature or ill-conceived they believe the choice to be. In the old institutional family, the authority was vested in the head of the family, the oldest male, who also controlled the property of the family. While his authority was great, so were his responsibilities. As head of the family he was called upon to support the fundamental traditional values of the society and to provide for the present and future security of his family to the best of his ability.

173

Although the institutional family permitted little individualism, it did offer a high degree of security and well-being to its members. The large family was a system of institutionalized relationships which covered most of the vital areas of human behavior and which led to a stable social organization and order. The institutional family contained the nuclear unit—husband, wife, and dependent children—which characterizes the American family of today. The institutional family is held together by legal and social obligations which support the fundamental values of the family unit and the society. These are forces which are external to the individual. The companionship family is held together by the affectional and emotional needs of the individual members. These are internal factors. No family is completely one or the other. What is more important is the position, privileges, and responsibilities of the individual members. The highly institutionalized family socializes its children to a point of view which Americans find inconceivable. This was illustrated by an incident which happened in one of the author's classes several years ago. A very charming and intelligent young Indian girl had made a report on marriage in India. Our American students thought it inconceivable that she could approve of her parents choosing her husband. Her very serious and sensible reply was that "marriage is too serious a thing to be left to the judgement of the young and immature."

The American companionship family is the small or nuclear family composed of the husband, the wife, and their dependent children. The kinship group is, of course, much broader, but most Americans have little knowledge or concern about relatives beyond uncles, aunts, and grandparents, and these are increasingly less important. The American nuclear family is characterized by a high degree of autonomy. When children marry, they are expected to establish a new household that is functionally independent of parents on both sides. Both wives and children have liberties that in other societies would be unbelievable. The companionship family, as the term implies, is held together largely by personal relationships. Most of the other functions which formerly held the American family together have been transferred to other institutions.

Family functions. The lives of the Eskimo, the New York banker, the Bantu tribesman, the Japanese business man, the Australian aborigine, and the Dutch farmer have more in common than one would think. Families everywhere and at all times perform certain functions which are the bases for family organization. These functions are: reproduction, care, status, and socialization. It is entirely possible that any one, or even all, of these functions could be performed outside the family. But, apparently some form of family organization is the best pattern of human association to carry out these functions.

The matter of reproduction is so important to the survival of any society that it cannot be left to chance. It is true that individuals do not give much consideration to reproducing offspring in the interest of society. Their motives are personal. But any society which is threatened by lack of population replacements will become seriously concerned and will usually formulate some policy to increase reproduction. The long period from birth to maturity makes the child an absolutely dependent creature. This long period of dependency is one of the most basic determinants of family organization. The third function, placement or status, determines the position the individual will occupy in the society into which he is born. He will have the status of his parents at birth, but he may change this later in life. The purpose of socialization is to produce an individual who can function effectively within the society. He learns to do the things which must be done in the ways they are expected to be done. The four functions mentioned above cannot be transferred to other institutions without destroying the family. Both the Russians and the Chinese tried to remove some of these functions to institutions outside the family only to give way under the pressure of parents.

An integrated society dominated by the family is very largely a society dominated by the institutional family. In the industrial era, other institutions have become increasingly autonomous, much less subject to the dictates of the family. The society of the Middle Ages was highly integrated under the domination of the Church. Today both the school and the church, as more or less autonomous institutions, play considerable roles in the process of socialization.

EUROPEAN BACKGROUNDS

Religious dissenters and the colonies. The modern American family is the result not only of its environment but of deep roots in its Anglo-Saxon and Judeo-Christian backgrounds. The principles founded in New England became generally accepted throughout the colonies. These principles were derived from the rising English middle classes who were predominantly of religious dissenting sects, especially Puritans. The Puritans wished to separate the church and the family, making the family secular and making marriage a civil affair. The Protestant dissenters had come to accept Martin Luther's and later Calvin's view that marriage was a divine institution but not a sacrament, and that it was subject to dissolution just as any other civil contract. This idea was put into the law by Cromwell in the Matrimonial Act of 1653, but the aristocracy had it abolished immediately upon the Restoration of Charles II in 1660. The New England Puritans made marriage a civil contract controlled by public officials.[1] But because there were no definite canons regulating marriage,

---

[1] Clifford Kirkpatrick, *The Family as Process and Institution*, 2nd ed. (New York, Ronald, 1963), p. 279.

confusion prevailed throughout most of the colonial period. In 1646 Massachusetts passed a law forbidding other than civil marriage; the other New England colonies followed this practice. In the South where the Church of England prevailed, marriage was viewed not as a sacrament but as a divine institution and therefore within the domain of the church.

The Medieval Church gains control over the family. The ancient world had always considered marriage a private and civil affair. It was the purpose of the Medieval Church to establish a universal authority which was capable of sustaining law and order. As tribal organizations disintegrated, their functions were transferred to the political and church authorities. In this long, drawn-out process the conception of marriage as a sacrament became established and the Church acquired control over it. Divorce was considered a violation of a sacrament and a sin, and it was therefore forbidden by the Church. By the beginning of the twelfth century, the ecclesiastical courts in England were in complete control of church matters and church officials. Because of its power the Church was able to transform the tribal "bride price" into the idea of a dowry. It eliminated most of the economic considerations from marriage, and it determined that marriages were to take place with the consent of the persons marrying rather than at the decision of their parents. The purpose of these changes was to take marriage completely out of the hands of the family and place it completely under the Church. This also achieved another change in marriage. Previously a marriage became effective when the agreement to marry was made and the bride price was paid; the ceremony that followed was merely a ritual publicizing the marriage and was not necessary to its validity. The new arrangement reversed the significance of these two practices and required marriage by a Church official. From this time until the Reformation, the Church through the ecclesiastical courts enforced its doctrines on all persons, thus creating the "universal" Church and the concept of the "Christian family." How much this era influenced the entire society of Western Europe is difficult to say, but its influence on the American family is still in evidence in the practice of church weddings, even though they are not necessary to the validity of the marriage.[2]

Common law and the family. One other inheritance from the English tradition which influenced the American family was the common law. In the middle period of English history, the "itinerant judges" who applied the king's law uniformly, overlooking local differences, developed a set of precedents which became the foundation of English common law. Common law recognized the validity of marriage without benefit of either clergy or civil ceremony. The Catholic Council of Trent in 1563

2 *Ibid.*, pp. 109–119.

prohibited such marriages and the British Parliament forbade them in 1753. They were common in the American colonies and during the nineteenth century on the frontier. Although generally frowned upon, they are still legal in about half of the states today. Another aspect of the common law was the legal position of women and, of course, this involved the question of ownership of property. Under the common law, when a woman married, both she and her property became the legal possession and responsibility of her husband. In England it was still the legal privilege of a husband to beat his wife, and this, though little practiced, carried over the American colonies. Although American women are probably the freest in the world today, they are not yet completely free of these former bonds, and state legislatures still hear the pleas for further extension of women's rights. To what extent the Christian religion is responsible for women's position is subject to debate. The early church did, however, stress monogamy and did take a strong stand against abortion, infanticide, and divorce by mutual consent. The Christian leaders also, despite the low esteem in which women were held, insisted that women were on an equal spiritual plane with men. This was a radical doctrine because of its implication for eventual equality in other areas.

THE EARLY AMERICAN FAMILY

New England, Southern, and frontier families. The story of early American family life is one of the most interesting but least known aspects of our history. Arthur W. Calhoun's *A Social History of the American Family,* though old, is still the best source available on the subject. While there were interesting variations in the New England, Southern, and frontier families, their similarities were much more important. At the end of the colonial period, approximately 80 percent of all Americans were of English descent, 7 percent were Scottish, 5.6 percent were German Protestants, and less than 2 percent were Irish. They were all mostly small farmers. Even in New England, with its commerce and industry, small farmers comprised 90 percent of the population. The same proportion of the farms in the plantation South were small farms.

The Puritans in New England had brought their families with them from the beginning and family life was held in high esteem; despite the generally stern picture of the Puritans, family life was on the whole dignified, comfortable, and at times companionable. Although early New England prohibited holiday revelry so common to cavalier Englishmen, not all of their needs to break the monotony of work were met by religious services. Militia training was an occasion for holidays, and was accompanied by much eating, drinking, and outdoor sports; the launching of ships, house raisings, and other common efforts were also occasions for merriment. The records indicate there was much illegitimacy and that drinking was common at all social gatherings. Although hard work and a rather drab existence was certainly the rural pattern for much of the colonial period, cities like Boston were hardly the gloomy places they have frequently been pictured.

In all colonies, hunting and fishing were common outdoor sports, and drinking, smoking, and gambling the ordinary vices. In the Southern colonies, horse-racing and cock-fighting were common diversions of the wealthy. Possibly the most widespread of all colonial amusements was dancing. In the later colonial era, formal dances became very elaborate, long-drawn-out affairs, frequently lasting all night. In the South where the Church of England prevailed, there was a more cavalier attitude toward life and a kind of romanticism developed among the upper classes. Women were placed on a "pedestal"; at the same time they were thought to be mentally inferior and in great need of protection. Isolation and self-support were conditions on the plantation which made for family companionship and strong family ties, and the home rather than the church was the setting of most weddings, christenings, and funerals. Here it was, too, that the plantation became the counterpart of the English manor. The plantation owner was the nearest equivalent in America to the feudal lord. The plantation aristocracy set the social standards and dominated the politics of the South. The lives of the indentured whites, the slaves, and the small upland farmers were in stark contrast to the grandeur of the aristocratic life of the planter family.

The frontier tended to strengthen the family ties; it also tended to bring about basic changes in the family. Women generally worked at physical tasks along with their men and thereby achieved a degree of equality. Frontier Protestantism also tended to promote equality of women. Self-reliance and independence were the most evident personal characteristics resulting from frontier life. As families moved westward, their ties were broken with the larger family they left behind. The old patriarchial relationship between father and son disappeared as the availability of new lands made it easy for sons to establish themselves. The nuclear family became more firmly cohesive. The vast undeveloped resources of the frontier tended to make the measure of a man his potential rather than his past accumulation of wealth.[3]

The American environment and the family. The vast amount of hard labor necessary to carve out a good future in the new and raw environment explains the origin of the glorification of work. The scarcity of labor and the abundance of cheap land made large families desirable. Children married early and it was not uncommon for mother and daughter to give birth to babies about the same time. As the frontier advanced from the Atlantic to the Pacific, those beyond the settled regions were always in a

[3] Don Martindale, *American Society* (New York, Van Nostrand, 1960), pp. 271–272.

struggle against the elements of nature as well as the Indians, and the nuclear family became increasingly self-reliant. Other institutions were weak or even non-existent. Even in the settled areas, the establishment of institutions other than local government and the church took a long time. Children were made to work at an early age, and women worked along with men. The family was a producing unit, and the cooperation of each member was essential. The farmer was necessarily a man of many skills. He had to be skilled in the cultivation of crops, in repairing wagons and farm tools, in making shoes and harnesses, in caring for his sick or wounded livestock, in building a house. His wife had to do as varied a job—she had to do all the household duties, make the clothing, and nurse the members of her family when they were sick. Although other things had their place in rural American life, the problem of conquering the wilderness and acquiring economic security was dominant. That America became known as a materialistic society is understandable in terms of this historical development.

Private tutors or teachers of parochial schools supplied most of the formal education for the middle and southern colonies. Public education was first established in New England. In 1637, Massachusetts required the establishment of public elementary and high schools. Even so, educa-tion for most colonists was mostly in the hands of parents. Where schools did exist, as along the Eastern seaboard, they mainly taught the three R's; the socialization process was largely left to the family. Children received vocational and domestic training within the family as a part of their contribution to the work of the family. Religious worship and ritual were also family functions. Sometimes family religious training was all that was available. Because of the isolation of farm life, the many family activities accustomed the members to companionship and recreation among themselves. Thus as family functions expanded in both number and variety, each family tended to become a self-sufficient social unit.

Characteristics. The early American family was neither an institutional nor a companionship family in a strict sense. It was a large nuclear family with many practices much nearer to the institutional than to the present companionship family. It is estimated that the average family size in 1790 was 5.7 as compared with 3.6 in 1962. The great number of children is also indicated by the fact that the median age was 16 in 1790, only 19 in 1880, and 30 in 1950. The average size of 3.6 of the American family in 1962 includes those families who never had children as well as those whose children were no longer at home. These two groups together comprised about 43 percent of the population. Until the industrial era, children were an economic asset. The early custom of "bride price" and other economic considerations were compensations to the bride's parents for the loss of an economic asset. While the American colonies did not follow these practices, the economic consideration in marriage was paramount. The successful marriage was judged more on the basis of permanence, fertility, and economic considerations than upon the affection of the mates, and this persisted well into the nineteenth century. The question asked was not whether a man loved his wife, but whether he was "a good provider." The bonds which held this older institutional family together were law, custom, duty, and public opinion.

Colonial capitalism manifested itself in trade and land speculation; manufacturing was thwarted by mercantilist restrictions as well as English industrial superiority. The Americans first developed household manufacturing; the members of a family all worked to make cloth and clothing, furniture, household utensils, and many other things for their own use or for local sale. The protestant ethic, so dominant in the New England Puritans, fostered work as an end in itself and economic prosperity as an indication of divine approbation.

CHANGING FAMILY FUNCTIONS

From a producer to a consumer unit. The American family had been a joint productive team or unit before the industrial revolution took production out of the home and placed it in the factory. Members of a family now work as individuals in different places and at different kinds of work. They frequently have only a vague notion of what each other does. The modern family can be called a consuming rather than a producing unit. Their general well-being depends upon their money income and the security of their jobs.

Change in family roles. The change from a rural to an urban society brought about changes in the roles played by the members of the family. The fact that women generally no longer make the clothing for their families or do their own baking, has made it possible for them to work outside the home. The money economy has made it advantageous for them to work for money and buy what they need rather than supply it themselves. In 1964, 36.5 percent of all women over fourteen years of age worked outside the home—women have become more than one-third of the labor force in the United States. Women have always done most of the teaching; now they are entering other professions in small numbers. Children have ceased to be of much importance in the labor force. Compulsory school attendance laws have left few children under eighteen years of age in the working force. The work of men, other than farmers, has changed. It is increasingly limited to the performance of quite simple and usually monotonous tasks. The elimination of children from useful labor and the extremely long period of schooling have made children a heavy financial burden on the family.

In the simple agrarian society, the roles of various members of the family were well defined. In the present urban society, the role of the husband is still reasonably well defined. He is still the main source of income for the family, although he may have lost control over most of its expenditures. The role of the wife has undergone great change and a great deal of conflict and confusion exists. Her earlier role was well defined: her place was in the home. Today she has many roles, somewhat depending on the social class and the nature of her husband's work. She is expected to be an efficient household manager and to assume the major share of responsibility for the children. But she is also expected to be the family purchasing agent, the representative to the PTA, a den mother for Cub Scouts, the family taxi driver, the arranger of the family social life, a charming hostess, a glamour girl as well as a companion to her husband. She may also work outside the home. These are by no means all of the duties which the wife is expected to assume. When these are all added together, it is easy to understand some of the problems which confront the wife in today's world. But the great changes in the role of the wife are reflected in the roles of other members of the family. Husbands today perform domestic duties which in the old days men would have considered menial and degrading to masculinity.

Shift in family authority. Early America was a man's world. When a woman married, she lost her separate legal identity. She could retain her property but her husband acquired control over it and received whatever income it produced. She could not vote, hold office, or serve on juries. She could not perform legal acts without her husband's consent, and he was the sole guardian of their children. Today most of the legal inequities have been removed and the trend toward equality of the sexes extends far beyond the law into the area of customary behavior. Not only have women gained greater freedom in marriage, they have also gained greater freedom from their parents both before and after marriage. The increase in education for women and the development of the democratic idea have also promoted equality of the sexes. Much of the distinction based on sex has disappeared. Women now vote, hold office, and serve on juries, attend coeducational institutions, participate in most of the same recreational and leisure-time activities as men, and work in nearly all the occupations open to men. The two areas in which there is substantial inequality are in income and political leadership. Very few women hold public office. With only a few exceptions, women hold lower paying jobs. Of all men and women employed in the United States, the median income for women is around one-third that for men. In many cases women doing the same work as men receive lower wages. The Federal Civil Service and some states require equal pay for men and women for comparable service. The authority in economic and family matters is generally shared by husband

and wife. Children are also allowed great freedom and sometimes share in the decision making. The patriarchial family is rapidly being replaced by the equalitarian family. Even so, the husband retains some measure of authority because his employment is the chief determinant of place of residence, and family decisions are made with his career taking precedence over other considerations. This is understandable in view of the fact that the status of the family still largely rests on the occupational status of the husband and father.

The family and socialization. We mentioned above the four universal family functions: reproduction, maintenance, placement, and socialization. Although the family still retains these functions, the conditions under which they are performed are greatly changed. Placement or status ascription has been greatly weakened because our society places so much emphasis on achieved status. Even so, achieved status on the average does not differ very much from the ascribed status derived from one's family. Since a child's most formative years are spent in very close contact with his family, his personality characteristics are largely formed by his family. Under pre-industrial conditions, the socialization process was largely carried out by the family. There were few influences, other than the physical environment and the family, to affect the socialization process. Under modern conditions, other institutions, especially education, play a much greater part in the process. The American public is generally agreed that the school should train "the whole child," even to the extent of teaching him honesty, fair play, good manners, right and wrong, consideration for others, and civic and patriotic responsibility. Much attention is given to the last through the social-studies classes and through the celebration of holidays with patriotic songs, poems, and speeches.

Religious training has to a great extent been given over to the churches and Sunday schools, and secular training to the school. A child receive his informal education largely through his experiences in the family and in his peer groups. This part of his socialization is fundamental, and it is doubtful that schools can do more than support the personality development already begun in the home. The function of secular education —formal training—has been very largely transferred to the schools. The motivation, study habits, and other personality traits so necessary to success in school are, however, formed almost completely in the home. In other words, the socialization process is still largely achieved through the informal experiences of the child in the family.

The protective and welfare functions. One area in which the family has lost most is the broad area of protective activities. The early American family was largely self-sufficient. Its physical, spiritual, social, protective, health, and recreational needs were mostly supplied in the home. Now, most of the protective functions are performed outside the family. Today firemen and policemen protect our lives and property; municipal, county, state and federal governments protect our health and afford us recreational facilities. Social Security, Medicare, unemployment compensation, and workmen's compensation protect the aged, the unemployed, and those who are injured. There are all kinds of insurance, private welfare, and charity organizations. All of these institutions have replaced the security that the early family provided for itself. When the westward movement ended, private charity relieved those in distress from death, accident, sickness, and unemployment. The government had begun to deal with these problems before the 1930s, and governments at all levels continue to provide more and more protective and welfare services for the individual American.

Recreation and play activities. Play is characteristic of life of people everywhere and at all times, and early Americans were no exception to the rule. The more common forms of recreation of the rural American family were reading aloud, visiting, family reunions, church socials, husking bees, hunting, fishing, dancing, and singing. Most of these brought two or three generations of the family together, or included the whole family in an intimate neighborhood group. Recreation has always varied according to social classes, and this has been, and still is, true in America. Country music and grand opera do not appeal equally to all classes of people. Of course there are regional differences too. Prior to the industrial revolution, recreation was centered in the home, and was participated in by the family as a group. Most of these recreational activities would today be considered at a low level of skills. This, however, was unimportant. It was the participation which fostered a feeling of intimacy and solidarity. It was this intimacy, this feeling of belonging, which gave the rural American family of the past its feeling of security and stability.

Today recreation, like economic production, has been removed from the home. It is not designed for family participation, but for individuals and couples. People do not actively participate; they take their recreation sitting down, vicariously. It has been argued that the automobile and television have brought the family closer together. This is at best a dubious claim. The automobile is the chief means of scattering the various members of the family to their individual activities, and television programs are studiously tailored to appeal to different age and sex groups. Group participation for the sheer pleasure of participation is largely a thing of the past. Small boys still play ball for no other reason than that they enjoy it, but most of us now prefer to see professionals. Play has its value to the individual for its physical, social, emotional, and educational benefits, and to society through the social integration of play activities. Play and recreation are social necessities, and recently there has been a growing attempt both publicly and privately to develop the play life of urban people. In fact, the American people spend over $20 billion annually on recreation of one kind or another, and even this is not enough. As leisure time increases, and as the number of elderly people and unemployed young people increases, still more and better organized recreational programs will be a necessity.

From the earliest times, the division of labor between husband and wife has been a major integrating factor in marriage. The change in the economic functions of the family has greatly weakened this bond. The former economic interdependence has been drastically altered by advanced technology, and the modern family depends more and more on leisure activities to keep them together.

Mobility and the companionship family. One of the most important factors in shaping the modern American family has been its mobility. The advancing frontier or westward movement which constituted a three-hundred-year sweep from Plymouth and Jamestown to the Pacific coast was an extremely prolonged and extensive wave of migration. The equal economic opportunity which the frontier afforded always beckoned to those whose fortunes had not prospered at home, the young and adventurous, the immigrant, and even the criminal and unscrupulous. It was an opportunity to rise in the social order. It was Frederick Jackson Turner's most important conclusion that the frontier promoted both individualism and democracy and that its organization was based on the family.[4] The traditional type of early American family, much as its European ancestors, depended upon a continuous settlement in one place. Many European families could boast of having lived in the same place—frequently in the same house—for four or five hundred years, and some even longer. Under such conditions the patriarchial family prevailed. The westward movement destroyed the old patriarchial family in America to such an extent that only a few vestiges of it remain in the back country where colonial folkways still survive.

Movement from one place to another without changing one's social status is called horizontal mobility and movement up or down in social status is called vertical mobility. Changing one's place of residence is generally made with the expectation of bettering one's social position. The westward movement with its vision of romance and wealth was the foundation of the "American Dream." Conditions of frontier life made individualism not just a possibility but a necessity. It leveled class distinctions and promoted individual choice in courtship, marriage, and family relationships. This emphasis on individualism eventually brought about an unstable family, a family where tradition, pride, and sacredness

---

[4] Frederick Jackson Turner, *The Frontier in American History* (New York, Henry Holt and Company, 1920), pp. 22–30.

count for little. The old idea of family solidarity and the principle of individual choice are incompatible. Young members of the family today usually find their jobs far removed from their parents, marry someone the family does not know or does not know well, visit with other members of the family only occasionally, and frequently find that they have more in common with certain people whom they have known only a few years than they do with members of their own family. Most people are reluctant to admit the degree to which this is true. The welfare of the family as a unit has ceased to be more important than that of any single individual member. Today the family exists for the satisfaction of the individual members; when that satisfaction ceases to exist the parents do not hesitate to separate and break up the family regardless of their children or other kin.

Out of this mobile society with its individual-centered family has come a great need by the individual for affection and intimacy that can come only in marriage. The early American man had a most utilitarian need for a wife to cook and sew and bear his children, and a satisfactory family life did not depend upon the romantic relationship between them. Today those dependencies have weakened, leaving affection as the tenuous thread which holds the family together. The family is no longer held together either by compulsion or contract but by the affection and loyalties growing out of satisfying associations within the companionship family.

The companionship family and instability. The American family today is called the companionship family because of its emphasis upon intimate interpersonal associations. Its egalitarian, democratic, and individualistic character places a heavy strain upon the ties of affection. That the strain has been too heavy is indicated by the comparative divorce rate which was 2.7 per 1,000 population in 1967 as compared to 0.3 per 1,000 in 1860, or an increase of over 900 percent. With our excessive individualism within the family, the continuously younger age at marriage, the increasing secularization of marriage, the increasing democratization in other areas of society, and the almost complete dependence upon romance to hold the family together, the present instability of the family is to be expected.

The "romantic fallacy" which pervades America and many other industrialized societies is one of the greatest hoaxes ever played upon unsuspecting youth. They go into marriage in splendor à la Hollywood, expecting to fold up in each other's arms and "live happily ever afterwards" only to find that this was only the prelude to sick babies, dirty dishes and diapers, and such mundane matters as earning a living in a highly competitive world. Of course there was romance "when knighthood was in flower," but it had nothing to do with the family. The age of chivalry contained elements of mere sex exploitation, and that is inimical to family life. In American marriage today physical attraction has become a highly valued characteristic, but it is not a sound basis on which to build a stable family. Romance should be understood for what it is. It is a good way to get married but an impossible basis for a lifetime of marital happiness. If older people acted as romantic as do our youth of today, they would be thought silly or childish, and that would be right. Romance is for youth. It would seem that intelligent young people could observe from the experience of their parents and grandparents that it is such personal characteristics as unselfishness, integrity, fidelity, kindness, and cooperation which make a happy marriage rather than the intense infatuation of youth. The unsophisticated rustic of yesteryear understood this and properly termed it "puppy love." The trouble comes from equating love with romance or infatuation so that when romance fades it becomes necessary to find some other, more stable basis for affection. Many never make it. But romantic love has evolved as a part of our democratic way of life, it is an essential part of our family pattern, and any attempt to eliminate it is out of the question.

Social classes and the family. An understanding of the family in a society requires some explanation of the relationship between the class structure and the family. The family into which one is born gives him his initial position or status in the society. It also determines such things as where he will live, his race, religion, political views, the amount of education he will receive, whom he will marry, his style of life. People do change their status, but they do so less frequently than is generally believed. Some of the advantages of being born into an upper class are better health, medical care, and nutrition as well as better opportunity for education, travel, and other experiences which guarantee one's remaining in a superior social position, or even improving it. On the other hand, one who is born into a lower class has none of these advantages and has to fight his way against all kinds of odds to move up the social ladder.

When we speak of class structure we do not mean that there are well-defined classes and that everyone knows exactly to which class he and others around him belong. The fact is, however, that we all rank people either consciously or unconsciously into those who are our equals, our superiors, or our inferiors: those with whom we would feel free to dine, those with whom we would like to dine but will likely not have the opportunity, and those with whom we would not like to dine. Or, there are those families with whose children we would like our children to associate and eventually to marry and those with whom we would not want our children to associate and certainly not to marry. The basis on which such ranking is made is the prestige or esteem in which the individual is held by other members of the community. We all know people at various levels who are ranked very high by the vast majority of people.

We also know some who have done nothing to be recognized and who are so devoid of personal qualities which the public values that they are at the bottom of the social scale. We also know great numbers in between these two. Roughly speaking, these classifications represent upper, lower, and middle-class positions.

The position or status that a family holds is largely that of the father and husband. When a girl marries, unless she has made a name for herself by her own achievement, she adopts the status of her husband. Children have the status of their parents. Status, in other words, is a family matter. There are numerous criteria by which ranking is determined, and these vary in different societies. In American society, money or wealth is of basic importance. The poor and uneducated are in a position to achieve very little that will raise their social status. A certain amount of money is essential to secure an education, which is the broadest channel to improvement of status. It is not education per se which gives the individual status, but the position he can achieve with his education. One may become a Supreme Court Justice, a great physician, a great scientist, a great inventor, but only because he could afford the requisite education. The criteria for achieving status are interrelated. The best single criterion for identifying the status of an individual is his occupation. It is common knowledge that members of the Supreme Court, Senators, and governors rank high because of the political positions they have achieved. Physicians, college professors, ministers, and lawyers also rank high. On the other hand, farm hands, restaurant waiters, janitors, garbage collectors occupy positions near the bottom of the social scale.

Studies have been made showing the status of most of our occupations. A few of the conclusions show the following: that "big businessmen" were ranked as upper class with a few exceptions in the middle class; that more than half of the doctors and lawyers were ranked upper class and nearly all of the remainder middle class; that more than half of the school teachers were ranked middle class and about one-third lower class; that more than half of the office workers were ranked lower class and most of the others middle class; that factory workers were rated as lower class with a few middle class; and that janitors were almost entirely ranked lower class. W. Lloyd Warner's "Yankee City" study showed that only about 3 percent of the population were ranked upper class, about 38 percent middle class, and about 59 percent lower class.[5] On the basis of family income, probably the most important factor in the style of life, the differences are somewhat shocking. The lower classes do not agree that America is an "affluent society." In 1964 there were some 9 million families and 5.3 million unattached persons—over 34 million people—with less than $3,130 annual income per family, or half that for single indi-

[5] W. Lloyd Warner, *American Life*, rev. ed. (Chicago, University of Chicago Press, 1962), p. 77.

viduals. Another 14 million families and unattached individuals—47 million people—had incomes between $3,130 and $6,000 annually. This represents a total of some 81 million Americans in over 21 million families, about half of whom live in poverty and the other half in varying degrees of deprivation, based on the above standards. Put in another way, the lowest 20 percent of the families in the United States had only one-eighth as much income per family as the highest 20 percent.[6]

Family income is also related to occupation and education. In 1960, the families in agriculture and forestry, personnel services, business and repair services, retail trade, entertainment and recreation services, and construction, with annual incomes of less than $4,000, ranged from 67 percent of the families in agriculture to 25 percent of those in construction. On the other hand, families in professional and related services, wholesale trade, finance, insurance and real estate, transportation and communication, manufacturing and public administration, with annual incomes of less than $4,000, ranged from 19 percent for professional and related services to 8 percent for public administration.[7] The same discrepancy in income holds for variations in the educational level. In 1958, of the wage earners with less than an eight-grade education, 65 percent were at the poverty level and 20.5 percent were at the deprivation level. Of the high school graduates, 23 percent were at the poverty level and 32 percent were at the deprivation level. Of the college graduates, on the other hand, only 9 percent were at the poverty level and 25 percent were at the deprivation level.[8] Another low income group is the aged. In 1960, of the 6.2 million families headed by people aged 65 or over, nearly 10 percent had incomes of less than $1,000 annually, almost one-third had incomes of less than $2,000 annually, and about two-thirds had incomes of less than $4,000 annually.[9]

While social class is not altogether a matter of money, money or education or both are generally necessary for one to improve his social status. Since a social class is composed of those who feel they belong together, what is more important is that its members have the same attitudes, values, and way of life. There is nothing, however, which influences these factors more than the level of income and education in the family. As the Lynds so cogently said in *Middletown*, there is nothing so important as "the mere fact of being born upon one or the other side of the watershed"[10] in determining how one will think and what he will

[6] Leon H. Keyserling, *The Role of Wages in a Great Society* (Washington, Conference on Economic Progress, 1966), pp. 21–22.

[7] *Poverty and Deprivation in the United States* (Washington, Conference on Economic Progress, 1962), p. 48.

[8] *Ibid.,* p. 63.

[9] *Ibid.,* p. 53.

[10] Robert S. and Helen M. Lynd, *Middletown* (New York, Harcourt, Brace, 1929), pp. 23–24.

do all of the days of his life. Each social class has its own behavior patterns, values, and way of life. The lower-lower-class child in the ghettos of our large cities—where hardly anyone has a steady job, where being on relief has become a way of life, where filth and lack of privacy dominate the scene, and where parents are likely to be uncooperative with school and other officials—is as conditioned to follow the behavior patterns and values of his environment as are the sons of bankers, businessmen, and lawyers. Such is the process of socialization. In other words, the class system operates through socialization to prepare most children for a class status similar to that of their parents. When sociologists speak of classes as subcultures they mean that the normal experiences of those in one class differ from those of other classes. This is obvious in regard to such activities as personal ambition, self-discipline, care and discipline of children, food habits, topics of conversation, religious practices, sex behavior, reading habits, work habits, and appreciation of the arts.

THE AMERICAN FAMILY TODAY

Sociologists generally agree with Arthur W. Calhoun who stated nearly half a century ago that the American family "has been . . . a product of the ascendancy of the bourgeois class, the dominance of a virgin continent, and the industrial revolution."[11] The American family today is the end product not only of its more recent native environment, but also of its cultural heritage. The rise of the middle class, industrialization, and urbanization have changed the whole physical environment, and beginning with the Renaissance and Reformation, the individual has increasingly become the center of our ideological system. The development of democracy has also tended to promote individualism. Many critics of the present family see instability as a process of disorganization which will ultimately destroy the family. On the other hand, most authorities on the family see the present condition as a process of reorganization—a transition to meet the changed needs of a new environment. There is also much evidence that family life in America is not on its way to extinction. A larger proportion of the population is married and living together than at any time in our history; and those who are divorced marry again in greater proportion than widows or than those who are single. It is true, however, that second marriages do not generally work out as well as first marriages.

Critics who believe the family is in a process of disintegration base their conclusions largely on the rising divorce rate, the falling birth rate, and the loss of family functions. These objective facts, however, in no

[11] Arthur W. Calhoun, *The Social History of the American Family,* Vol. 3 (New York, Barnes & Noble, 1945), p. 332.

way minimize the importance of the family. In keeping with the trend in all other areas of American society, family functions have been largely reduced to specialization in socialization and affection among its members. It can hardly be argued that to reduce the divorce rate and to increase the birth rate to what they were a hundred or so years ago would be compatible with these goals. Since individual happiness is the primary goal of present-day marriage, it is not difficult to see why a divorce rate much higher than in the past is inevitable. Furthermore, it cannot be scientifically established that it would be better for either the family or society if American families had more children than they now have. These are judgements which some Americans hold; but they do not alter the fact that in general Americans are committed to the small family. The approach to the solution of present family problems is not a return to some earlier stage of family development but to a positive approach to new solutions.

Many efforts are being made to aid the family. Some of these efforts are to remove the causes of the problems, others are only ameliorative. Government at all levels has done much. There are state welfare departments whose activities are largely carried out at the local level. States also have mental and physical health services; services and care for tubercular, indigent, and crippled children; unemployment insurance, workmen's compensation, vocational rehabilitation; veterans services; and public recreation programs. At the federal level, Social Security covers some nine-tenths of all workers; public assistance is provided the aged, the needy, blind, disabled, and dependent children; there are programs of child welfare, vocational rehabilitation, public health, veteran's services, Medicare, aid to hospitals, and public housing. The complete list would cover several pages. Most churches have programs of one kind or another, especially for their youth and young married adults. In addition to social-work schools, colleges and universities everywhere are offering courses in marriage and the family. Public schools also deal with family life. Beyond all of this there are professional counsellors such as psychologists and psychiatrists and many private agencies in the community which support the family in many ways. There are also many national organizations under what has been called "the family life movement" which are devoted to the problems of children, marriage, and the family. This is the most promising approach because it is apparent that specific problems must be considered in relation to the whole family. Among the best known organizations of this "movement" are The Child Study Association of America, The National Congress of Parents and Teachers, The American Home Economic Association, The Planned Parenthood Federation of America, and The Family Service Association of America. There have also been many "national conferences" and 'White House conferences" on various problems of the family.

Evidence is abundant that the values emerging in the companionship family are in keeping with its goals. A few of these goals are:

1. *The satisfaction of the affectional needs.* Today's family does not generally remain intact unless the affectional needs are met. This accounts in part for the high rate of divorce. Since many of those who are unhappy do become divorced, and since happiness is a good criterion of marriage, it is a fair conclusion that there is greater happiness in the family today than in the past.

2. *The equality of spouses.* In a society in which women are accepted as equals in education, politics, and economic activities, it is consistent that the same should be true in the family.

3. *The greater freedom of children.* Probably no area of change in the family has been more sweeping than that of the position of children in the family. Today's family life is largely centered around the activities of its children. They are not only permitted but encouraged to participate in family decisions, especially concerning themselves.

4. *Personality development.* One of the chief tenets of modern education as well as family training is the fullest development of the personality potential of the individual child.

5. *Greatest happiness in the family.* In the institutional family, happiness was more a by-product of its other activities than a direct goal. It is true that members of the institutional family felt greater security than do members of the present family, but this does not prove that they were happier. They probably were not. As life's daily activities become more and more specialized and monotonous, individuals look increasingly to the family for their personal satisfactions. These values are placed squarely in the psychological area because today the personal relationship is becoming the main aspect of marriage.

BIBLIOGRAPHY

Anshen, Ruth Nanda, *The Family: Its Function and Destiny.* New York, Harper, 1949.

Baber, Ray E., *Marriage and the Family.* New York, McGraw-Hill, 1953.

Blitzen, Dorothy R., *The World of the Family.* New York, Random House, 1963.

Burgess, Ernest W., and Harvey J. Locke, *The Family: From Institutional to Companionship.* New York, American Book, 1953.

Calhoun, Arthur W., *The Social History of the American Family.* New York, Barnes & Noble, 1945.

Cavan, Ruth Shonle, *The American Family.* New York, Crowell, 1953.

Christensen, Harold T., ed. *Handbook of Marriage and the Family.* Chicago, Rand McNally, 1964.

Kenkel, William F., *The Family in Perspective: A Fourfold Analysis.* New York, Appleton-Century-Crofts, 1960.

Kirkpatrick, Clifford, *The Family as Process and Institution.* New York, Ronald, 1963.

Ogburn, W. F., and M. F. Nimkoff, *Technology and the Changing Family.* Boston, Houghton Mifflin, 1955.

Sirjamaki, John, *The American Family in the Twentieth Century.* Cambridge, Mass., Harvard, 1953.

Stroup, Attlee, L., *Marriage and the Family: A Developmental Approach.* New York, Appleton-Century-Crofts, 1966.

Turner, Frederick Jackson, *The Frontier in American History.* New York, Henry Holt, 1920.

Winch, Robert F., *The Modern Family,* rev. New York, Henry Holt, 1963.

10

Education

PRIMITIVE societies had little formal education and certainly had nothing which we would call schools. Most learning was accomplished informally in the family and other primary groups. The individual learned the language, manners, customs, and other patterns of behavior from his elders. Through verbal statements and experience he learned the behavior which was expected of him in regard to work, play, religion, the family, his tribe, his enemies. This knowledge was acquired in an informal way. There were no complex, organized programs of studies, no particular individuals designated as teachers, and no assignments of authority outside the family for carrying out the learning activities. As a greater amount of learning was required, education became more and more organized, more formal. We shall use the term "education" here in the sense of formal education—education that involves programs of study, specialized facilities, teachers, and books.

Ancient societies such as China and Greece had formal education only for special social classes. Education had different purposes in different societies. In ancient China, formal education was limited to teaching classical literature and poetry to those who were to become the ruling intellectual aristocracy. It was so successfully done that Confucian China has been called "a kingdom of philosophers." The highest aim was the cultivated, moral man, and this ideal dominated not only Chinese education but the whole of Chinese social thought for 2,500 years, down to 1911. Modern China demands a different kind of education, one based on science and technology rather than on literature and philosophy. Ancient Greek education stressed service to the state, individual initiative directed toward patriotism and social welfare. Until recently the great masses in all societies had little or no formal education; the performance of their roles did not require it.

The great masses of people, even in Western Europe and America, before the nineteenth century, required little if any more formal education to perform their societal roles than was required by the Chinese or Greeks two thousand years ago. The rise of the commercial-industrial societies and the middle classes changed the roles of people so radically that family training was no longer adequate preparation for the tasks they would be called upon to perform. The Division of labor and specialization require mechanics, machinists, typists, stenographers, photographers, accountants, engineers, lawyers, doctors, teachers, and hundreds of other people with specialized training. Along with the long development of the industrial revolution came the development of formal education. The greater the degree of industrialization, the more formal education is required. This relationship is important. It is no mere coincidence that states such as Russia and China which try to change their institutions radically in a very short time attempt to do so largely through institutions of formal education. The masses have to be taught their new roles and, because they are more complex, greater formal education is necessary.

European backgrounds and nationalism. European education during the early Middle Ages was mainly in the hands of the Church. After the beginning of the eleventh century, the rediscovery of the classical writings and thought of Greece and Rome opened the way for the Renaissance and eventually the loosening of the hold of the Church on education. The classical influence on European and American education has been deep and long-lasting. Catholic institutions still stress classical studies, and many other schools and colleges offer Latin and Greek languages and literature in their curricula. The "great books" idea is also in the classical tradition. The foundations of the modern scientific and secular tradition started with the rise of "humanism" as represented by Petrarch, Boccaccio, and many others in the fourteenth century. It was more specifically influenced by Copernicus, Brache, Kepler, Galileo, Descartes, Francis Bacon, Isaac Newton, and others during the sixteenth and seventeenth centuries. Today the classics have been largely replaced by the social studies, modern languages, literature, and the natural sciences, all of which deal more with the present than with the past.

Another influence giving shape to modern education in the Western world was the rise of nationalism. National languages took form during the Middle Ages; by the sixteenth century, there was a great demand for a national literature in the Vernacular. The newly invented printing press supplied numerous copies of the classics as well as grammars and dictionaries. The stage was set for national libraries, national literatures, and national education.

Some German states, particularly those of the Protestant faith, building upon the efforts of Martin Luther to establish a public religious system of schools, developed what might be called the first national systems of education. Their primary aim was to give children the proper background for understanding their religion. In 1787 Prussia established a ministry of education and took the supervision of the schools out of the hands of the clergy. By the nineteenth century, the aim of education, throughout Europe, had become the indoctrination of students with patriotism and religion. Elementary schools were established for the masses and secondary schools for the upper classes. The early national systems of education did not essentially interfere in the relationship between the church and the state. The church continued to dominate the schools; the Catholic Church in particular remained in virtual control of education in the Catholic countries.

THE EMERGENCE OF PUBLIC SCHOOLS IN AMERICA

English backgrounds. The early American settlers brought with them the ideas of education prevalent in the mother country at the time. Education was still mainly the responsibility of the parents. The well-to-do learned to read at home or in private schools. They then went to Latin grammar schools for seven or eight years. The English Latin grammar school was a product of the Renaissance; it had replaced the older secondary monastic and cathedral schools. Most of the education in these grammar schools was devoted to learning to read and write Latin and some Greek. When a student had acquired proficiency in Latin he was admitted to one of the colleges at Oxford or Cambridge. Certain opportunities were provided for bright boys who were unable to pay the regular fees. This type of education well served the needs of those who would enter the service of the Church or the professions. Private masters gradually established schools where middle-class children could learn the basic skills. The poor were generally apprenticed to master craftsmen for a term of years while they learned a trade. Many conscientious masters taught their apprentices to read and write.

Education in New England. Education in the colonies varied. It was in New England that public, tax-supported education first took root. The Boston Latin School, in the tradition of the English Latin grammar school, was established in 1635. In 1643, it became publicly supported, and soon after the neighboring towns began to establish their own public schools. In 1642, Massachusetts made it compulsory for parents to make some provision for the education of their children, and masters were required to teach their apprentices reading and religion. In 1647, towns with fifty or more households were required to establish schools to teach all children to read and write; those with one hundred or more households were required to maintain schools where boys could be prepared for college. By about 1675, there were many private schools teaching such subjects as advanced arithmetic, modern languages, bookkeeping, and navigation. Toward the end of the colonial period many private secondary schools called "academies" began to appear. They were designed mainly to prepare students for college, but their curriculum was much broader than that of the old Latin grammar schools.

As the frontier moved westward, the settlements became more dispersed, and the town school and town church suffered a decline. As the Congregationalists lost their religious monopoly, their interest in maintaining the school as the means of religious indoctrination weakened. Independent public schools, many of them small country schools, began to appear in community areas or districts. This was the beginning of the district system as a tax-supported, democratic organization. It became characteristic of schooling throughout the country—the small, one-room country school became the symbol of rural American education.

Education in other areas. During the eighteenth century only New England had public schools in any numbers. Practically all schools in the Middle Atlantic and Southern states were private institutions controlled by religious denominations or individual schoolmasters. In the colonial South the most common was a private school where a group of neighboring families would cooperate to erect a building and employ a master to teach their children reading, writing, and arithmetic for a few months in the year. The teacher was required to have a license. This was the only control the government exercised, and it did it perfunctorily. Most of the teachers were Anglican clergymen or lay readers of the parish. The plantation system made the distances between neighbors a serious handicap to both religious and educational activities. Most wealthy parents employed tutors for their children, and a few sent their children to England to be educated. During the early colonial period, most of the tutors came from Oxford or Cambridge; during the eighteenth century, they came mostly from Harvard, Yale, and Princeton, and some from the universities of Scotland. Girls as well as boys received instruction. For the poor there were a few endowed free schools and a few charity schools maintained by the Anglican Church. The apprenticeship system was the most important institution for providing elementary education. The majority of the poor received no formal education at all.

In the early colonial period both New York and Pennsylvania had public schools which later gave way to private and parochial schools. The excellent schools maintained by the Dutch deteriorated after the English took over New York, and in Pennsylvania the great hopes of William Penn for public education were soon dashed. The Quakers, however, maintained among the best elementary and secondary schools in America. Because of the many religious and national groups in Pennsylvania, schools varied both in type and quality. The Scotch-Irish were very interested in education, and one of the most notable secondary schools in Pennsylvania was William Tennent's Log College which taught not only the fervent evangelism of the early Presbyterians, but also the traditional subjects of the classical curriculum. Tennent was a graduate of the University of Edinburgh and, in addition to training his own four sons to the ministry, trained some twenty other extraordinary preachers. In the interior and more isolated areas, the schools were more likely to be poor quality neighborhood schools.

The Latin grammar school was eventually established in all sections of the colonies. It was intended primarily to prepare students for college. Although it taught other subjects, emphasis was placed on Latin. This type of school was not well suited to a new country where Latin was of little use, and in the course of time it was superseded by the academy. The academy grew out of private efforts by schoolmasters to establish secular schools which would offer subjects useful to the growing commercial and trade classes along the eastern seaboard. The academy made its appearance at the end of the colonial period and was most firmly established around the middle of the nineteenth century. Massachusetts had 17 academies in 1800; by 1860, the number had grown to 154.

Public education. Despite the many setbacks to public education, public education was gradually extended from New England to other states. This was due in part to the growing conviction that democratic institutions and universal male suffrage demanded an enlightened public. It was also promoted by the tremendous migration of Yankees who had grown up with the institution. By the time of the Civil War, most of the states in the North had established democratically controlled, tax-supported public schools. Public schools came to the South only after the Civil War. The South was not, however, as far behind the rest of the country as it might appear. The proportion of white children attending school in the South in 1860 was only slightly less than elsewhere.

The New England district school with its board of trustees gradually spread throughout the states. The struggle was long and sometimes bitter. The idea that every property owner, whether he had children or not, should pay taxes to support the education of all children was a radical innovation and a bitter pill for the conservatives. In the development of the public school system, the cities were more progressive than the rural areas. Once the public schools were accepted, the problem of how to improve the quality of education arose. Under the early district system attendance was generally poor, uniformity in standards nonexistent, supervision negligible, facilities shabby and lacking in sanitation, teachers poorly paid and often poorly trained. Good schools, then as now, cost money, and bitter controversy at the district level often ended at the expense of the schools. But how dear it became to the hearts of Americans is indicated by the fact that there still exists a great deal of nostalgia for the "crossroads schoolhouse." As late as 1930 there were still nearly 150,-

000 one-teacher elementary schools; by 1962, the number diminished to 13,333.[1] These schools were not always poorly run. Many of the teachers were men and women of excellent character and sound, if limited, training who gave more individual attention to their pupils than was possible in many of the overcrowded urban schools.

In 1860 there were only a hundred or so public high schools in the whole country, mostly in New England and the Middle West. The number had grown to 2,500 by 1890, and by 1963, to over 25,000, with nearly 2 million high school students. This great growth can be due to middle-class demands for status and a more practical education and by demands for a higher level of technical and specialized education created by industrialization. During the last half of the nineteenth century, free elementary education had become the right of every child; it was the second quarter of the twentieth century before high school education gained the same status. In 1900 only some 10 percent of the children of high school age attended school; today, over 95 percent do, and more than half of all high school graduates go to college.

THE EMERGENCE OF HIGHER EDUCATION

Universities in the Middle Ages. The Renaissance awakened an interest in elementary and secondary education as well as in the colleges and universities. During the Middle Ages, centers of study were formed by noted teachers and their students. Some cathedral and monastic schools such as Oxford, Paris, and Bologna acquired widespread fame. These were the centers around which universities developed. By the year 1200, the teachers and students at these centers were beginning to form associations or guilds for mutual protection and advantage. They secured charters from either the pope or the king. The word university originally meant an association. By the end of the twelfth century, such associations or universities had been established at Salerno, Bologna, and Reggio in Italy; Paris and Montpelier in France; and Oxford in England. By the end of the thirteenth century, eight more had been established in Italy, three more in France, five in Spain and Portugal, and one—Cambridge—in England.[2] By 1600, there were 108 such universities in Europe. This great revival of learning was the intellectual counterpart of the rise of the town economy and the middle classes.

By the fourteenth century, the medieval universities had four faculties: liberal arts, law, medicine, and theology. Each faculty had a dean and each university a rector and a chancellor, whose position was more

[1] *The U. S. Book of Facts, Statistics and Information for 1966* (New York, Herald Tribune, 1965), p. 106.
[2] Wallace K. Ferguson and Geoffrey Bruun, *European Civilization*, 2nd ed. (Boston, Houghton Mifflin, 1947), p. 305.

honorary than administrative. In order that only those who were qualified taught, the chancellor was empowered to grant licenses to students who had passed examinations. These examinations led to a fixed curriculum of studies on which candidates were examined. When a student had finished the first stage, a four-year elementary liberal arts program, and had passed the examinations, he was granted a Bachelor of Arts degree which entitled him to be an assistant teacher. The Master of Arts degree usually took two more years of study; having passed the required examinations, the student became a master teacher and a member of the governing body of the university. For the Master of Arts degree the student was usually required to prepare a thesis and defend it against his examiners much as the journeyman presented his masterpiece to the guild members as proof of his proficiency. This six-year program was required of all students. It consisted of the seven liberal arts which were divided into the trivium: grammar, rhetoric, and logic; and the quadrivium: arithmetic, geometry, astronomy, and music. Having become a Master of Arts, the student wishing to specialize in one of the professions could pursue a course of study leading to the doctoral degree and admittance to the faculties of theology, medicine, or law.[3]

The university was essentially a clerical institution. Both students and teachers were considered clergy and were exempted from ordinary civil jurisdiction. As a corporation, the university was also exempt from the jurisdiction of the bishop, and disciplinary power was vested in the faculty, subject only to the pope. The continental universities were very cosmopolitan. There was no language barrier since proficiency in Latin was the primary entrance requirement. If the records are true, some of the students were rich, some poor, some diligent, some lazy, and some just enjoyed a long vacation away from home. In fact, they were apparently very much like students of modern times except that they were undoubtedly more undisciplined, probably given to greater drunkenness, violence, and immorality.[4]

Science and mathematics. The seventeenth century has been aptly called the Century of Genius. It was at this time that the two basic "habits" to which science owes its great success came into practice. These were the habit of translating all calculations when possible into mathematical terms, and the habit of basing all conclusions on observation and experiment. Libraries, laboratories, and observatories, and such inventions as the telescope, microscope, barometer, and air pump helped scientific investigation. The Royal Society of London was founded in 1662, and the Academie des Sciences in Paris in 1666. These and other academies pub-

[3] *Ibid.*, pp. 306–307.
[4] *Ibid.*, p. 307.

lished journals and collected funds to promote scientific activities.[5] The eighteenth century was well-called the Scientific Renaissance. Less than a century after Galileo had been threatened by the Inquisition for his scientific ideas, Sir Isaac Newton was buried in 1727 "with honors befitting a king." During this era, logarithms, analytical geometry, and calculus were invented. Great progress was made in physics, chemistry, and zoology; astronomy, anatomy, biology, geology, and mineralogy were introduced as scientific disciplines.

The educational institutions in Halle, Germany, in 1695 were the first to break with the classical tradition. History, geography, the study of animal life, writing, counting, music, and religion were added to the elementary school curriculum. The secondary school added history, geography, music, science, and mathematics to Latin, Greek, and Hebrew. The University of Halle, established in 1694, was the first modern university founded in the spirit of the new science and mathematics. It was a revolt against the orthodoxy of Lutheranism. Latin was replaced with German, and Descartes and Bacon replaced Aristotle as authorities. The university encouraged free investigation and research based on academic freedom.[6] The University of Berlin, founded in 1810, expressed the new conception of a university whose ideals were dedication to original research and the contribution to knowledge. The revolution of university education both in Germany and other parts of the world followed.

Early American colleges. Only two colleges were established in America during the seventeenth century: Harvard, by the Puritans in 1636, and William and Mary, by the Anglican Church in 1693. Yale was established in 1701 by the Congregationalists. Between 1740 and 1769 six colleges were established: Princeton by the Presbyterians in 1746, King's College (Columbia) by the Anglicans in 1754, Brown by the Baptists in 1764, Rutgers by the Reformed Dutch in 1766, Dartmouth by the Congregationalists in 1769, and the College of Philadelphia (University of Pennsylvania) in 1755.[7] It will be observed that all of these except the College of Philadelphia were denominational. At the same time that these colleges with their rigid curricula and orthodox ideas were being established, a different concept of education was forming in Europe. Not only was the eighteenth century the age of the scientific renaissance, it was also "the age of reason and enlightenment." The "enlightenment" was best expressed in the thoughts of Rousseau and Voltaire. It was a reaction against absolutism in government, mercantilism in economics, authoritarianism

5 John Geise, *Man and the Western World* (New York, Hinds, Hayden, and Eldridge, 1947), p. 673.

6 R. Freeman Butts, *A Cultural History of Western Education* (New York, McGraw-Hill, 1955), pp. 297–298.

7 Nelson Manfred Blake, *A Short History of American Life* (New York, McGraw-Hill, 1952), pp. 88–91.

in religion, the doctrine of original sin in human nature, the rigid class system, and the domination of intellectual life by medieval conceptions of truth. It represented a growing faith in the common man and in human and scientific reason. This intellectual revolution was neither sudden nor violent, but it revolutionized intellectual values, unshackled men's minds, and turned their thoughts from the past to the future.

America was not untouched by this movement. The more liberal intellectuals favored a complete system of education under the supervision of the state. In keeping with this idea they attempted to transform the private denominational colleges into state institutions. This attempt began as far back as 1750 in a battle over the founding of King's College. Representatives of the Anglican Church and the Tory classes wanted the college to be founded by a royal charter; representatives of the Presbyterian, dissenting, and democratic forces wanted it established by an enactment of the legislature, thereby bringing it under government control. Jefferson's attempt to convert William and Mary into a state institution in 1779 failed, as did attempts at Yale and Dartmouth. In the case of Dartmouth, New Hampshire attempted to abrogate the charter. The case went to the Supreme Court of the United States which handed down the now famous Dartmouth College decision in 1819, stating that the charter was a contract and could not be set aside by the state. This ended the efforts to convert the older colleges to state institutions and encouraged the establishment of many other private colleges.[8]

The number of colleges established is indicative of the interest in higher education. By 1860 there were 173 new colleges which had survived and several times that many that had failed. From our vantage point the situation appears ridiculous. Of the 173 only 17 were state universities. The number of church colleges were as follows: Presbyterian, 49; Congregationalist, 21; Methodist, 34; Baptist, 25; Episcopalian, 11; and Catholic, 1. Ohio had 17 of these colleges; Pennsylvania had 16; New York, 15; Illinois, 12. The number was far in excess of demand. At the time Harvard and Yale had only 400 to 500 students, and the small colleges had 200 or less. Largely dependent upon student fees, none of these institutions could afford adequate faculty or equipment and their standards left much to be desired.[9]

State Universities. The proponents of state-controlled higher education, having failed to take over the older denominational colleges, turned to the establishment of the first state universities. New York moved toward state control when the legislature created the Regents of the University of New York in 1784 as a private corporation which could found colleges, give them the right to grant degrees, and inspect their conduct. Although

---

[8] *Ibid.,* pp. 304–305.
[9] *Ibid.,* p. 306.

Columbia was included, it was given special privileges. After the non-sectarian College of Philadelphia came under Anglican and Tory control, attempts were begun to convert it into the University of Pennsylvania; this was accomplished in 1791. The University of Georgia was chartered in 1785, North Carolina in 1789, Vermont in 1791, Ohio in 1804, and South Carolina in 1805. Most of these schools did not get under way for several years, and the state's control over them was indirect and negligible. Financial support came from private gifts, tuition fees, and endowments. In Virginia, Jefferson worked for years to establish state control over William and Mary but the conservative opposition prevailed. Turning to the legislature, he secured the creation of the University of Virginia in 1819. Jefferson was given great freedom in planning the campus, organizing the curriculum, and selecting the faculty. The result was an institution unique to the American scene and probably the accomplishment of which he was most proud. The campus itself was unique, the faculty was carefully recruited from England, and the curriculum omitted theological courses and emphasized modern languages, government, political economy, and science. The University of Michigan, following the pattern of the great German universities, was the first true university established before the Civil War.

Along with the growth of higher education came the development of professional schools. Medical schools were established at the College of Philadelphia, King's College, Harvard, and Dartmouth between 1765 and 1798, and several others early in the nineteenth century. Professorships of law were instituted at several colleges before 1800, and the Harvard School of Law was established in 1817. The majority of doctors and lawyers, however, still gained their training through apprenticeship. Later other professions such as engineering and teaching came into the curriculum.[10]

Since the early aim of higher education, aside from limited training for the professions, was mental and moral discipline, the fact that the subject matter of the curriculum was largely irrelevant to early nineteenth-century life disturbed only a few critics. The standard required curriculum meant that those who were preparing for business or law took the same subjects as those preparing for the ministry. A good many subjects were listed, but only Latin, Greek, mathematics, and philosophy were emphasized. A little science, economics, and political science might be included along with some phase of philosophy. Almost completely neglected were English literature, modern history, and modern languages. By 1860, some recognition had been given to these newer subjects but their status was so low that they were frequently given as extra subjects at unusual times in the schedule and did not count toward the B. A. degree.

10 *Ibid.*, pp. 304–308.

The break with the classical tradition. It was only after the Civil War that the new industrial age demanded and began to get an education more suitable to its needs. The new demands made on the college curriculum were met in three different ways. Some schools added courses which could be taken instead of the classical courses. In this way the traditional classical curriculum remained intact, and most educational and religious circles still regarded it as the true liberal education. The B. A. degree was jealously reserved for those taking the classical curriculum. The B. S. degree came into being for others. Some independent technical schools were established. The best known of these were the Rensselaer Polytechnic Institute, and the Massachusetts Institute of Technology. Education was no longer the prerogative of a wealthy elite, but the necessary occupational training for mechanics, farmers, and businessmen, as well as all of the professionals. The third response to the demand for curriculum change was the establishment of "schools of science" separate from the regular college. Only a few of the older colleges tried this approach. The departure from the traditional college education was also aided by the Morrill Act which Congress passed in 1862 to promote agricultural and mechanical colleges. This movement virtually vocationalized higher education, and to a considerable degree secondary education.

The final break with the classical tradition came when the colleges accepted the idea that they should offer courses in all phases of knowledge to meet the needs of the growing industrial society. President Eliot strove to make Harvard a university in which all branches of knowledge could be taught and investigated. The old liberal arts college had grown into a university with not only a school of liberal arts or arts and sciences, but also schools of engineering, architecture, education, business, and fine and applied arts. The large university today offers 75 to 100 or more majors leading to degrees, from 25 or 30 different departments grouped into five or more schools. Higher education in America has become almost completely utilitarian—the indispensable prerequisite to jobs with high status and income, and the acknowledged privilege of all high school graduates who are able and want to do the work.

German influence. A surprising number of American students went to the German universities during the nineteenth century. By 1850, several hundred had already studied in Germany; by the end of the century, ten thousand had studied in German universities and returned home, many with Doctor of Philosophy degrees, to become college or university research scholars and professors. They had acquired not only knowledge, but new methods of investigation and teaching, and a devotion to learning and its application which American institutions were unable to give them. Among the noted men who studied in Germany and came home to influence American education were Horace Mann, Calvin E. Stowe, G.

Stanley Hall, and George Tichnor. The greatest number went to the University of Berlin, but Leipzig, Heidelberg, Halle, Bonn, and others also attracted students. The great number of German immigrants who came to this country during the middle of last century also had its influence. Some specific areas in which German influence was felt were the seminar method, the Doctor of Philosophy degree, teacher training, physical education, music education, the kindergarten movement, the study of psychology, and vocational education. Probably most important was the German example and teaching methods which transformed American colleges into universities which emphasized graduate research training provided by laboratories and seminars. The first well-organized and adequately staffed graduate school was Johns Hopkins, established in 1876. In the course of time the great private schools such as Harvard, Yale, and Columbia, and the state universities, especially in the Middle West, steadily built up outstanding graduate schools.[11]

CHANGE IN THE AIMS AND FUNCTIONS OF EDUCATION

Nature of aims. The aim of education in any society is to create the kind of adults that the society considers desirable. This may be the religious man, the patriot, the businessman, or the humanist, or some combination of these. Americans believe in education for citizenship. One of our current problems is that school authorities and teachers frequently have aims which are not shared by parents and students. Even some parents may have aims not shared by their own children as students. This in large measure accounts for our dropouts. The middle-class aims of school boards and teachers are frequently incompatible with the aims of lower-class or underprivileged children in our schools. For aims or goals of education to be effective in making the kind of adults society idealizes, these aims must be internalized, they must become the personal goals of the students.

In our early agrarian society this was a simple problem. For the vast majority the aims were simple: they needed to read, write, spell, and be able to do simple accounts. They wanted and needed to read the Bible, write on occasion, and do simple figuring and record-keeping. At a higher level the simple aims were those of preparing for the professions or for the life of an upper-class gentleman.

As in the previous discussions of our economic, political, and familial institutions, it is necessary to distinguish between individual and societal aims. Individual aims are personal and may or may not be compatible with those of society. Fortunately, they are in harmony for most of the people most of the time. In our society, as in any other, there are prob-

---

[11] Laurence R. Veysey, *The Emergence of the American University* (Chicago, University of Chicago Press, 1965), pp. 125–133.

lems which are common to all of us. The problem of family life, discussed above, is one of them. The problem of health or physical well-being is another—it requires much more than the efforts of the individual, or even the family. The same is true of the problems of occupational preparation, training for social and civic responsibility, caring for those who cannot care for themselves, and provision for increased leisure time as industrialization continues to make for shorter and shorter working hours and early retirement. These and other common problems, in addition to a common language, institutions, customs, and values, make for a basic cultural unity which is reflected in the schools.

Formal aims. Several good lists of educational objectives have been drawn up by various commissions and committees, and they have served a useful purpose for many teachers. In 1918, the Commission on the Reorganization of Secondary Education presented the seven "cardinal principles" of education: health, command of the fundamental processes, worthy home membership, vocational efficiency, civic participation, worthy use of leisure time, and ethical character. Some twenty years later the Educational Policies Commission of the National Education Association presented the following list: self-realization, human relationships, economic efficiency, and civic responsibility. More recent statements have been presented by Sidney Hook, by the White House Conference called by President Eisenhower in 1955, by Frederick Mayer in 1956, and others. The idea of "teaching the whole child" has led to a tendency to make educational objectives cover the whole range of child development. There is widespread criticism, apparently justified, that there is a serious lack of direction among teachers generally, not because the objectives are poor, but because of their general nature and the remoteness of their ultimate achievement. Some of the stated objectives are guidelines toward which to work; they cannot be immediately applied. These general aims in no way imply that either teachers or students may not have their own private aims in addition to, or even in place of, these or any other list. It is obvious that these extensive aims are far more complex and far-reaching than the simple ones with which our educational system started.

Change in aims and functions. Today the school accepts responsibility for a part of the socialization process of the children in its charge. This extends into such personal areas as developing sensitivity to the needs of others, cooperativeness, leadership, and good manners. While this aim of "good" social adjustment is particularly accepted at the elementary level, it is recognized at all levels, and even beyond the college where business executives say that getting along with others is of the utmost importance. It has even led to the use of sociometrics as a diagnostic device for measuring certain aspects of student interaction to further promote social adjustment among students. One of the most important functions of present-day education is that of increasing the upward social mobility of those who receive it. In early America education for most children was, if at all, only incidentally related to improved occupational status. Today education is the most important requisite to occupations and incomes which carry one up the social ladder. All occupations with high prestige require an adequate education.

Another function of modern education, although not stated as such by either parents or school officials, is that of institutional baby-sitter. Schools continue to take children at an earlier age, keep more of them at every stage all the way through college, and keep them for longer hours. The only people whose hours and labor have not been reduced by our industrial society are the school children. Some politicians and school executives are placing such pressures on schoolchildren that they are in danger of creating a nation of neurotics. The attempt to make our schools more efficient is both understandable and necessary. The transmission of the cultural heritage is largely a function of our educational system, and it becomes an increasingly bigger job as knowledge continues to grow at a fantastic rate.

CHANGES IN THE CURRICULUM

Nature and importance of the curriculum. In attempting to analyze changes in the educational institutions, it is well to keep in mind the relationships of the various components. The aims or objectives of education determine in a general way what education is expected to achieve. Given the aims, plans to carry them into effect require a curriculum, a detailed plan of what will be taught and in what sequences. This is the content of education. The number of possible curricula is almost infinite. The industrialization of American society has increased the number of occupations available from a few dozen to over 25,000. It is apparent that the extension of education beyond the academic into preparation for occupations represents a changing concept of both the aims and content of education.

Standardization of the curriculum. At the end of the Civil War only a few high schools existed, mostly in New England and the Middle West; it was the turn of the century before the high school reached maturity. There was no model or set of standards to guide high schools in the addition of new courses. The result was chaos and confusion as far as the curriculum was concerned. To eliminate this confusion a Committee of Ten was appointed by the NEA in 1892. From the work of this committee and others that followed, the subject-matter areas and units of high school work gradually became standardized. These subjects and units eventually became the basis for accreditation and college entrance requirements. At the turn of the century high schools were still offering a strictly academic curriculum—English, foreign languages (mostly Latin), mathematics, natural science, history, and geography.

The impact of rapid industrialization forced new aims upon secondary education. Among the new aims were occupational competence, social and civic responsibility, healthful living, and worthy use of leisure time. To fulfill these goals, scores of new courses were introduced into the curriculum. From 1900 to 1930, the average number of high school courses more than doubled. Among the subject fields that grew most rapidly were fine arts, industrial arts, physical education, household arts, and commercial studies. Of the old academic subjects, social studies and English grew rapidly. By 1930, nonacademic courses were over 20 percent of all courses taken by high school students. Enrollment in foreign languages dropped to less than half of what it was in 1890, and mathematics and science also lost ground to the nonacademic courses. The tendency to introduce vocational subjects into the high school curriculum continued down to World War II. The increasing number of high school graduates now going to college will no doubt re-emphasize the academic courses.

An even greater transformation has taken place at the college level. In 1850, the three important subjects of the college curriculum were still classical languages, mathematics, and philosophy. By the end of the century, literature, modern languages, the sciences, and the social sciences had found their places in the curriculum. Since 1900, the increase in the number of subjects offered has been phenomenal. Courses in the older subjects such as English and history have multiplied possibly tenfold or more. Large universities and colleges list between 75 and 125 courses in English and 75 to 100 in history. The same is true of all other older subjects. The new fields such as education, business administration, engineering, physical education, home economics, art, music, architecture, agriculture, and social service have scores of courses. As new knowledge becomes available, new courses are created to teach it. Society demands that training be provided in the new professions and, in fact, in almost all areas of life in which people are interested. College education has come to be almost completely directed to preparing students for occupations. This has happened because of the increasing number of high-status and high-income jobs which require a college degree. In other words, the vast growth that has taken place in the number of courses is in response to the demands of society for specialized training, and it is likely that this will continue as more and more specialized knowledge becomes available through our scientific research and technological development.

AMERICAN EDUCATION TODAY

Mass education in a mass society. It is difficult to realize how far education has come in America in the past hundred years. We have already observed the development and changes in objectives and curriculum; a few comparisons in enrollment will help to clarify the picture. In 1870, the largest colleges and universities had only a few hundred students and the total school enrollment was less than 17 million, mostly in elementary school. High schools had around 200,000 students. In 1964, public school enrollment reached over 41 million, college enrollment was nearly 5 million, and enrollment in public and private educational institutions totalled 53 million.

By 1966, there were 55 million students in school; in 1967, about 6 million were enrolled in college; in 1969, there were 7 million students in college. A still more dramatic picture is shown in the following statistics. In 1870, only 7 in 1,000 students of high school age entered high school; in 1957, a staggering 930 entered, 667 graduated, and 357 entered college.[12] Today these numbers are considerably larger. In 1960, of all the children between 5 and 20 years, 81.8 percent were in school. The greatest changes have come in the numbers entering high school and college. Between the years 1920 and 1960, we find these startling increases in percent of school enrollments: for 18 years olds, from 21.7 to 50.6; for 19 year olds, from 13.8 to 32.8; for 20 year olds, from 8.3 to 23.5.[13] The total expenditure for education in 1966 was $54.5 billion. Even this sum was less than 8 percent of the GNP. The great increases in enrollment were especially reflected in high school and vocational courses and in the professional and graduate schools.

Gross figures in numbers of schools and numbers of students enrolled are rather meaningless unless one knows something of the size of individual schools. In the public schools, the number of students per school is kept reasonably low; as the number of students increases, new schools are established. This is not as true at the college level, and individual college enrollments have become fantastic. Many large universities now have as many students as would have populated a good sized city at the turn of the century. The Middle West universities, mostly founded between 1840 and 1875 are among the large schools. For 1967 some of the enrollments were as follow: University of Minnesota, 46,000; University of Michigan, 29,500; Michigan State, 37,400; University of Wisconsin at Madison and Milwaukee, 45,600; University of Indiana, 37,400; University of Illinois, 40,400. In other parts of the country, enrollments for the same year were: Pennsylvania State, 29,200; University of Texas system, 42,800; University of California system, 91,500; City University of New York, 64,900; New York State University system, 139,500.[14] The

12 *Information Please Almanac for 1965* (New York, Dan Golenpaul Associates, 1964), p. 331.

13 *The U. S. Book of Facts* . . . , p. 109.

14 Dr. Garland Parker, Vice Provost for Admissions, University of Cincinnati, quoted in an Associated Press release, December 11, 1967.

immediate cause for the great increase in school enrollment at all levels was the rapid increase in population due to improved medical care and increased production of food and other goods resulting from improved technology. The needs of industrialization is the second cause.

These gigantic educational centers contain masses of human beings, each functioning in his own little world, more or less oblivious to the myriad activities of the total institution. This is the mass society in operation, the educational factory system. It is the ultimate in division of labor and specialization. It is a system that requires a high degree of standardization, red tape, impersonality, uniformity, and conformity. As we have said, this is more characteristic of college than of public schools. It is, however, the condition under which our teachers get their training. The major question that concerns us is whether our factory system of education will educate our children so that as adults they will be able to function to society's and to their own best advantage.

What kind of education? We can expect that many of the skills now being taught will, within a decade or so, become obsolete. This is already happening where automation is taking place. The problem of the individual's adjustment to his job has taken on a new emphasis. In the past, the individual acquired a skill and settled into a job more or less permanently; in the future, he will require the kind of education which will serve as a foundation on which he can acquire new skills when his old ones become obsolete. In other words, education can no longer be a short-range matter.

The question of an adequate education becomes an increasingly complex and difficult problem. The sheer amount of knowledge in any field is staggering. At the higher levels, the degree of specialization requires longer and longer years of training in narrower and narrower fields of study. To compensate for the narrowness of specialization at the college level, there has been an effort to require a broader general education, even for the most specialized fields. This should and no doubt will be extended much farther, and will require more years to complete the training program than at present. Since the Middle Ages, four years has been the time required for a B. A. degree. The present need for better education would well justify extending this to six or seven years.

The amount of education, however, is not the only problem. Quality is just as important. The Germans were a highly educated nation, but this did not save them from Nazism. Despite our great progress in science and technology, our ability to solve our problems in the field of social thinking lags far behind. We have not solved the problems of crime, poverty, or race relations, to say nothing of the overwhelming problem of war and peace.

It would obviously make more sense for people the world over to spend their energies and resources on education, relieving poverty, suffering, and illness than to spend them on wars and weapons of destruction. But as long as nationalism governs state policy, including education, no such ideal is in sight. Some prominent individuals believe the solution to this problem lies in the field of religion, but the evidence of history is against them. Whatever the answer to these and other such problems, a part of it is found in the educational system. As old and as trite as it sounds, education must teach our children how to think, abstractly and independently. The field of education needs the same kind of theoretical foundation to guide its activities as is found in the field of science. Whether the problems are personal, community-wide, national, or international, we have to think our way out of them. The problem of education is not simply the dissemination of knowledge but also the wisdom to know what use to make of it.

RELIGION AND EDUCATION

Private and parochial schools. Private education includes both parochial and other non-tax-supported schools. In 1960, private schools enrolled about 6.5 million or 15 percent of the elementary and secondary school children. Of this total approximately 4.8 million children were enrolled in Catholic schools, and 1.7 million were distributed among other denominations and private schools.[15] Some 3.3 million Catholic students were enrolled in public schools. Few problems have arisen over private schools because they were a relatively insignificant part of the total, and because those who attended them were largely from classes that were able to afford it. One of the main problems arises between the Catholic hierarchy and those who oppose public support to private education of any kind. Most Protestant denominations and a few Catholic clergy as well as unaffiliated individuals and groups do oppose it.

Recently another and probably more controversial problem has been that of religious instruction in the public schools. As we have indicated, early American schools were largely supported by denominational groups and for religious purposes. But as industrialism changed the nature of society—ways of living, methods of acquiring wealth, prestige and power —education took on two other functions which have come to overshadow its original aim. It came to be looked upon as essential to the operation of a democratic society and to the vocational or professional preparation for one's life work. The growing pluralism in religion, especially the growth of the Catholic Church from less than one percent of the population in 1790 to one-fourth of the total, and its demand for church control

[15] *Annals of the Academy of Political and Social Sciences* Vol. 332 (November 1960), p. 96.

of education, brought the problem of the relationship between religion and education into both the public and political arenas. The political problem arose over the demands of the Catholic hierarchy for participation in proposed federal aid to public education.

The problem and its implications. Emphasis on religious training largely disappeared from the public schools, not so much because of the First Amendment or any other legal barrier but because it was voluntarily abandoned. Some religious practices of one kind or another have always been widely practiced in American public schools and, despite the recent controversy and court decisions, they still are. The First Amendment was meant as a guarantee of religious freedom; many of those today who oppose any kind of government aid to parochial schools do so believing that such a policy is better for both society and religion. Americans, including Catholics, do not hold for an established religion or church. Their disagreements hinge on what "separation of church and state" means, and the problems arise over specific issues such as whether federal aid should be extended to parochial schools or whether the Bible should be read in the public schools.

While federal aid to parochial schools is only one of the problems, the recent tendency in Congress to increasingly appropriate funds for programs in which parochial schools participate, if carried to great lengths, is fraught with potentially dangerous consequences. If carried far enough, Protestant denomination and private schools would, no doubt, feel compelled to compete for such funds. The pressures brought on Congressmen, and the passions generated by such competition are potentially ominous. It could be detrimental if not destructive to the public school system. While many of the religious conflicts that have flared up in the schools are not over the issue of federal aid, they are symbolic of the much greater problem of the conflict between religion and public education in American society.

In some American communities where the majority of the population is Catholic the issue of school control has become more than a theoretical problem. In North College Hill, Ohio, in Dixon, New Mexico, in twelve public-school districts in northern Michigan, and in parts of North Dakota and Illinois, Catholic majorities have elected Catholic school boards. Claiming the right of self-determination, these boards have closed the public schools and used tax funds for the support of parochial schools. Of course secularists, modernist Protestants, and Fundamentalists vigorously oppose such action. *The New York Times* of November 16, 1952, quoted Dr. James B. Conant, then President of Harvard University, as proposing that all education should be in the hands of the state because of the divisiveness of parochial schools. Whatever the merits of the controversy, it is in the public schools that the youth of America, regardless of creed, family fortune, or cultural background, come together with the one best prospect of creating unity in our national life.[16]

If there were no differences between parochial and public education, there would be no point in having parochial schools. The differences in aims are basic. Tendencies in American secular culture are at odds with traditional religious values. The secularist drive is toward a wholly autonomous secular society and public education is the most significant means toward this end. Religion, on the other hand, must insist on the sacred or transcendant aspect of reality. These differences in aims can probably never be resolved and there is no particular reason why they should be. A free society admits differences in aims among its members, and in order that it be understood it must also admit the teaching of facts about religion in the public schools. No individual or group should attempt to use the public schools to propagate its own doctrines. Religion, however, is one of the most significant aspects of American culture and to attempt to exclude the subject from the public school curriculum is to admit that Americans cannot face up to the real facts of life—their differences. But we have done so in the past and there is good reason to believe that we will do so even better in future. There are, of course, those at both extremes who violently disagree with this point of view.

As a pluralistic society we can expect religious controversies to continue to rise and spill over into the schools. Controversies have arisen in the past and will, no doubt, do so in the future when religious groups involve themselves in secular matters. This is something all large denominations do. They maintain lobbies or pressure groups in Washington, and some at the state and local levels. The activities of these organizations vary widely from furnishing information to their parishioners to expert lobbying to influence government action. At the local level their efforts consist chiefly in sporadic propaganda and pressure campaigns—calling meetings, passing resolutions, and sending letters and telegrams. Many of these activities in one way or another involve education. Controversies have arisen over the curricula and programs of public schools in such areas as family planning which involves birth control, health programs which include innoculations and other things objectionable to certain groups, and the teaching of evolution. Controversies have also arisen over religious holidays, saluting the flag, the glorification of war and war heroes, the reading of books banned by the Catholic Index, and released time programs. No doubt new problems will also arise in the future.

A great deal has been written about a solution to the religious conflicts and the problems they cause in our society. The obvious solution would be for religious groups to withdraw from participation in secular affairs. But that this has been too much the case in the past is the chief

[16] Thomas Ford Hoult, *The Sociology of Religion* (New York, Dryden Press, 1958), p. 339.

criticism of religion in America today. Most churchmen reject the notion that faith can be sealed off from the rest of man's activities. Neither Christians nor Jews believe that they can afford to be indifferent to what is going on in the world around them. The contention today is that religion, to be more meaningful, must become more relevant to the secular problems of its environment. Furthermore, where religious liberty flourishes, religious pluralism seems inevitable, and incompatible differences unavoidable. While we may lament the jeopardy to the public schools and the injury to the community in which conflicts arise, this is a part of the price a free society in which religious pluralism exists must pay.

The reduction of religious controversy in the schools is not a matter of driving religion from the classroom nor of building more impregnable walls between religion and education. In our society all religions must live together and make their contributions to society. This can obviously be done better if they understand and appreciate each other. Isolation and walls of separation breed prejudice and suspicion. With the Constitution as the mediator, and with greater tolerance on the part of parents and outside individuals and groups, the school can become the means to better understanding and greater respect and cooperation among groups whose religious beliefs and practices are different. This is the genius of a free and democratic society.

BIBLIOGRAPHY

Bartky, John A., *Social Issues in Public Education*. Boston, Houghton Mifflin, 1963.

Bell, Robert R., *The Sociology of Education: A Source Book*. Homewood, Ill., Dorsey Press, 1962.

Brim, Orville G., Jr., *Sociology and the Field of Education*. New York, Russell Sage, 1958.

Brookover, Wilbur V., *A Sociology of Education*. New York, American Book, 1955.

Butts, R. Freeman, *A Cultural History of Western Education: Its Social and Intellectual Foundations,* 2nd ed. New York, McGraw-Hill, 1955.

Callahan, Raymond E., *An Introduction to Education in American Society,* 2nd ed. New York, Knopf, 1960.

The Center for the Study of Democratic Institutions, *Religion and American Society: A Statement of Principles*. Santa Barbara, Cal., The Center, 1961.

The Center for the Study of Democratic Institutions, *Religion and the Free Society*. Santa Barbara, Cal., The Center, 1958.

Cremin, Lawrence A., *The Transformation of the School: Progressivism in American Education*. New York, Knopf, 1961.

Drake, William E., *The American School in Transition*. Englewood Cliffs, N. J., Prentice-Hall, 1955.

Edwards, Newton, and Herman G. Richey, *The School in the American Social Order*. Boston, Houghton Mifflin, 1947.

Good, H. G., *A History of Western Education*. New York, Macmillan, 1960.

National Society for the Study of Education, *American Education in the Postwar Period,* 44th Yearbook, Part II. Chicago, University of Chicago Press, 1948.

Pound, Ralph L., and James R. Bryner, *The School in American Society*. New York, Macmillan, 1959.

President's Commission of Higher Education, *Higher Education for American Democracy*. New York, Harper, 1948.

Russell, James E., *Change and Challenge in American Education*. Boston, Houghton Mifflin, 1965.

Stanley, William O., et al., *Social Foundations of Education*. New York, Dryden Press, 1956.

Veysey, Laurence R., *The Emergence of the American University*. Chicago, University of Chicago Press, 1965.

Whitehead, Alfred North, *The Aims of Education*. New York, Macmillan, 1929.

11

Religion

HAVING already discussed the structure and functions of our economic, political, familial, and educational institutions, we turn to the one institution whose ultimate values are in a different category—religion. Like the family and other institutions, religion is clearly a universal aspect of human behavior. Every culture includes a set of beliefs which for its people answer the questions for which there are otherwise no answers—the ultimate explanations of life, death, evil, and so on. Among the many different societies, there are great varieties of customs and practices such as human sacrifice, bodily mutilation, communion, fasting, and feasting; most anthropologists and other students of religion believe that there are some characteristics which are shared by all religious systems.

Religion is an integral part of the culture in which it exists; its origin is lost in antiquity and can only be a matter of speculation. The nature of the relationship between religion and society has been called "sociocultural compatibility." The inference is that religion as well as most of the other institutionalized aspects of human life have common cultural backgrounds. This accounts for the fact that religions generally uphold the other dominant values of the societies in which they exist, and that the nonreligious institutions generally frown upon religious behavior which does not accord with other cultural values of the particular society. This is a simple matter of socialization. That religion is learned is obvious. If it were otherwise, all efforts at religious training and missionary work would be purposeless.

THE NATURE OF INSTITUTIONAL RELIGION

We have termed institutionalization that process of change whereby relatively formal and permanent organization was affected, along with the change in values, relationships, and procedures. Religion has gone through this process. Although most primitive societies had a priesthood, they lacked a formal theology and a distinct religious organization, or church, which could be isolated from the other aspects of the social organization. Christianity has gone through the religious institutionaliza-

215

tion process; it evolved from small groups of persecuted individuals to the highly organized medieval church with a vast hierarchy of officials, a sacred literature, and highly developed creeds, myths, and rituals; sacred music, masses, chants, and invocations; marriage, birth, death, and baptismal rites—a dominant institution in the medieval world. A more recent example of the institutionalization process was the rise of Methodism. It started as an offshoot of the Church of England and rapidly developed into a full-fledged denomination. Examples are numerous and there are more than 230 cults, sects, and denominations in the United States today. These are institutions if they have become organized, that is, if they have a slate of officials, a set of rules and regulations, committees, and fund drives.

Religion has been defined as a system of beliefs and practices through which a group of people seek the answers to the ultimate questions of human existence. The questions are those for which science has no answers. Such questions involve the meaning of life and death, suffering, and tragedy. Religion is, first, a system of beliefs concerning the supernatural. It posits the existence of supernatural forces which control man and his destiny, and to which man must adapt himself. It also includes a conception of the nature of godliness and the means through which man establishes his proper relationship with the supernatural. The second aspect of religion includes certain acts of reverence and propitiation such as prayer or communion. But religion is not narrowly confined to the relationship between the individual and the deity. It also deals with the relationship between individuals. This leads to the third aspect of religion which defines certain human actions as violations of divine law and hence sinful. This relationship is expressed in the Christian religion in the Great Commandments, St. Matthew 22:34-40. The fourth aspect of religion is salvation or deliverance from what is regarded as evil. In Christianity it is deliverance from the bondage and consequences of sin through the atonement of Christ. While the spiritual goals of the major religions are similar, the provisions for their attainment, the kinds of rewards for good conduct, and the kind of punishment for bad all take many forms.

Religion is also understood in terms of its universal functions. As stated by the functionalists, institutions are not to be understood in terms of their remote origins, but in terms of the functions they perform. One of the most important of these is to give men comfort and peace of mind in the face of tragedy and frustration. Religion also defines man's relationship to the cosmos which enhances his self-importance. Religion is a means of cohesion in societies; it provides a common body of moral rules and values. When there are conflicting forms in the same society, however, religion may be a deadly divisive factor, as in the case of Hindus and Moslems in India. Religion also generally furnishes individual guidance, and, as an institution, aids society in social control and frequently acts as a welfare agent to the unfortunate.

Religion as an institution may also be analyzed by considering its structural components. As outlined in Chapter 1, an institution must have: (1) an ideology, (2) structure or organization to carry out the ideology or purpose, (3) usages, rules, and laws to govern its action, (4) usually some sort of facilities such as buildings and other material things, and (5) functionaries or personnel to carry out its work. The Christian churches have this structure. The Christian beliefs or ideology came into being with the teachings of Jesus and his followers, a small group of radical and atheistic dissenters from the prevailing Judaic religion. Because of its peculiar beliefs and communal organization, the authorities looked upon it as subversive and attempted to suppress it. In the course of time more and more groups came into being, especially with the missionary work of the Apostle Paul. These groups became formally organized into churches and, by the middle of the second century, had compiled the New Testament, which became the accepted guide to the religious faith of all Christians. Eventually Christianity became the accepted religion of the Roman Empire and, by the thirteenth century, the dominant institution in the Western world. In this process the Christian Church developed many doctrines and rituals to govern its action. It also built many churches, cathedrals, and monasteries, and developed an organized hierarchy of the priesthood to carry on its work.

EUROPEAN BACKGROUNDS

The Medieval Church. During the thirteenth century, the Roman Church and the papacy were inseparable, and the papal monarchy was the most imposing institution in existence. The church organization, the number of officials, and the amount of church property are almost incomprehensible from our vantage point. The hierarchy of officials ran in ascending order from the lowliest country priest to deacons, archdeacons, bishops, archbishops, and finally the Pope. In addition, there were cardinals who were distinctly administrative officials of the papacy, and priors and abbots of the monasteries. The original church system was based on the Roman imperial form of administration; all Christendom was divided into dioceses each governed by a bishop. Above the bishops were the archbishops whose jurisdiction corresponded to some former province of the Roman Empire and included several dioceses. Below the bishop were the priests of the parishes, and at every cathedral or seat of the bishop was a chapter of canons—clergy of varying degrees—who assisted him in administration. The head of the chapter was a dean elected by the canons.[1] In

[1] John J. Van Nostrand and Paul Schaeffer, *Western Civilization: A Political, Social, and Cultural History*, Vol. I (New York, Van Nostrand, 1949), pp. 347–350.

addition there were ecclesiastical courts which administered ecclesiastical or canon law. The bishop claimed jurisdiction over all persons who were classed as clergy, including students, widows, orphans, and crusaders, as well as deacons who had not been ordained. They also claimed authority in a variety of cases not involving the clergy which were of religious or moral in nature. Such cases included marriage, business transactions sanctioned by oath, violations of church property, heresy, and blasphemy. Cases could be appealed to the papal court at Rome. During the twelfth century, France alone had over seven hundred monasteries. The Church also maintained cathedral and monastery schools. In fact, the church pretty well enveloped the whole life of the individual.

As time passed the popes gained greater and greater power at the expense of the bishops. By the thirteenth century, they had centralized authority to the extent that they were able to draw income from the clergy in all parts of Roman Christendom. In addition to the tithe or tax of one-tenth of one's goods or property value, required from all ecclesiastical benefices, the popes collected the first year's income from all important clergy appointed to office, the income from all vacant offices, lucrative income from appeal of ecclesiastical causes from the bishops' courts, and many other sources.[2] The church was in fact a superstate. It owned one-quarter to one-third of all real property in Western Europe, collected rents and imposed taxes, produced goods and employed labor on a large scale, and was involved as merchant, banker, and mortgage broker. Through its secular involvement the Church had become deeply feudalized, and became the most powerful temporal as well as spiritual institution.

The authority of the Church and the power of the clergy rested on the sacramental system. The doctrine of the sacraments had developed slowly from the early days of Christianity until, by the twelfth century, there were seven sacraments: baptism, confirmation, extreme unction, penance, the Eucharist, marriage, and ordination. With the exception of baptism, only the ordained clergy could administer the sacraments. In fact, the clergy held a monopoly that made their position secure, since they alone could offer to the people the gift of salvation. Disobedience could be met by excommunication which cut the offender off from all hopes of salvation. Despite its power, the Church was continuously beset by temporal enemies from without and by heresy from within.

The extent to which the Church was willing to go to maintain its power and doctrine is indicated by the extirpation of the Albigenses, a heretical sect in Southern France. The established Church had no more taste for the doctrine of "apostolic poverty" which the Albigenses preached than it did for their denial of Christianity. All other methods having failed to bring them to abandon their religion, Pope Innocent III

[2] *Ibid.*, p. 353.

ordered their extirpation in what is known as the Albigensian Crusade. Philip Augustus, King of France, opposed the crusade but was unable to restrain the movement. There were in fact two crusades in 1209–1215 and 1223–1226. The leader of the first crusade was the notorious Simon de Montfort whose fire and sword devastated southern France from the Rhone to the Pyrenees—he destroyed almost every town, burned crops and vineyards and poisoned wells. Thousands were slaughtered; at Minerve alone he burned 140 persons alive. The smaller fiefs of the region were distributed among his followers, he took for himself the huge county of Toulouse, and gave to the Pope the city and county of Avignon. In order that heresy be completely eradicated the Inquisition was established. Inquisitors with special courts were set up to search out and eradicate heresy. In these courts trials were secret and the name of the accuser kept secret. Counsel was ineffective and sometimes denied, and torture was used to extort confession. Penalties ranged from confiscation of property to life imprisonment and death. Because of church doctrine, the torture and executions were carried out by civil authorities.[3] The Inquisition was dissolved when it had succeeded in stamping out open heresy, but it was revived in 1478 in Spain to stamp out the remnants of the Jews and Moors, and again during the Counter-Reformation of the last half of the sixteenth century. The Inquisition was a reign of terror which succeeded in stamping out all open signs of heresy in Italy and Spain.

When Pope Boniface VIII died in 1303, the power of the Church appeared to be impregnable. That this was not the case, however, was soon to be shown when the King of France ordered the new Pope arrested and brought to France for trial. He was arrested and, although not taken to France, died in shock and humiliation a month later. The temporal supremacy of the papacy had ended and the papacy was now brought definitely under the influence of the French King. The next pope moved the papal court to Avignon and there ensued a bitter struggle within the Church which lasted for over one hundred years. For much of the period there were two popes, and for part of the time three. Each pope declared the other to be anti-Christ and devout Christians were in doubt about which pope was the legitimate successor to St. Peter. The Council of Constance, 1414-1417, finally settled the issue. One of the popes had resigned and the other two were deposed bringing "the great schism" to an end. In the meantime serious heresy had taken root in England with an Oxford professor, John Wycliffe, and the Lollards, and in Bohemia at the University of Prague by John Huss and his followers. The doctrines of Wycliffe and Huss were basically the forerunners of later Protestantism. The Emperor had guaranteed Huss safe conduct to the Council of Constance where he had been summoned to answer the charge of heresy, but

[3] *Ibid.*, pp. 355–357.

the order was disregarded by the Council and he and a disciple were found guilty and burned at the stake. This did not, however, end the movement and the Hussite wars continued in Bohemia until settled by compromise at the Council of Basle in 1441. This council also tried to reform the Church but after an eighteen-year struggle with the popes was dissolved without success.

The Renaissance and Reformation. The Renaissance, covering the fourteenth, fifteenth, and early sixteenth centuries, was the expression of forces which were destined to change not only the secular but also the religious aspects of the Western world. It brought the Middle Ages to an end and introduced the period of modern history. It was also a time of chaotic change filled with intellectual, social, and political ferment. The Renaissance was made possible by the great increase in wealth through commerce and industry, the rise of towns and the middle classes, the great revolution in education wrought by the rise of the universities, and the spread of secular literature written in the vernacular. The most significant feature of the Renaissance was a new outlook on life. With the decline of feudalism, the rise of towns, and the lessening of ecclesiastical authority, a spirit of individualism emerged. The increase in commerce and industry and the rise of sophisticated distractions and cosmopolitan interests replaced religion and thought of the future. With this change, the Church and the papacy lost the great esteem in which they were held during the thirteenth century.

It is no mere coincidence that the height of the Renaissance and the low point of the Church both came at the first quarter of the sixteenth century. The only medieval institution which stood unchanged, although shaken to its roots and under continuous attack, was the Church. The common abuses and worldliness of the Renaissance Church are common knowledge and the ferocity with which it fought off its attackers is illustrated by the trial and execution in 1498 of probably the most pious monk of all, Savonarola. After trumped-up charges, a secret ten-day trial, and fourteen tortures, a confession was extorted, Savonarola was hanged and burned.[4] It will be remembered that this was at the beginning of the great era of exploration and discovery and six years after the discovery of America.

The unity of Western Christendom had been broken, but the Roman Church still claimed universal sovereignty, and the clergy still held a monopoly on salvation through the sacramental system. It was principally this monopoly against which Wycliffe, Huss, and Luther rebelled.

[4] To quote Ralph Roeder, "When the embers, soaked in a slow deglution of blood and vicera, cooled, the faithful gathered and grubbed in the cinders in silence; and the women, rising suddenly, spirited away the heart, which was found whole." *The Man of the Renaissance* (New York, Viking, 1933), p. 130.

The conviction of Luther, Calvin, the Anabaptists and other Protestant sects that faith alone was necessary for salvation, and that the Church's doctrine of good works, fasts, pilgrimages, the sacraments, and the services of the clergy and the Pope was unnecessary became the barrier to any reconciliation with the Roman Church. This bitter, irreconcilable conflict led to a series of religious wars in Europe which covered the period from 1517 to the end of the Thirty Years' War in 1648, and to the Restoration of the monarchy in England in 1660. While the Roman Church through the Council of Trent, 1546–1563, did much to reform the objectionable abuses of the Church, its statement of doctrine only drew the lines of demarcation between Catholicism and Protestantism more sharply.

The religious wars were contemporaneous with the early period of American colonization. The earliest results of the Reformation were three great church systems—Lutheran, Reformed or Calvinist, and Anglican. They were all closely allied with the nationalistic development in their countries and were in effect, establishment churches. They were neither religiously tolerant nor concerned with social reform. In fact, Protestants as well as their Catholic adversaries persecuted all dissenting opinion. The Reformation in England was at first chiefly political and liturgical; doctrinal questions which troubled Luther and Calvin were relatively unimportant. England passed through the Reformation period without a civil war, only to be involved in the Puritan Revolution as the Thirty Years' War came to an end. England was not, however, without its religious problems.

Although Henry VIII separated England from the Catholic Church in 1534, no important doctrinal reform took place until the time of Edward VI, 1547–1553. This change was instituted by the Act of Uniformity which made the Book of Common Prayer mandatory. Queen Mary succeeded to the throne in 1553, and Protestantism was disestablished and Protestant worship forbidden; 31 heretics were burned in London and 44 in the provinces. In 1555 Archbishop Cranmer, under whose guidance the Book of Common Prayer and the Forty-Two Articles were written, and bishops Ridley and Latimer were executed. Mary married Philip II of Spain, the arch-enemy of Protestantism. After reigning only five years, Mary died and Queen Elizabeth came to the throne. Protestantism was re-established; and as the Dissenters or Non-Conformists increased in number, they were more severely persecuted.

Besides the three large church systems of the Protestant religion, there was a left wing of the Reformation. The best known of these more extreme groups were the Anabaptists. Although varied, these groups looked upon the church as a fellowship rather than as an organization, and believed in personal "regeneration" as a prerequisite to membership as a communicant. Their organization was generally of the congregational type, and they opposed an established church. Their strength resulted from their extreme piety and stern discipline. Their influence was widely felt in Europe, especially among the lower classes; and in America their doctrines eventually superseded the idea of an established church.

The results of this long religious struggle were the establishment of the three major branches of Protestantism—Lutheranism, Calvinism, and Anglicanism—as state or established churches. The more radical groups such as the Anabaptists, who opposed infant baptism and whose cardinal tenet was the complete separation of church and state, had by the end of the Reformation, developed into denominations, the best known of which were the Mennonites, the Baptists, and the Moravians. The Catholics, through the vigorous use of the Index, the Inquisition, and the armies of the states where they were dominant, turned back the Protestant revolt and retained control. This occurred in the Latin countries and in about half of Germany.

FIRST PHASE OF THE TRANSFORMATION

Traditional and radical groups. Religious developments in Europe directly influenced religion in the American colonies. The right wing of the Reformation—Lutheran, Reformed, and Anglican—claimed to be the true heirs of the Church's faith, and it was this group that dominated American organized religion during the colonial period. The greatest change in organized religion came with the elimination of established churches at the time of American independence. In the meantime, a great religious ferment had been taking place outside the more or less formal structure of established churches. It should be remembered that until about 1825 the lower classes were little influenced by organized religion and that only a small percentage of the population were members of any church.[5]

The traditional Protestant churches tried in varying degrees to retain the medieval conception of the church with an elaborate and formal theology and formal worship enforced by an organized church body. They viewed the state as the appropriate agency to enforce the religious and moral tenets of the church. Radical groups, such as the Anabaptists, the Baptists, and the Quakers differed widely among themselves, yet they were in agreement that church administration should be separate from the state, and that churches should be congregations of "true believers" rather than elaborate, wealthy establishments. In the England of the seventeenth century, political and religious radicalism went hand in hand, and the doc-

[5] H. Sheldon Smith, Robert T. Handy, and Lefferts A. Loetscher, *American Christianity, An Historical Interpretation with Representative Documents,* Vol. I (New York, Scribner, 1960), pp. 143–150.

trines of the Baptists and Quakers struck at the very foundations of both the state and church organizations. In America these groups were also generally considered radical and dangerous. They were in direct conflict with the Established Church and the Act of Uniformity which the Stuarts attempted to enforce during most of the seventeenth century. Establishment and uniformity were principles which all major branches of Protestantism as well as the Catholic Church tried to enforce at this time. Most Puritans in both England and America believed in the union of church and state, but there was a small branch known as "Separatists" who, although Puritan in other respects, believed in congregational autonomy based on the doctrine of a covenant with God and with each other. This doctrine became basic to the later Congregational churches in America. The "Congregational Way" became firmly rooted in New England quite early.

In the American colonies, religion generally adhered to the traditional or classical orthodoxy until the end of the seventeenth century. The religious ferment in England which had resulted in the Puritan Revolution largely ended with the Glorious Revolution—the establishment of a limited monarchy in 1688 and religious toleration for all but Catholics in 1689. Pluralism in England had become an accepted fact. After this date the British government moved consistently to transform all American colonies into royal provinces directly under the Crown; by the time of the American Revolution, only Maryland, Pennsylvania, and Delaware remained proprietary colonies. Gathered around the royal governors was an aristocratic colonial elite who were, at least nominally, Anglicans. In increasing opposition to this elite were the middle classes who were other than Anglican and who were coming to dominate the colonial legislatures. A sharp cleavage between the social classes ran through all of the colonies. Along the seaboard from Boston to Charleston was a well-to-do class whose style of life set them apart from the poorer classes. There was also a growing economic and social cleavage between the North and the South. This cleavage presaged a greater sectional and social differentiation in religion in the future.[6]

The Great Awakening. By the beginning of the eighteenth century, the fervor which had so marked early colonial religion was rapidly giving way to indifference. Economic improvement—the growth of commerce, the Navigation Acts—helped to focus attention on materialistic interests. Also, several factors tended to increase the diversity of religious groups and to change the character of religion in general. There was a great influx of Germans, most of whom were Lutheran, many of whom were Reformed, and some of whom were more radical Mennonite and Moravian. More numerous and more influential were the Scotch-Irish from Northern Ireland. Fifty-four ships from Ireland landed at New England

[6] *Ibid.,* pp. 193–194.

ports alone, mostly at Boston, between 1714 and 1720. Most ships landed in Pennsylvania. Scotch-Irish immigrants made their way from Pennsylvania to Maryland, Virginia, the Carolinas, and Georgia, and they arrived in sufficient numbers in all the colonies to make their influence felt. In years to come, they and their descendents played an important role both in the religious and in the political life of the frontier.

Also important in changing the character of religion in America was the Great Awakening. The second quarter of the eighteenth century saw an extraordinary outbreak of religious enthusiasm. This revivalism occurred with the rise of Pietism in Germany and the Netherlands and with the Wesley revival in England. A new generation of ministers, shocked at the complacency of the churches, stirred the emotions of their congregations with their descriptions of the future punishment of the damned. Under the preaching of these powerful ministers, such as Frelinghuysen of the Dutch Reformed Church, Gilbert Tennent of the Presbyterian Church, Jonathan Edwards of the Congregational Church, religion in many communities took on an emotionalism that bordered on the psychopathic. People shrieked, shook, moaned, and fainted, and a few committed suicide.[7] The great following of the Baptists and Methodists began to grow several decades later; it flowered with the westward movement, increasing in momentum to the middle of the nineteenth century. The Great Awakening was the early manifestation of the great change which was ultimately to reshape religion in American life.

The Great Awakening revived religious fervor. Religious practice had declined until the churches were almost stagnant; the potential for religious enthusiasm, however, had never disappeared. The apparent stagnation concealed a dissatisfaction with the established churches and with their powerful officials. As church authority passed from the hands of the church officials to the hands of the lay congregation, religious interest and participation increased. To a certain extent, however, religion in America had always been in the hands of laymen. For one thing, there had never been an Anglican bishop or any single church head in the colonies. Also, authority in church matters had gradually shifted to groups of officials within individual churches. Since the individual churches were in fact independent, the Anglican state churches simply collapsed. The state churches of New England survived a generation longer. It is very probable that early Americans, especially the lower classes, were never more than nominally Christian. Colonial state churches were sustained at public expense as they were in Europe. There, the ruler decided what the religion of his people was to be—he could change his mind, and often did. In America the preoccupation of the churches has been to try to win back a people who abandoned the church

[7] Nelson Manfred Blake, *A Short History of American Life* (New York, McGraw-Hill, 1952), pp. 74–77.

when support ceased to be compulsory. Today "voluntarism" is the basic principle of American religious association. Religion is considered a purely personal matter. This is a long way from the state-enforced religious conformity which dominated most of the colonial era.

It would be a mistake to assume that this religious change was a self-contained movement. In New England and in the other Eastern states, the educated, well-to-do elite dominated the established churches. They not only opposed the emotional excesses of the "Enthusiasts," but succeeded in excluding emotionalism from religious practices. The conservatives succeeded in dismissing Jonathan Edwards from his Northampton pastorate, and the Harvard faculty, endorsed by the Yale faculty, rebuked Whitefield's methods and message in a fifteen-page pamphlet.[8] The frontier and rural America, on the other hand, were uncongenial to a formal or rational religion; the conditions there encouraged evangelism. The evangelical movement throughout the country not only split the Congregationalists and Presbyterians into the New Lights and the Old Lights, but began a process of religious differentiation which eventually led to over 230 denominations and religious sects in the United States. This diversity in American religion has been instrumental in promoting religious toleration, an "activistic" spirit, and denominationalism.

Deism. Any study of factors shaping American religion cannot ignore the "intellectual revolution." The rapid growth of science and philosophy in the seventeenth and eighteenth centuries, the establishment of the Royal Society of London in 1662 and the Academie des Sciences in Paris in 1666, the rise of natural philosophy and the decline of theology, the rise of rationalism, deism, and skepticism in Europe had their influence on the educated classes in America. Cotton Mather, elected to the Royal Society in 1713, was the first of many Americans who were directly touched by the intellectual revolution. Many well-to-do Americans were educated abroad and many of the colonial ministers were Scotch, English, and Dutch. Students at Yale were studying Locke and Newton as early as 1717, and 1752, Chief Justice Paul Dudley, a Fellow of the Royal Society, left an endowment to Harvard with which to inaugurate a lectureship with special attention to the merits of natural and revealed religion. No doubt the educated ministry, whether from abroad or from American colleges, felt the impact of the new scientific and philosophic learning. The spirit of rationalism grew during the seventeenth century and by the latter part of the eighteenth had profoundly influenced the development of science, religion, philosophy, and social and political theory in both the old and new worlds.

One aspect of the intellectual revolution as it affected religion de-

[8] Smith, *op. cit.*, pp. 312–315, 329.

serves special consideration. This is Deism. It was a movement among the highly educated which grew out of rationalism. Much of the thinking of John Locke was deistic, but it remained for Lord Herbert of Cherbury to formulate its basic doctrines in his *Religion of the Gentiles* in 1645. It was elaborated during the seventeenth and eighteenth centuries and reached its peak around 1800.

Deists drew a distinction between "true" and "historical" Christianity: true Christianity consisted of the teachings of Jesus, historical Christianity consisted of later additions and interpretations. The Deists accepted true Christianity and rejected historical Christianity. English Deists were not anti-religious, but they were opposed to the institutional forms and practices of traditional religion. This was also true of such leading American Deists as Franklin, Jefferson, and Washington who were, in fact, favorable to religion. The most radical of all Deists was Voltaire whose fearlessness, irreverence, keen wit, and great intelligence made him one of the most influential intellectuals of the eighteenth century. Deism in America was confined to a small, highly educated class along the Eastern seaboard. It was eclipsed by the rising tide of evangelism in the early nineteenth century. In its rather extreme challenge to orthodoxy, it had a considerable influence on the rise of Unitarianism, Universalism, and other nonritualistic religious groups immediately prior to and following the American Revolution.

The churches and the Revolution. It has been estimated that at the outbreak of the Revolution there were some 3,100 churches in the colonies. Of the total, approximately 650 were Congregational, mostly in New England, 550 were Presbyterian, 500 Baptists, 480 Anglican, 300 Quaker, 250 Reformed, 150 Lutheran, and 50 Catholic.[9] During the Revolution, Methodism was still a movement within the Anglican Church and Wesley's strong loyalty to the King was a source of embarrassment to his followers in America. The Methodist Church was not formally organized outside the Church of England until 1784. The independence of America did not create problems of reorganization for those denominations who were already independent of European ties—Presbyterians, Congregationalists, Baptists, Lutherans, and Quakers—but it did create problems for the Anglican and Catholic churches. Both eventually had American bishops appointed. The American bishop was the highest authority in the Episcopal Church, the Catholic bishop was responsible directly to Rome.

Prior to the Revolution, the ministers were the most important group to shape and control public opinion. Congregational, Presbyterian, Dutch Reformed, and Baptist ministers were overwhelmingly on the side of the Revolution. The Anglican Church was most loyal to the King and

9 William Warren Sweet, *The Story of Religion in America* (New York, Harper, 1950), pp. 172–173.

suffered most from the Revolution[10] despite the fact that two-thirds of the signers of the Declaration of Independence were Anglicans. In the South and Middle colonies, the majority of ministers supported the Revolution. In New England, they were most loyal to the Crown. Anglican laymen were seriously divided in their allegiance. With the religious settlement growing out of the Revolution, the great milestone of religious freedom had been achieved. It was significant because it marked a complete break with a tradition of church-state relations that began in the Middle Ages and had grown to be a major aspect of Western civilization. Western Christendom had firmly believed that a nation should have one religion with one church and that the church should be maintained by the state. The early colonists made strenuous efforts to maintain the ideal. Steps toward religious toleration were also being taken in Europe. The Toleration Act of 1689 in England placed her far ahead of the colonies in matters of religious freedom, but the achievement of full religious liberty was first completed in America.

This change did not, of course, happen immediately with the Declaration of Independence. It is significant that Jefferson considered the passage of the Virginia Statute for Religious Liberty in 1786 one of the most important achievements of his career. The facts are enlightening. When independence was declared in 1776, petitions immediately flooded the Virginia Legislature both for and against the disestablishment of the Anglican Church. The majority of Virginians were dissenters but the majority of the Legislature were Anglicans. Even though Jefferson became governor in 1779 and worked toward complete religious freedom, it was not accomplished until 1786. It was the Baptists and Presbyterians who made the most of the political crisis to overthrow the established Church. In New England the final settlement was much longer in the making. In the election of 1817 in Connecticut, the Baptists, Methodists, Unitarians, Universalists, Quakers, and Episcopalians supported the Republican Party; the Congregationalists supported the Federalists. The Republicans won the election, but disestablishment did not occur until 1833. Other New England States soon followed.

THE RESHAPING OF RELIGION IN AMERICA

The extent to which religious thinking in America had changed by 1787 is indicated by the fact that the separation of church and state was written into the Constitution without serious controversy. This is understandable when we consider the diversity of religion among the colonies. Most of the original state constitutions, however, denied the right to public office to Catholics, Jews, Unitarians, or atheists, and most of the Puritan clergymen in New England were supported by taxes for several

[10] Smith, *op. cit.,* pp. 430–431.

decades more. Only four states—Virginia, Maryland, Pennsylvania, and Delaware—early abolished the old laws and allowed Roman Catholics equality with Protestants. It was not until 1834, when Massachusetts removed tax support from the Congregational Church, that the American principle of separation of church and state became fully established.

All of rural society was composed of people who were activists with little formal education or sophistication. Their isolation from the rich European historical heritage made it inevitable that their religion, like other of their institutions, would develop characteristics peculiar to their cultural environment. As any religious movement becomes older and more established, it becomes more formal and ritualistic. It tends to stress rules and organization rather than inspiration. William Warren Sweet in his book, *Religion on the American Frontier,* quoted an observer who said about the Episcopalians that "their whole system of worship is incongruous to the people of Arkansas. They have too much formalism to do much good or harm here."[11] The same was true of the New England Congregationalists, the largest denomination at the end of the colonial period and the group with the greatest numbers in the westward movement. Neither Episcopalians nor Congregationalists made any headway on the frontier. Presbyterians succeeded where Congregationalists did not. The educational standards required for Presbyterian ministers, however, proved to be a serious handicap. The "book learning" of many of them was not suited to a wild and crude frontier society. Furthermore, the strict Calvinistic doctrines of human depravity and predestination were incompatible with the chief characteristics of individualism and self-reliance which the frontier demanded. Although they were successful at first, Presbyterians could not adapt to the demands of frontier life and, in the end, gave way to the Methodists and Baptists. The Catholic Church in this country was no more successful in gaining followers than the established Protestant denominations, although the number of Catholics increased with the expansion of the country into Louisiana, Florida, Texas, and California. Membership in the Catholic Church increased most with the immigration from Ireland and Germany in the two decades prior to 1860.

The evangelization of religion. Revivalism at the time of the Civil War was part and parcel of the American dream of "manifest destiny." In 1800 the population of the nation was slightly over 5 million; by 1860 it was over 31 million—over a sixfold increase. At the beginning of this period, it is estimated that only 7 to 10 percent of the population were members of any church. The unsettled and arduous nature of frontier life and the frontiersmen's great hopes for success and fortune made for a folk romanticism and a susceptibility to religious revivalism.

[11] William Warren Sweet, *Religion on the American Frontier, 1783–1840, The Presbyterians* (New York, Cooper Square, 1964), p. 698.

Historically, the early missionaries found it necessary, in converting the tribes of Western Europe to Christianity, to convert only the tribal chiefs. When the Reformation changed the religion of the national states in Europe, it was done through the chiefs of state. But the conversion of "unchurched" Americans was an individual matter, it had to be done through individual persuasion. The most successful denominations were those which were least encumbered in meeting the religious needs of a mobile frontier society. Historians generally ascribe the success of the Methodists and Baptists to their success on the frontier, and the failure of other denominations to their failure on the frontier. The ideal of individual Christians and voluntary churches had completely superseded the old ideal of a state religion.

The most spectacular aspect of the religious movements of this period was the revival meetings. They started as "camp meetings" and were eagerly adopted by the Baptists and Methodists. Itinerant preachers and the practice of ordaining ministers without formal theological training contributed greatly to the success of these denominations. Vestiges of these practices still exist in rural areas. One of the best known of the great frontier camp meetings was at Cane Ridge, Kentucky, in 1801. Over one thousand wagons covered the grounds, and an attendance of 25,000 was reported. The emotionalism was apparently as remarkable as the size of the crowd. The physical and emotional anguish that accompanied the conversion of many was a visible symbol of frontier evangelism. The more rational clergymen condemned this as an unhealthy hysteria. They were distressed that meetings attracted some dissolute characters and that, while many were saved, some souls were lost through intoxication and seduction.[12]

Revivalism was not limited to the rural West. A wave of revivalism had begun in a small Presbyterian college in Virginia in 1787. Timothy Dwight, President of Yale and the movement's outstanding leader, attacked Deism as the enemy from without and liberalism as the enemy from within. For half a century the battle raged in New England between rational, liberal Christianity and revivalist, conservative Christianity. It involved such great American ministers as William Ellery Channing, Ralph Waldo Emerson, Theodore Parker, Lyman Beecher, and later his son, Henry Ward Beecher. The controversy involved Harvard (liberal) and Yale (conservative), and was largely responsible for the establishment in 1808 of the Andover Theological Seminary to train conservative ministers. By 1825 the split of the Congregationalists had become complete. The liberal wing established the American Unitarian Association, which included all but twenty-five of the churches in Massachusetts, and nine of the ten in Boston.[13] Identified with the liberals were the leading

12 Blake, *op. cit.*, pp. 253–254.
13 *Ibid.*, pp. 263–265.

writers, educators, and statesmen who continued to oppose the emotionalism of revivalism and to promote their own cause through rational persuasion. In the course of time their influence spread among the cities
from Boston to New Orleans. Their success, however, was held in check
by revivalism in western New England and by proslavery sentiment in
the South. Their influence, though limited in scope, was profound. Its
spirit stimulated the first important era in American literature. It also
helped to soften the creeds of other Protestant groups. Its appeal was to
an intellectual class whose indirect influence, although not measurable,
has no doubt been great.

While religious sentiment of the nineteenth century seemed to be
primarily evangelical, many other religious feelings and ideas were emerging. The excesses of the camp meetings overshadowed the much more
important influence of the local and itinerant preachers and laymen
whose religious efforts, more than any other, helped people withstand
the harsh realities of the American frontier. It was this usefulness which
made the evangelical groups successful. Periods of revivalism are periods
of rediscovery of religious teachings. They are called, at the time of their
occurrence, "periods of awakening." "The first great awakening" was
marked by great preachers such as Jonathan Edwards and George Whitefield; "the second great awakening," by Timothy Dwight and Charles G.
Finney; and a third period, after the Civil War, by Dwight L. Moody,
and later others. Revivalism wins converts; holding them and maintaining church discipline are different and more difficult problems. Mass
evangelism means the maintaining of a steady and continuous effort to
win converts, not sporadic revivals. The efforts of the nineteenth century
required organization and brought into being both home and foreign
missions. All denominations attempted missionary work of one kind or
another. It was done mostly by separate denominations, but some interdenominational groups, such as the American Board of Foreign Missions,
the American Bible Society, and the American Tract Society, were successful. The organized efforts of various denominations and sects continues to the present time. Among the most aggressive at the present time
are the Mormons, the Seventh Day Adventists, and the Jehovah's Witnesses. Most, if not all, large denominations carry on foreign mission
work of one kind or another.

The rise of new denominations and sects. By 1870 the major branches of
the Protestant faith had become firmly established, mature institutions.
In their earlier years they had been sectarian, "dissenters," and generally
scourged by the established churches. In 1870 they had become solid,
middle-class, suburban-centered institutions that not only approved of
but considered themselves a cornerstone of the established order. In their
richly furnished new churches, with educated ministers and respectable

congregations, they began to lose their taste for their earlier enthusiasm and "hell-fire" sermons. They had made peace with the world and were, in their turn, decidedly cool toward the new groups who attempted to promote radical sectarian movements. There is nothing unusual about this change. It is, in fact, the history of all successful social movements. It is a paradox that to the extent to which they succeed, groups who begin by rejecting the status quo become themselves a part of the status quo.

Religious diversity is nothing new in history. The early Christian period had its sects. The Council of Nicaea in 325 began an attempt to settle the Arian heresy. It was not successful until the second ecumenical council in 381. Arianism was the most powerful threat to orthodox belief of the early Church. The Council of Nicaea decreed the doctrines of the Trinity and Incarnation—the union of Divinity and humanity in Christ— and condemned the Arians. Condemned and exiled Arianism skirted the borders of Christendom until it was revived with coming of the Reformation. The universality of the Christian Church was, of course, shat-

Denomination	Churches	Membership
Amana Church Society	7 (1967)	737
American Catholic Church (Syro-Antiochean)	1 (1967)	450
General Six-Principle Baptist	5 (1967)	190
Independent Baptist Church of America	2 (1966)	25
Seventh Day Baptist (German)	3 (1951)	150
Christian Catholic Church	5 (1965)	1,555
Church of God (Seventh Day)	7 (1960)	2,000
Church of the Gospel	4 (1965)	42
Church of the Revelation	5 (1968)	750
Eastern Orthodox Catholic Church in America	3 (1967)	225
Syrian Orthodox Church of Antioch	7 (1963)	25,000
Church of Daniel's Band	4 (1951)	200
Liberal Catholic Church	8 (1956)	4,000
Protestant Conference (Lutheran)	7 (1967)	2,400
Cumberland Methodist	4 (1954)	65
Lumber River Annual Conference of the Holiness Methodist Church	7 (1959)	360
Pentecostal Evangelical Church of God	4 (1965)	NA
Associate Presbyterian Church in North America	4 (1965)	650
The Schwenkfelder Church	5 (1967)	2,550
United Seventh Day Brethren	4 (1968)	NR
United Wesleyan Methodist Church of America	5 (1966)	550
Gospel Mission Corps	4 (1965)	200

tered by the Reformation, and the successful heresy of the three major branches of Protestantism serve as glowing examples for succeeding dissatisfied groups.

America became the most religiously diversified nation in the world. Some denominations and sects existed before 1800, but most of them are products of the nineteenth century. *The Yearbook of American Churches,* 1969 edition, listed 238 religious bodies and their memberships. Among the largest groupings were 32 branches of Baptists, 20 Methodists, 19 Eastern Churches, 13 Mennonites, 10 Pentecostals, 10 Lutherans, 11 Churches of God, and 10 Presbyterians. In addition to these, there were 8 groups of Quakers, 5 Reformed, 4 Mormons, 5 Adventist. There are many other smaller groupings and unit organizations, some with large memberships, among whom are the Churches of Christ with over 4 million members and the United Church of Christ with over 2 million members. Other large denominations include 3.4 million Episcopalians, 5.7 million Jews, 47.5 million Roman Catholics, and 330,000 Jehovah's Witnesses. Listed on the preceding page are those denominations with eight or less churches and their memberships.

There were 73 denominations with less than 5,000 members each, composed of 1,891 churches and a total membership of 131,206, or an average of less than 1,800 members per denomination and less than 70 members per church.

FROM EVANGELISM TO SOCIAL GOSPEL

Religious response to industrialization: the South. Until after the Civil War, American religion was the product of a rural, frontier society. In the light of our present way of thinking it was simple, sincere, overlaid with emotionalism, and extremely narrow and individualistic. Industrialization and urbanization created a challenge to this evangelism. Changes in the period have been referred to as "religion's response to the industrial age." The vast majority of the American people before 1900 were still rural, or new migrants from the farm to industrial centers. They were believers in the literal interpretation of the Scriptures. It should be observed, however, that despite the success of the periods of revivalism, church membership remained limited. From less than 10 percent of the population in 1800, church membership had increased to around 23 percent in 1860. It failed to keep pace with the growth of population and in 1880 was only 20 per cent. It rose to 36 percent in 1900.[14] Controversies and trends existed at this time which have eventually resulted in the present division between "fundamentalism" and what is now generally called "neo-orthodoxy."

[14] A. Ray Eckhardt, *The Surge of Piety in America* (New York, Association Press, 1958), p. 22.

American churches were, of course, caught up in the Civil War. Jefferson Davis, who was very diligent in invoking prayers and fasts on behalf of the southern cause, was praised by southern preachers as "our Christian President"; but to the northern ministers "the most unmitigated set of villains they have in the south are the Methodist, Baptist, Presbyterian and Episcopal Preachers."[15] It is obvious that the high Christian idealism of Abraham Lincoln and Robert E. Lee did not exist in the churches either during or after the Civil War. Unfortunately, the churches in the South remained identified with "the lost cause," while Radical Reconstruction was blessed with the righteousness of northern Protestantism. The degree to which religion can be influenced by its cultural environment is obvious from this example. This is, of course, no isolated case. In most major conflicts, both sides claim righteousness through Divine favor. One of the lasting and unfortunate results of this conflict has been, until recently, the failure of southern evangelicals, both Negro and white, to keep within the mainstream of religious, social, and intellectual developments of the times. The South is still the stronghold of fundamentalism.

There was a softening of evangelism after the Civil War period. To be sure, mass evangelism continued, but new techniques were introduced by those who turned away from the camp meeting. The harsh and threatening tone of the revival message of repentance was softened, and the terrors of the "awful day of judgement" were less emphasized. The avoidance by Dwight L. Moody of all reference to social issues was a betrayal of the great tradition of revivalism and mass evangelism. The rapid growth of the churches from 1880 to 1900 was probably both cause and effect in the lowering of traditional standards of church discipline. The newer denominations, those growing most rapidly, had built their membership on direct appeal, and had supported their work on a voluntary basis. In other words, the very success of mass evangelism meant the elimination of standards for membership. Efforts to maintain high standards became increasingly difficult. The early Methodist doctrine that differences in status ended at the door of the church could not stand up against the growth in numbers and the increasing middle-class affluence of its leading members. What was true of Methodism was also true of other major denominations. In fact, church discipline was largely abandoned in the early twentieth century. An important factor in this change was the development of science and technology.

The impact of science and technology. Science and technology transformed America into an urban society with a laissez-faire economy and a greater disparity between the rich and the poor. It also undermined evan-

15 Franklin Hamlin Littell, *From State Church to Pluralism* (Chicago, Aldine, 1962), p. 68.

gelism. As the major churches, with their educated clergy and middle-class congregations, gained a greater stake in society, they became less evangelical and even heartily disapproved of the newer dissenting groups. The most liberal groups in the major denominations were making inroads on the evangelicals by moving toward a social gospel. Another group of dissenters was moving in the opposite direction. These were the Adventist, pentecostal groups who withdrew from the traditional churches and looked toward the Second Coming of Christ. Others who made considerable inroads upon the traditional denominations were the Mormons, the Christian Scientists, and the most rapidly growing group of all, the Churches of Christ.

An impassioned debate, lasting from about 1875 to 1910, was brought about by the challenge to orthodoxy by the rise of science and the scientific method. The controversy over Darwin's *Origin of the Species* did not entirely subside until after the Scopes trial in Tennessee in 1925. The conservatives, or fundamentalists, saw the theory of evolution as a contradiction, and a threat, to the Biblical account of creation. Darwin tried to prove that the more complex animal species evolved from the simpler through the process of natural selection. He "demoted" man to a place in the animal kingdom and traced his descent from other species. Many scientists and educated clergy accepted Darwinism, but many did not. The vast majority of Americans were probably horrified at Darwin's ideas. The debates were acrimonious and feeling in the congregations and communities ran high. Some college professors lost their jobs and some ministers were tried for heresy and subjected to discipline. In the end, of course, the liberals prevailed.

The rise of fundamentalism can certainly be accounted for in part because of the major religious reorientation within the traditional churches. Extreme breaks with tradition, such as the readjustment of religion to the growth of both scientific knowledge and scientific method, always create a radical reaction by those who oppose the change. The conservatives, defeated and embittered, largely withdrew from association with "liberals" and liberal causes. Many of them joined new fundamentalist denominations. In the South where the traditional denominations were already essentially conservative, this division was largely avoided. Fundamentalists have continued to be strong, in the South and Middle West.

The rise of Biblical criticism. Darwin's theories provoked another challenge to the faith of the traditional churches. The challenge of Biblical criticism cast further doubts on the literal interpretation of the Scriptures. Many outstanding theological scholars, both in the United States and in Europe, examined the Scriptures with the same objective approach that the scientists were using. This examination was generally called the Higher Criticism. These profound scholars questioned the history, origin, and meaning of every aspect of the Old and New Testaments, even the Virgin Birth of Christ. Needless to say, this brought on acrimonious debate between those who denied the verbal infallibility of the Bible and those who accepted its literal interpretation. The liberals ranged from Colonel Robert G. Ingersoll, an aggressive agnostic lawyer and orator, to those who accepted institutional Christianity, among them, Washington Gladden, Dr. Lyman Abbott, John Fiske, Phillips Brooks, William Rainey Harper, President of Chicago University and a leading Baptist. The controversy begun by Darwin's theories continued to rage in all large denominations. Roman Catholics caught up in the controversy, however, were silenced by the encyclicals of Pope Leo XIII in 1893; another encyclical in 1907 closed the door of the Catholic Church to the acceptance of any "modernist" interpretations.[16] During this period, around 1880 to 1910, the attitudes of all leading Protestant denominations underwent a noticeable change in the direction of social gospel. The Presbyterian Church in 1902, for example, adopted a statement that conceded the possible validity of Biblical criticism, and acknowledged the more liberal attitudes found in many colleges and seminaries.

A different kind of evangelism. The nature of evangelism itself changed in the new industrial age. The new evangelism, with its extensive church facilities and social creeds, was far removed from the old Protestantism of Jonathan Edwards and Charles G. Finney. The earlier periods of revivalism were the results of the efforts of the denominations and of great denominational preachers. The most widely acclaimed revivalist between the Civil War and World War I was Dwight L. Moody, a poorly educated and unconventional orator. He had been a successful shoe salesman in Chicago, and despite his turn to preaching, he was never ordained—a very unusual circumstance. When Moody preached to crowds of 15,000 to 20,000 in Philadelphia, New York, and other cities throughout the country, he avoided the hysterical emotionalism of earlier revivalists. Many other revivalists of the period tried unsuccessfully to compete with him. The most successful in capturing public attention was the flamboyant Billy Sunday, a former baseball player whose picturesque slang and acrobatic gestures drew huge audiences in special tabernacles constructed for his meetings. The appeal of both Moody and Sunday was largely to the exploited poor of the cities. By 1914, their popularity was on the wane.

The social gospel and Christian socialism. The social gospel was a revolt of many leading churchmen against the horrible conditions created in the cities by industrialization. These churchmen attempted to replace

16 Blake, *op. cit.,* pp. 494, 499.

the rugged individualism of the Protestant ethic with an emphasis on social justice.

Mainstream opinion followed the conservative position that progress in alleviating social injustices should come through private channels, especially through organized charity. The deplorable conditions of the poor in the cities prompted a large segment of the most intellectual ministers of the period to raise serious questions of why there was so much poverty and degradation in a society that was prosperous and that boasted of providing equal opportunities for all. They no longer considered satisfactory the old answer that the poor deserved their poverty because they had wasted their opportunity through laziness or intemperance. The grinding poverty of the cities arose from conditions over which the poor had no control. Was it the fault of the wage earner that he could not support his family well, that he must live in poverty and degradation without medical care, education, or the most elementary physical necessities? Historically, Protestantism had been preoccupied with the salvation of men's souls and considered the matter of societal reform a secular question of no concern to preachers. The social gospel was a challenge to these conceptions. Its advocates saw all men as the children of God and looked upon Jesus as the prophet of social justice. Their gospel stressed concern with man.

The social gospel was not peculiar to America. In Europe, numerous social movements, especially Christian Socialism, found strong adherents among both Catholics and Protestants. The Christian Socialist movement was a religious response to the evils created by the Industrial Revolution. It grew to serious proportions during the last half of the nineteenth century. Its purpose was twofold: to eliminate the evils created by the rise of capitalism and to bring the workers back to the church, away from the anti-Christian socialist movements to which they were flocking. Among Catholics this dissenting movement was known as Social Catholicism. Its leaders were chiefly priests and aristocrats who hoped to check the advance of liberalism and socialism by improving the lot of the working class. It climaxed in an encyclical by Pope Leo XIII in 1891 which formulated the policy of the Church on social problems, and committed the Church to policies designed to advance the welfare of the working class. In England the movement found such stalwart advocates as John Ruskin, Thomas Carlyle, and Charles Kingsley. It was a revolt against the apathy of the Church in regard to the evils of the economic system. The English Christian Socialists denounced the teachings of classical economics as "moral atheism," they asserted that competition was a denial of brotherly love as preached by Christ and held that no true Christian could support a social order built on laissez-faire capitalism. In America, Walter Rauschenbusch, George D. Herron of Grinnel College, and W. P. D. Bliss, founder of the Church of the Carpenter of Boston, were socialists, as were many others. Bliss, with the assistance of the Reverend Francis Bellamy, organized a Society of Christian Socialists in Boston in 1889. The working class in the industrial areas were likewise influenced by the millions of European immigrants, mostly working class, who came to America during this period. Their brand of socialism was Marxian. Christian Socialism in America was never an organized movement as was Social Catholicism on the Continent. Its influence was, however, very great on the whole social gospel movement.

Outstanding representatives of the social gospel in America were Washington Gladden, an influential pastor of a Congregational Church in Cleveland, and Walter Rauschenbusch, a German-American Baptist professor at Rochester Theological Seminary. Gladden was among the boldest critics of contemporary society. He believed that a wage system based solely on competition was both anti-social and anti-Christian, and that workers had the right to organize and strike. Rauschenbusch was the most active of all of the promoters of the social gospel, both through his long tenure of teaching and through his widely read books such as *Christianity and the Social Order* (1907). He was also sympathetic with the ideas of Henry George. The impact of Christian Socialism was greatest on the Episcopal Church. Bishop Huntington became a member of the Knights of Labor, he helped to organize and was president of the Christian Social Union of which Richard T. Ely, professor of Economics at the University of Wisconsin, was secretary. The Christian Socialists did not advocate overthrowing the social system, but only removing the inequities. Most of them advocated the regulation of capitalism and a few of the more radical advocated the ownership of some of the means of production. They condemned Marxian socialism for its materialism and were in turn condemned by the Marxists for rejecting the class struggle and adhering to supernaturalism. The positions taken by the Christian Socialists were too advanced to win general acceptance, but many ministers preached the social gospel in a much less radical form, condemning both unregulated capitalism and socialism. A general change in attitude was shown by the General Conference of the Methodist Episcopal Church in 1908. It adopted a social creed that sounded more idealistic than the programs of the early labor unions. It was an almost verbatim statement of the creed of the newly founded Federal Council of Churches. The movement met with opposition from big business and the strong revivalistic groups, but it gradually gained status among the great evangelical churches, and soon the Baptist, Congregational, Presbyterian, and Disciples of Christ churches adopted social creeds and established agencies to put them into practice. A consensus had been established, and religion in America had made an important adjustment to the conditions of its existence.

The changes discussed here are important, but they did not by any means mark a complete break with previous trends and forces. It is doubtful, furthermore, that the majority of the laity accepted the social gospel in most of its implications.

FROM SOCIAL GOSPEL TO NEO-ORTHODOXY

The rise of fundamentalism. All great changes in American culture and social environment have required major religious reorientations. One of the problems of religion, as of any other institution, is that of maintaining it relevance to social needs. Each major religious reorientation has produced reformers working within the traditional denominations as well as a reactionary fringe. The reformers range from liberal to radical, the others from conservative to reactionary. Efforts to thwart change or to bring it about range from persuasion to use of government power. The fundamentalists in the South sought to sustain a religious belief by using the government—passing laws—to prevent the teaching of evolution in the public schools. They won the legal battle in the "monkey trial" in Tennessee in 1925, but failed to halt the acceptance of the scientific point of view by all major religious denominations in the United States. The fundamentalists have continued to promote their cause through two major organizations: the American Council of Churches organized in 1941, claiming 15 denominations and over 500,000 members in 1965; and the National Association of Evangelicals, the neo-fundamentalists, organized in 1942, and claiming in 1965 to represent 34 denominations and over 1.5 million members. The outstanding representative of the Evangelicals is Billy Graham. Both of these federations have established seminaries, publishing houses, and so on to promote their causes. The great majority of the 20 million fundamentalists, however, have refused to join these groups. The National Council of Churches represents 34 denominations and has over 41 million members. Although it represents the liberal consensus it is itself divided into liberal and conservative wings, and it is here that a more serious re-orientation is taking place.

Origin, influence and decline of social gospel. The social gospel movement arose from the deplorable conditions created by the industrialization process: long hours and low pay, the exploitation of child labor, the crowded, filthy, and dehumanizing living conditions of the poor. In glaring contrast to this unsavory side of American life was the glowing luxury and sumptuous living of the capitalistic classes. The social gospel was the religious response of liberal Protestantism to the human needs of the poor. As indicated previously, in Europe the response ranged from religious movements to Marxian socialism. In the course of time in this country, government regulations, successes of organized labor, and organized charity had ameliorated the worst of these conditions. The social gospel of the earlier period was strongly pacifistic. Later developments, however—the Sino-Japanese War, the intervention in Ethiopia by Mussolini, and the rise of Hitler in Germany during the 1930s—all ran counter to pacifism. The social gospel ran its course and gave way to neo-orthodoxy.

The Depression of the early 1930s had brought many religious conservatives to support the social legislation of the New Deal. The social gospel lost most of its support as such, but it did achieve widespread support for its most important tenet: that the churches be concerned with social realities and that public issues not to be divorced from religious conviction. This is one of the greatest single advances in American church history. The social gospel, which had been vigorously opposed by big business and all conservative groups, would henceforth guide the goals of the church. The church would no longer confine itself to "soul-saving," but extend itself into the social life of the community and into the public issues and problems of the day. This positive and aggressive approach marked a definite break with the past. The religious groups that had previously attempted to regulate morals through the use of laws regulating liquor, the teaching of evolution were, in comparison, mostly negative and restraining.

In his earlier years Reinhold Niebuhr was among the most radical of contemporary advocates of the social gospel, but by the 1940s he had become the most influential critic of its theories. He repudiated his earlier socialist and pacifist views, and, with the efforts of other influential Protestants, helped to reemphasize the supernatural in American religion. Changes in social and economic conditions also contributed to the decline of the social gospel. There was a rapid decline in the discussion of "Christian ethics" as the Depression subsided. After World War II the conservatives saw liberalism as a movement away from the American way of life under the influence of socialism and communism, and many still do.

Status of neo-orthodoxy. The swing away from the liberal Christianity of the social gospel era caused many to fear that neo-orthodoxy was becoming too conservative. Niebuhr and others attempted to mediate between the idealistic social gospel and the more hard-headed groups who placed power and self-interest above brotherly love.[17] While many of the elements of the social gospel, especially the socialist and pacifist aspects have largely disappeared, its emphasis on brotherhood, social justice, and peace have been accepted doctrinally by every major denomination. The concern of the National Council of Churches with such questions as racial equality, peace, and justice and the participation of ministers, both Protestant and Catholic, in the civil rights and other move-

[17] Smith, *op. cit.,* Vol. II, p. 508.

ments both indicate the degree to which religion in America is involved in the crucial issues of the day.

It is difficult to determine whether Americans are moving toward conservatism in re-emphasizing the supernatural, literal tenets of religion —as represented by neo-orthodoxy and fundamentalism—or whether they are moving toward a socially conscious liberalism. Theologians here and abroad battle over whether "God is dead," but very few of their congregations take the trouble to learn what the controversy is all about. Urban ministers are far more liberal than their congregations, and the "separation of pulpit and pew" constitutes a serious problem. Many ministers assert that the churches are now answering questions which are not being asked. Others insist that the churches are not confronting the problems of the postwar generation. Despite the assertions of involvement, it is obvious that the great majority of American churches are not intensely concerned with the great issues of the day. This gives weight to the argument of many theologians that the great problem of the church today is the relevance of religious beliefs and church activities. Neo-orthodoxy has been a movement limited to the liberal ministry; it has found little response among the masses of their membership. It has been mostly a concern of the theologians and one in which most Americans have had little interest. The old concept of religion as "an experience" which made an observable change in men's lives is obviously not adequate today.

THE ECUMENICAL MOVEMENT

The rise of ecumenism. In the Christian world, the liberal spirit has been growing. As far as the United States is concerned, the three most important outward aspects of this movement have been: first, the union among various Protestant branches of denominations, and to a more limited extent among the denominations; second, the cooperation among Protestant denominations in such far-reaching organizations as the World Council of Churches and the National Council of Churches; and third, the ecumenical movement within the Roman Catholic Church. More important than what has actually been accomplished is the spirit or attitude out of which this movement toward Christian unity has developed. It is a commitment to the effort to make religion relevant to a world in which science and an urban-industrial way of life have created a new cultural environment. Ecumenism is the beginning of a major reorientation. The controversy continues between the liberals who want to adapt the church to its modern environment and the conservatives who are reluctant to make drastic changes. The conservatives in general represent the areas where the industrialization process has been incomplete.

Among the most important unions that have taken place are: the United Lutheran Church in America, the United Evangelical Lutheran

Church, the Methodist Church, the United Presbyterian Church in the U. S. A., the Congregational Christian Churches, and the Unitarian Universalist Association. Each of these new churches represents a union of two or more branches of a single denomination or the combination of two or more denominations. The boldest of all interdenominational thinking came from Eugene Carson Blake, a Presbyterian and Secretary General of the World Council of Churches, in 1961 when he proposed the merger of the Methodists, Episcopalians, Presbyterians, and the United Church of Christ.

The second major line of ecumenical development began with such cooperative efforts as the YMCA, the Student Volunteer Movement for Foreign Missions, and culminated in the organization of the World Council of Churches in 1948. The National Council of Churches of the United States has already been mentioned. The significance of the Third Assembly of the World Council of Churches, held in New Delhi in 1961, was echoed in the words of Henry P. Van Dusen, President of Union Theological Seminary, who stated that "we are seeing right here one of the very early events of the second great Reformation of Christendom."[18] All major Christian denominations except the Roman Catholic were represented. Surprisingly, it did include the Eastern and Russian Orthodox Churches.

Ecumenism has its critics outside as well as inside the movement. Denominations whose doctrine does not permit recognition of other Christian bodies as true churches—Southern Baptists and Missouri Synod Lutherans, for example—are, of course, not free to participate in the movement. The most vigorous criticism, however, comes from the fundamentalists who have formed their own organizations: the American Council of Christian Churches and the National Association of Evangelicals.

In the early stages of ecumenism it was hoped that the Roman Catholics might take part in the movement, but the rigid doctrinal views of the Roman Church made this impossible. Within the Catholic Church there was, however, an increasing demand for Christian unity which eventually led to the issuance in 1949 of an "Instruction on the Ecumenical Movement." This was a distinctive "Catholic ecumenism" which did permit Roman Catholic unofficial observers to attend Protestant ecumenical meetings, which many have done. More significant still, for the first time in history, observers from Protestant and Orthodox churches sat in attendance and were sometimes consulted on issues under discussion when the Second Vatican Council met in Rome in 1962. Despite these achievements, the ideal of a single Christian Church is still a dream. The fact that Catholics and Protestants can overcome their historical enmity and meet each other and discuss issues in good fellowship is a tremendous gain. The appointment by the Catholic Church in 1960 of a

18 *Time* (December 8, 1961), p. 76.

Secretariat for Promoting Christian Unity, and the election of a Catholic as President of the United States the same year were not only signs of a deep change in attitude but also contributions to it.

Catholic growth and religious controversy. While the most visible results of the ecumenical movement have touched the Protestant and Eastern Orthodox churches, the attitude of the Roman Catholic Church toward ecumenism is of the greatest importance to Americans. In 1966 there were 45.6 million Catholics; they constituted over 37.5 percent of the total church membership. The U. S. Bureau of Census based on a 1957 census sampling reported that over 25.7 percent of the total population was Catholic. In 1790 there were probably not over 30,000 Catholics in a population of some 4 million, or less than 1 percent of the total population. By 1860 the ratio was approximately 10 percent. From about 1840 to 1860 Catholics immigrated in great numbers. Anti-Catholic animosity soon came to the boiling point. The Reverend Lyman Beecher was only one of those who wrote and preached about the Catholic menace. Inventor Samuel F. B. Morse warned of a papal plot to overthrow American institutions by capturing America through immigration.[19] The attitude and statements of some outstanding Catholics lent credibility, at least doctrinally, to the accusations. Monsignor Thomas S. Preston of New York pressed the idea that all good Catholics must seek the reestablishment of the temporal power of the Pope. Archbishop Corrigan, also of New York, held similar views and some of these conservatives attempted to curb the more liberal views of Father McGlynn, Cardinal Gibbons, and other liberal Catholics. The attack on Catholics was not limited to the printed page and the platform. Ursuline Convent near Boston was burned in 1834, two parochial schools and a seminary were burned in Buffalo in 1840, in 1844 anti-Catholic mobs in Philadelphia attacked convents and churches and thirteen persons were killed and fifty wounded in the rioting, and there was other violence. By 1860 the Catholic Church with 3 million members was the largest single denomination in the United States. The "nativism" which resulted was more than religious: it was Anglo-Saxon, white, Protestant. It was also aggravated by the hostility of laborers to immigrant labor competition.

Nativism in the form of the Know-Nothing Party arose in 1852 and by 1855 claimed many voters throughout the country; thirty-five states had Know-Nothing Parties and they controlled several states. But a more serious religious conflict was averted when the slavery controversy turned interest elsewhere. After 1860 the Catholic population doubled approximately every twenty years, reaching 16 million by 1910. This rapid expansion of Catholicism brought protests similar to but less serious than those before the Civil War. Fortunately, many prominent Catholic

19 Blake, *op. cit.*, p. 267.

churchmen of the period, including Father Isaac Hecker, Bishop Keane, Bishop Spalding, Archbishop Ireland, and Cardinal Gibbons, did much to adapt the Catholic Church to its American environment and to lessen anti-Catholic sentiment. Cardinal Gibbons took every opportunity to praise American democracy and even to defend the separation of church and state. This tendency among many important American Catholics to place less emphasis on doctrine and more on individual conscience and social work brought criticism from conservative Catholic clerics who influenced Pope Leo XIII to condemn "false Americanism."[20] This was, nevertheless, the beginning of the "Americanization" of the Catholic Church in this country. President John F. Kennedy made the most eloquent statement of the success of this adjustment in his pre-election appearance before the Protestant ministers in Houston, Texas, on September 12, 1960, where he made an unreserved commitment to religious liberty and to the separation of church and state. His record as President was in strict accord with this commitment. Early in his administration he went on record as opposed to diplomatic relations with the Vatican. The most striking illustration of his independence from the Catholic Church and its hierarchy was his staunch opposition to any direct federal aid to parochial schools. He sponsored a bill that was opposed to all direct aid to parochial schools as unconstitutional. His position was more opposed to that of the Catholic hierarchy than was that of his 1960 Protestant opponent, Richard M. Nixon, now President Nixon, or that of former President Lyndon B. Johnson, a Baptist.

There have been schisms among Christians from the beginning of Christianity, and many serious ones since the Arian Heresy, which began in the fourth century and separated Christians for many centuries. The "ecumenism" of the early Christian Church and of the Roman Catholic Church until recently had been an effort to regain the Christians who had separated from the Church. The present ecumenical movement is more a striving to find a common faith based on a commitment to Christianity. Catholic-Protestant cooperation in the United States, has been hindered by factors other than religious. The Catholic Church has been called an "immigrant church." Many of the immigrants lived in "ethnic islands," attempting to perpetuate their European religion as well as their Old World culture. The Catholic acceptance of authority, the rigid church hierarchy, and institutional mediation rather than direct, personal responsibility before God, are foreign to the general American orientation. Furthermore, such dogmas as the Assumption and Infallibility as well as the recent "liturgical movement" stressing the eucharistic core of Catholicism make more difficult the task of the ecumenical rapprochement. American Protestants are more oriented to left-wing Protestantism. Despite these difficulties, much has been accomplished in the acceptance

[20] *Ibid.,* p. 494.

of a common brotherhood, as can be seen when Protestants, Catholics, and Jews appear together in common causes, as they frequently do.

Catholic ecumenism. The Vatican Council of 1962–1965 had as its job the modernization of the Catholic Church. The recent removal of the ban on meat on Friday, the liturgical reforms permitting the mass in the vernacular, participation of the congregation in oral response and singing at mass, and the priests facing the congregation have all, to a degree, brought American Catholicism into the mainstream of religion in America. Two major problems still confront the Catholic Church: birth control and divorce. A Gallup poll in January 1965 showed that 78 percent of Catholics favored making birth control information available. The national figure was 81 percent. Catholic marriages break up in a ratio of about one out of five to the national ratio of divorces of about one out of four. The Catholic divorce rate is somewhat lower than the Protestant, but the separation and desertion rate is higher. It is obvious that Catholics are moving in the direction of other major denominations in the United States. Edward Wakin and Father Joseph F. Scheuer have said that "Because of the tensions in the American Catholic identity, because of the Anglo-Saxon and Roman confrontation, American Catholicism is evolving and transforming itself. . . . . In twenty-five years we shall not recognize the Roman Catholic Church in America."[21]

RELIGION TODAY

We have attempted to trace the steps in the transition of religion in America up to this point. Listed below are a few characteristics of religion at the present time.

Pluralism. Few members of any religious group want a way of life different from that of other Americans. The mass society of today makes impossible a community dominated by a religious atmosphere. Protestants, Catholics, and Jews all participate in the American way of life.

Secularism. Secularization is a trend away from the sacred and mystical interpretation of life and a trend toward rational and naturalistic interpretation. Secularization is one of the most profound changes in our history; it forms the basis for our scientific and technological civilization as well as our modern democratic government. A few examples will clarify the process. Not too far back in our history kings were thought to hold their thrones by "divine right" and to represent God's will to their subjects. In some places this is still true, and some rulers are even thought to

---

[21] Edward Wakin and Father Joseph F. Scheuer, *The De-Romanization of the American Catholic Church* (New York, Macmillan, 1966), p. 291.

be divine themselves. In our society the rulers are mere men who represent us without any claim on divine authority. A second case is education. Early education was essentially for religious purposes. Today it is intended to train for democratic citizenship and economic competence. Another case is marriage. Early American marriage was entirely a religious affair. Today it is a civil rite even though the ceremony may be religious.

Scientific orientation. Scientific knowledge and scientific method have become so pervasive in our society that they overshadow the older method of referring to custom or to the supernatural as a basis for interpretation. Most, if not all, religions have a cosmology, or explanation of the creation and existence of the universe. Science has created a new cosmology based on empirical knowledge. Modern science has brought about profound changes in the conception of the nature of God. Dietrich Bonhoeffer stated this view cogently when he said that, in the modern secular world, science, politics, morality, philosophy, and even religion need no God to explain and justify themselves. This does not mean that Bonhoeffer was irreligious. He was, in fact, a modern day Christian martyr who was executed by the Nazis in 1945.

Doctrine, denominations, and liturgy. With the decline of Calvinism among Congregationalists and Presbyterians, doctrine among American Protestant groups has become increasingly less important. Protestantism has no unifying doctrines such as have supported the Catholic faith. This doctrinal weakness also weakens denominationalism, making it easy for Protestants to shift from one denomination to another or to form new groups with little or no feeling of remorse. Despite the differences among Protestants and Catholics, they have an overall Christian tradition and a common way-of-life orientation. Theology seems to be thought of as reflection on religion rather than as authoritative pronouncements of divinely revealed truth.

Churches vary widely in the use of ritual and symbolism. They have generally been divided into liturgical and nonliturgical. The Catholic Church has always been highly liturgical, and the Lutheran and Episcopal churches have not departed widely from the Catholic service—lighted candles, crosses, robed choirs, pastors in full vestment, elaborate rituals. Early American denominations, except Anglicans and the few Catholics and Lutherans, were left-wing Protestants who had revolted against the formalism of the church. Churches are, of course, not either liturgical or nonliturgical; there is a continuum from the most informal holiness sect to the most formal high-church Episcopal. The formality of religious services among Protestant groups tends to be proportional to their social class. The historically disinherited are usually associated with the sectarian groups where emotionalism is at its height; successful business and professional groups are usually associated with churches that have more formal services.

Many outstanding theologians contend that the American way of life has become the religion of Americans, and some of them are warning against the dangers of a culture-religion. They correctly point to the pietistic support of the churches on both sides of the Civil War, where Lincoln's spiritual statue stood above the pietistic religious denominations on both sides who prayed to God as some kind of tribal deity. They also point to the excessive pietism of the Third Reich under which Nazism arose. Pietism is a kind of religion without creed or church discipline. It represents a kind of revolt against institutional religion and emphasizes personal religion rather than conformity to external standards. Those who approve of the growing pietism point to the American spirit of mission. American Protestant churches have never been strong on creed or doctrine, and they are increasingly less so. With the evangelization of religion the churches lost their discipline over their membership so that today they have neither a strong doctrine nor a church discipline to support their faith. In the process of de-Romanization, the Catholic Church will, no doubt, follow in the steps of the Protestant churches.

In 1900 the church membership in the United States was 36 percent of the total population; in 1930 it was 47 percent; and in 1963 it was 63.4 percent. While in our affluent society it may be true, as some contend, that belonging to the church is a sort of status symbol, it cannot all be written off as such. The vast amount of money contributed and the great amount of time and effort given to religious work of one kind or another indicate that this is not the whole truth. The sermons of a better educated clergy are more secular than formerly, and other religious services such as young peoples' services and evening services are also more secular. Churches have added many secular programs such as nursery schools, recreation, group discussions of important questions, reviews of important books, and dozens of other secular activities. Also, as previously indicated, religious groups of all kinds are working together with an increased sense of common purpose on common problems. It is also evident that churches are more liberal, and that they are moving in the direction of accepting greater social responsibility in a search for greater relevancy to the urban-industrial environment in which they exist.

BIBLIOGRAPHY

Abell, Aaron Ignatius, *The Urban Impact on American Protestantism, 1865–1900*. London, Archon, 1962.

Blake, Nelson Manfred, *A Short History of American Life*. New York, McGraw-Hill, 1952.

The Center for the Study of Democratic Institutions, *Religion in a Free Society*. Santa Barbara, Cal., The Center, 1958.

Cox, Harvey G., *The Secular City*. New York, Macmillan, 1965.

Eckhardt, A. Ray, *The Surge of Piety in America: An Appraisal*. New York, Association Press, 1958.

Herberg, Will, *Protestants, Catholics, Jews*. Garden City, N. Y., Doubleday, 1956.

Hoult, Thomas Ford, *The Sociology of Religion*. New York, Dryden Press, 1958.

Knudten, Richard D., ed., *The Sociology of Religion: An Anthology*. New York, Appleton-Century-Crofts, 1967.

Littell, Franklin Hamlin, *From State Church to Pluralism: A Protestant Interpretation of Religion in American History*. Chicago, Aldine, 1962.

Marty, Martin E., *The New Shape of American Religion*. New York, Harper, 1958.

Moberg, David O., *The Church as a Social Institution: The Sociology of American Religion*. Englewood Cliffs, N. J., PrenticeHall, 1962.

"Religion in America," *Daedalus,* Vol. 96, No. 1 (Winter 1967).

"Religion in American Society," *Annals of the American Academy of Political and Social Science,* Vol. 332 (November 1960).

Salisbury, W. Stewart, *Religion in American Culture: A Sociological Interpretation*. Homewood, Ill., Dorsey Press, 1964.

Smith, H. Shelton, Robert T. Handy, and Lefferts A. Loetscher, *American Christianity: An Historical Interpretation with Representative Documents,* 2 vols. New York, Scribner, 1960.

Stokes, Anson Phelps, *Church and State in the United States,* rev. ed., New York, Harper & Row, 1964.

Sweet, William Warren, *The Story of Religion in America*. New York, Harper, 1930.

Tavard, George H., *Two Centuries of Ecumenism: The Search for Unity,* trans. by Royce W. Hughes. New York, New American Library, 1960.

Wakin, Edward, and Father Joseph F. Scheuer, *The De-Romanization of the American Catholic Church*. New York, Macmillan, 1966.

Whitman, Lauris B., ed., *1969 Year Book of American Churches*. New York, Council Press, 1969.

12

Stratification and class structure

PEOPLE in all societies rank those around them as their superiors, equals, or inferiors. More important, the distribution of worldly goods is largely made on this basis. Those in positions of leadership are usually ranked at the top and constitute only a small minority. Positions of great responsibility that require long periods of training are ranked next. Those at the lower levels have tasks that are mostly routine and that demand only a low level of skill. As we descend the population pyramid, the number of individuals in each stratum increases and the prestige of the position decreases. The United States is an exception to this rule; the number of people in the lower-lower class is smaller than the two above it. The division of labor and the ranking of prestige are generally related in some way to the economic life of the society.

THE IMPORTANCE OF STRATIFICATION

Social stratification is based on the distribution of wealth or income, the types of occupations, the social standing, group identification, level of consumption, and family backgrounds of the various groups within a society's population. A stratified society is one in which the distribution of wealth and power is unequal. Stratification, then, is the ranking of individuals into hierarchies based on a superiority-inferiority valuation. Any large group is likely to have some degree of stratification.

The desire of individuals to gain prestige, and to pass the advantages of their status on to their children, makes even an open class system difficult to maintain. As noted by observers of society from Plato to Robert Michels and C. Wright Mills, there is a tendency toward aristocracy and rigidity of class structure. In some societies, this has resulted in a caste, or closed class system; in others, classes have become more or less rigid. At the other extreme is the open class system where movement up or down the social structure is based strictly on personal effort and ability. In the United States, the graduated income tax, the inheritance tax, and public education have tended to equalize opportunities for children of all status levels and thereby blur the lines of demarcation between classes.

As we noted in Chapter 1, *status* is the position one occupies in a group, and *role* is the function he is expected to perform because he occupies the status. For example, an army captain is expected to give orders; if the new recruit tried to give orders, he would be attempting to play a role which was not in keeping with his status in the army. Most of our activities are governed by our roles. The activities of a minister, husband, corporation president, or student are determined by his status and role as a minister, husband, etc. Social systems, then, provide direction for individual behavior through established patterns of conformity determined by positions or statuses and roles. In this respect the status system is an important factor in regulating the behavior of individuals and thus maintaining the organization and functioning of the society.

In feudal society there were three well-defined social classes: the clergy, the nobility, and the peasantry. The duty of the clergy was to conduct worship services, administer the sacraments; the duty of the nobility was to govern, preserve the peace within their realms, and repel invasion from without; the duty of the common people or peasantry was to work to support themselves and the two upper classes. Feudal society was said to be composed of "those who work, those who guard, and those who pray."[1] There was no doubt as to which class an individual belonged. His rights and duties, his standards of behavior, his dress, his education and his general style of life were all determined by his class. The feudal classes were sharply separated. The classes of modern Western societies are not. Modern society has a great diversity of culture patterns, an immense number of statuses or jobs to be performed, a high degree of specialization, and a great diversity of interests. All these characteristics tend to blur the lines between the social classes. Status is still partly a matter of ascription in Western societies, but it has come to depend to a great extent on achievement, especially in the United States. Also, egalitarian values conflict with the concepts of social classes. The United States Constitution struck a blow against the traditional class system by prohibiting laws of entail and escheat. Although stratification in American society is a fact, the social classes are not very clearly defined.

The determinants of stratification. The stratification of society has been considered from two points of view by social analysts. It has been conceived, first, as a continuum of degrees or levels of wealth, income, education, occupation, and so on. Although a continuum can be constructed within each of these categories, the continuum, or the information it contains, cannot in itself reveal patterns of social stratification. This would be true even if the continuum were to be arbitrarily marked

[1] John Geise, *Man and the Western World* (New York, Hinds, Hayden, and Eldridge, 1947), p. 425.

off at different points. All college graduates in the United States, for example, or all people with annual incomes of $10,000 to $20,000, do not per se constitute social classes. No continuum includes all the categories necessary to define a social class. Social classes are defined partly by objectively measurable factors and partly by such immeasurable factors as class interaction, class consciousness, and value orientation.

Stratification is also conceived not as a continuum but as a ranking of discrete categories. Communities, for example, are composed of many smaller groups and associations which contain different statuses and roles. The groups within a society with essentially the same status are social classes. This structural differentiation is not a statistical construct, but the observation of repeated experiences of class differentiation, discrimination, and antagonism. Persons in the same class are aware of their common interests, attitudes, and opinions. Common economic interests alone, however, do not create a social class. They are the bases from which social interactions arise. These patterns of social interaction—companionship, marriage, entertaining—make for class distinctions and enable analysts to define those classes. As a social system becomes larger and more complex, a greater amount of coordination becomes necessary. Coordination in the community is achieved through the interactions of individuals.

There are many definitions of class. A class can be defined as a stratum of people of similar social positions; or, as those groups within a society having essentially the same status; or, as aggregations of persons whose positions of power, privilege, or prestige are similar; or, as those people who are ranked by members of the community into socially superior and inferior positions.

Social stratification is directly related to the division of labor. As societies grow larger, their social structures become more complex and the problem of differentiating between classes becomes increasingly difficult. The breakdown of the feudal system occurred when the status based on heredity was replaced by a status based on wealth. Sir Henry Maine noted that there had been an evolution from status to contract in legal relationships among persons; Karl Marx emphasized the rise of new economic classes in Europe. Max Weber, one of the most discerning of modern social analysts, placed "the possession of goods and opportunities for income"[2] at the heart of the definition of class. Most American sociologists have also considered economic factors the main determinants of social class.

Wealth is probably the most important factor in the social structure of American society. But wealth and the size of income are factors in social stratification only insofar as they affect the behavior of individuals so that they act in a way similar to others with comparable income.

[2] H. H. Gerth and C. Wright Mills, eds., *From Max Weber: Essays in Sociology* (New York, Oxford, 1958), p. 181.

What people do for a living has much to do with their class position. It is probably the best single criterion for determining an individual's social status, and both income and education are correlated with it. Individual occupations themselves can be ranked. One of the most widely known occupational rating scales is by North and Hatt. Social class cannot be determined by such rating scales alone, however.

Income, occupational, and educational statistics are studied extensively by sociologists in their analysis of class structure. These statistics enable them to make some generalizations about the different social levels of the community. Education is eagerly sought, not so much for its intrinsic value, but because it most frequently enables people to improve their status. Higher education brings not only occupational skills but also changes in values, goals, and class orientation.

The various determinants of social classes are usually analyzed separately, but they are in reality inseparable. The relative importance of the different variables that determine class structure is still subject to question, but there is no doubt that society is stratified or that the stratification is basic to social organization and the orderly functioning of modern mass societies.

The functions of stratification. We have observed that the degree of statification is related to the size of the community or society and its division of labor—the more complex the society, the more groups it has. In the pre-industrial village there were few positions or statuses to which people could aspire; the stratification system was relatively simple. Even so, it was essential that those positions on the village council, church offices, guild councils, and so on should not only be filled, but that they should be efficiently administered. As villages grew into cities, hundreds of new functions or services were required and these added new statuses to the social structure. As the number of statuses increased, the stratification of society increased. In industrial societies it is extremely complex, and the statuses at the extremes of the spectrum are very widely separated. Thus, stratification is a necessity for placing and motivating individuals within the social structure. In order to properly fill the various statuses or positions, society must offer rewards in accordance with them. Those positions that have the greatest importance to society and require the greatest training or talent have the highest prestige and offer the best rewards.

Briefly, social stratification functions as a device for arranging individuals, families, and groups into a social system of unequals. If it functioned perfectly, every individual would be perfectly placed. In reality, statistics show that people's statuses are generally proportional to their social achievements and proficiencies. This means that society's division of labor does take advantage of people's unequal abilities to integrate them into a cohesive society.

THE AMERICAN CLASS STRUCTURE

Community studies and the class structure. In the past several decades many studies have been made of the class structure of individual communities. Robert S. and Helen M. Lynd in their books on "Middletown" divided the population on the basis of occupation into two classes, the working and business classes. Richard Centers, with a subjective approach, divided the community he studied into four classes, the upper, middle, working, and lower classes. He questioned members of the community as to which class they belonged. The responses he got indicated that 51 percent were working class, 43 percent were middle class, 3 percent upper class, and 1 percent lower class. August B. Hollingshead used a five-class distribution in his "Elmtown" study to arrive at a distribution of 3 to 4 percent in the upper class, 6 to 8 percent in the upper-middle class, 35 to 40 percent in the lower-middle class, around 40 percent in the upper-lower class, and 12 to 15 percent in the lower-lower class. It is obvious from a comparison of these two studies that few Americans rank themselves lower class even when objective criteria place them there. W. Lloyd Warner and his associates in their "Yankee City" studies used a six-class distribution. They divided the upper class into upper-upper and lower-upper; the other four were similar to Hollingshead's divisions.

The sizes of the communities studied are varied. James West's "Plainville" is a village community of only 275 persons; "Yankee City" is a long-established industrial-commercial city of a population of 17,000. It is difficult to come to any generalizations about American society as a whole from an examination of these community studies. Each of the studies used different criteria and different methods for distinguishing between one class and another. The conclusions of each of them are based on one set of criteria and methods, and are thus difficult to compare. Furthermore, each community had its own set of symbols and ways of expressing them. Almost everything of social significance was drawn into the evaluations—education, religion, morality, family, marriage, friendships, ethnic origins, attitudes, values, social participation, responsibility. But even with their differences, these studies serve very useful purposes. They each provide a view of class structure, and through a more descriptive, intimate view of class differences make the concept of social class more realistic. The communities studied are very much alike in their class structure. Perhaps most important, these studies reveal the extent to which behavior is "class" behavior. The course of conflicts between labor and management, for example, is strongly influenced by the general class interests, loyalties, and outlook of the groups in conflict.

In general, American sociologists do not agree on a description of the American class structure. What is true of the community studies mentioned above—their lack of agreement as to criteria for deciding what exactly a class is and their differences in methodology—is generally true of sociologists whose concern is society as a whole. Because communities and regions vary widely in social structure and style of life, and because our open class society has a high degree of social mobility, it is even more difficult for sociologists to reach agreement about the American class structure.

The national class structure differs from the community class structure not only in size, but also in the kind of factor that must be considered. The national economy and the federal government have their own special functions. "Nationalism," "national loyalty," or ideology is also a factor.

Style of life. Despite the difficulties in analyzing our class structure, sociologists have been able to describe the style of life of the different classes. This "style of life" is described in terms of the behavior of individuals and is expressed as beliefs and attitudes.

Style of life is largely acquired through the experiences of childhood and is therefore a result of socialization. In large cities the most wealthy— 3 or 4 percent of the population—are numerous enough to form large urban or suburban neighborhoods. They are a cohesive, organized social group, not merely a statistical category. They belong to exclusive clubs, the men sit on the boards of directors of businesses, banks, other corporations, universities and so on, and in general make the important decisions in our society. Their children attend private schools, their sons the "prestige" universities, and their daughters the exclusive women's colleges.

There are two fairly distinct categories within the upper class. One, generally called upper-upper, is based on inherited wealth and position. The other, the lower-upper, is composed largely of those who have recently risen from the middle class; many members of the lower-upper class have as much or more money than the upper-upper class. There are many stories of highly successful business executives who fought their way to the top only to be humiliated by refusals to the exclusive clubs of the upper-upper class; there are even more stories about their wives and daughters, who were more society-minded than themselves. The men, however, have much in common since they frequently have business dealings with each other, sit on boards of directors together, and work together on such common things as community chest drives. The children of the two groups may not play together in each other's homes, but they may attend the same schools, meet later in social and recreational activities, and eventually intermarry.

F. Scott Fitzgerald observed in *All the Sad Young Men* that this upper-upper class is "different from you and me," and deep in their hearts they think that "they are better than we are." Newcomers, regardless of their wealth, cannot hope to emulate their style of life easily. Upper-upper class families place great significance on family line. They are "the old families" of the community, mostly Anglo-Saxon and Protestant. The fathers and grandfathers of the upper-upper class were pillars of social power and respectability, and they themselves grew up in an environment of permanence, gracious living, opportunities for travel, and the best of private education. To them ostentation, boastfulness, aggressiveness, and display of wealth appear crude and boorish; they are conservative, dignified and proper in their relationships. To them education is part of their style of life, not a channel to improved status as it is for other classes.

The lower-upper class has acquired to some degree many of the characteristics of the upper-upper, but it is more aggressive, more ostentatious, more money-minded, more status-conscious, and less inclined to patronize the arts.

Upper-class families have the smallest number of children and the largest number of older people, especially widows and spinsters. W. Lloyd Warner says that 11 percent of the upper-class families are children, 28 percent in the other classes; 39 percent of the upper-class families are over 60 years of age, 11 percent in the other classes.[3] The upper-middle class, which constitutes 6 to 8 percent of the populations in the community studies discussed here, is in many respects both like the upper classes to which it aspires and the lower-middle class from which it seeks to emerge. It is largely composed of heads of families who are professional people, large industry officials, and large businessmen who hold more college degrees than any other class.

The lower-middle class is one of the two largest classes; it constitutes 35 to 40 percent of the total population of the communities studied. It is composed of heads of families of white-collar workers, semi-skilled workers, skilled workers, the lower levels of business and the professions, foremen. This class holds most of the memberships in churches, fraternal organizations, associations, and political organizations. It also holds most of the political offices, although major policies are often determined by the members of the upper classes. Its style of life is markedly different from that of the classes above it. The older members of this class generally attended high schools not designed to prepare them for college entrance. The younger people are now enrolling in colleges in tremendous numbers. It is still too early to tell what effect this new enrollment will have on the class structure.

Warner calls the lower-middle and the upper-lower classes, 75 percent of the population, "the common-man level"; he calls the lower-lower class, 12 to 15 percent of the population, "the level below the common

[3] W. Lloyd Warner, ed., *Yankee City*, abr. ed., Vol. I (New Haven, Yale, 1963), p. 241.

The differential fertility rate is another factor in mobility. Poorer families tend to have more children than richer families. This means in general that each level of employer recruits from the class below it. This was especially true in the upper levels where there seems always to be a shortage of capable executives and specialists. The tremendous growth in population and the unprecedented increase in our level of living resulted in a phenomenal growth in industry; and the bureaucratic organization which we have previously described created more jobs at higher levels. It also greatly increased the need for personnel engaged in the professions and service industries.

Several other factors in American society have tended to create equality of opportunity. Egalitarianism has been a dominant theme in American history and, while the myth has been more pervasive than the reality, we as individuals have been disturbed by the disparity. Political action and other means have been attempted to make the ideal a reality. There are many examples: compulsory education, child labor laws, laws prohibiting discrimination in employment, graduated income taxes. Many adult education programs and in-service training programs of corporations have aided many young men to improve their social status as well as their occupational status. Some efforts have been made to remove "the culture of poverty," but with relatively little success. Here the great hope has been and still is a better equalization of the opportunity to get a good education.

Education and mobility. Every society must have some means of training people and for placing them into positions according to their training. In rural societies this training took place largely within the family. Industrial societies have depended on formal education for this purpose. Prior to the industrial revolution, formal education played little part in either the socialization or the job preparation of the great majority of people. Until the nineteenth century, and then only in the industrialized countries of Western Europe and the United States, education beyond the rudiments of reading and writing was reserved for the upper classes or for the upper-middle classes who were able to pay for it. While the schools that existed served primarily to aid the upper classes in maintaining their established positions, they were forced to admit some of the more influential of the bourgeoisie. During the nineteenth century, when the middle classes were rising to power in England, these so-called public schools tended to fuse the values of the two classes. The working classes were largely excluded from the schools. At the same time in the United States, education also served mostly the upper classes. Only in the latter part of the century did it become an important factor in the advancement of relatively large numbers of the middle classes, and only in this century did its influence become pervasive.

In pre-industrial societies, higher education, except for the traditional professions of law, the ministry, and medicine, was a liberal-arts
education; the more practical subjects were suspect. In present-day industrial societies, both the production and distribution of goods are
increasingly handled by large corporations, and the growth in both their
size and complexity has caused colleges to devote their curricula to the
practical fields such as engineering, business administration, public administration, commercial art, fine arts, social work, the sciences, and
teacher training. This has probably been carried farther in the United
States than anywhere else. In the last few decades there has been a great
proliferation both in the number and kinds of schools and in the numbers who attend the schools. Because of this change, high school and college curricula have largely eliminated those subjects that have no connection with the recent mobility demands and have added scores of those
that do. Society has demanded that educational institutions adjust to
what it believes are their major functions. Social scientists have repeated
what many youth and employers knew for a long time—that the rewards
of higher education are gains in occupational prestige and income.

It has been well established that advancement in occupational prestige and income are directly related to the degree of education. In this
country the bachelor's degree is a prerequisite to entrance into the occupations and professions that provide a middle or upper-class way of life.
High school education is required for most technical and white-collar
jobs, and semi-skilled or unskilled jobs await those who drop out of
school before graduation. It is very clear that one's placement in the
occupational hierarchy depends upon the amount and kind of education
he receives. Viewed in this light, educational inequality is one of the
greatest barriers to mobility. Hence the poorly educated are consigned
to statuses of low prestige and income with all of the economic and cultural disadvantages that are attached to these positions. The economic
inequalities are, at least in many instances, less a barrier to educational
equality for the poor than is the lack of motivation. Sociological research
indicates that the sons of professional and upper classes nearly all go to
college and eventually enter jobs at the higher levels; very few sons of the
unskilled classes go to college and the majority of them enter jobs at the
unskilled level.

The change in aims of education from that of the cultivated mind
to that of social mobility has had some rather obvious results. To most
present-day youths, learning for its own sake has given way to learning
as a step-by-step process to a job. Since the turn of the century, parents
have instilled in their children the idea of the need for an education to
get ahead, and this has normally been interpreted in terms of monetary
income. Teachers have appealed to children in the same terms. In recent
decades trained counselors have been established in schools to aid stu-

dents, but this is essentially curriculum and occupational counseling. Because much of the subject matter of high school and college courses is so remotely related to the student's objective, many students fail to see their importance; they want a diploma but they are little interested in learning. This is true in spite of the fact that many high school and most college programs are designed to lead to jobs. In short, education as an intellectual pursuit has largely been replaced by education for occupational and social mobility.

Consequences of mobility. Social mobility has always been thought essential to the fulfillment of individual personality, and as a contribution to society. The pre-industrial craftsman felt secure in his status. There was little chance that he would rise beyond his own craft, and little chance that he would fall. His satisfaction derived from his security and his craftsmanship. The lack of division of labor and specialization gave his ingenuity free play and afforded an opportunity for pride in workmanship. The present division of labor and standardization have largely eliminated worker ingenuity, satisfaction derived from work, and the pride in workmanship. Industrialization has, beyond doubt, tended to break down class rigidity and to increase social mobility. But the chance to rise is also the chance to fail. The vast numbers of highly educated professionals, technicians, experts, unskilled and white-collar workers are all scrambling for the symbol of status. The American tradition has always expected children to rise above the status of their parents, and the pressure of this aspiration has caused anxiety among those who have succeeded as well as among those who failed. Failure to achieve expected goals frequently leads to frustrations which are internalized, resulting in varying degrees of mental illness ranging from mild frustration and dissatisfaction to complete nervous breakdown. On the other hand, frustrations may be turned outward by rationalization and the blame for individual failure placed on some ethnic or minority group or other external cause. This may be the basis of much prejudice toward minority groups.

For those who succeeded in gaining higher status, it would seem that both they and their families should be happy. This is not always true. With each visit home, children often find that they have less and less in common with their parents; children are frequently reluctant to have their new friends meet their parents. Successful promotion frequently means either moving to a new city, uprooting one's family, establishing new friends and a new style of life, or altering one's present authority relationships and friendships. It means one may drop one's old friends and establish new, more formal, relationships with former associates who were left behind. Not only the individual, but his whole family becomes implicated in the strain of adjusting to a new role. Many marriages are threatened in this very situation. It may also happen that the individual's new standard of living places him in a worse financial position than he was before his supposedly successful move. It seems that in a competitive society, both success and failure are fraught with psychological pitfalls with which a great many individuals are unable to cope. Personal relationships often become functional, temporary, and superficial. Business relationships are more legal and formal. Justice has become largely a matter of staying within the letter of the law, and many other relationships are on the same basis. Because of the complexity of economic and social organizations, justice seems more difficult to determine. For many new relationships, there are few precedents or well-defined norms, and hence behavior is more permissive and more rational. Values have shifted from an emphasis on work to an appearance of being successful.

BIBLIOGRAPHY

Barber, Bernard, *Social Stratification: A Comparative Analysis of Structure and Process.* New York, Harcourt, Brace, 1957.

Bendix, Reinhard, and Seymour Martin Bendix, eds., *Class, Status, and Power: Social Stratification in Comparative Perspective* 2nd ed. New York, Free Press, 1966.

Beshers, James M., *Urban Social Structure.* New York, Free Press, 1962.

Centers, Richard, *The Psychology of Social Classes: A Study of Class Consciousness.* Princeton, N. J., Princeton, 1949.

Cuber, John F., and William F. Kenkel, *Social Stratification in the United States.* New York, Appleton-Century-Crofts, 1954.

Gordon, Milton M., *Social Class in American Society.* Durham, N. C., Duke, 1958.

Hollingshead, August B., *Elmstown's Youth.* New York, Wiley, 1949.

Kahl, Joseph A., *The American Class Structure.* New York, Rinehart, 1957.

Lipset, Seymour Martin, and Reinhard Bendix, *Social Mobility in Industrial Society.* Berkeley, University of California Press, 1959.

McKinley, Donald Gilbert, *Social Class and Family Life.* New York, Free Press, 1964.

Lynd, Robert S., and Helen M. Lynd, *Middletown.* New York, Harcourt, Brace, 1929.

Mott, Paul E., *The Organization of Society.* Englewood Cliffs, N. J., Prentice-Hall, 1965.

Reiss, Albert J., Jr., et al., *Occupations and Social Status.* New York, Free Press, 1961.

Reissman, Leonard, *Class in American Society.* Glencoe, Ill., Free Press, 1959.

Warner, W. Lloyd, *American Life: Dream and Reality.* Chicago, University of Chicago Press, 1962.

Warner, W. Lloyd, *Social Class in America: A Manual of Procedure for the Measurement of Social Status.* New York, Harper, 1960.

Williams, Robin M., Jr., *American Society: A Sociological Interpretation.* New York, Knopf, 1960.

13

The national community

THE term mass society is frequently used in an evaluative sense. Our concern, however, is with the transfer of social participation from the local community to the national community. The mass society is characterized by mechanization, specialization, mobility, competition, impersonality, status-mindedness, anonymity, bureaucracy, and more or less superficial and transitory relationships. The following is an attempt to deal with a few of the major institutions and social values of American society as a national community.

American society with its mass production, mass consumption, mass advertising, and mass systems of transportation and communication has increased many times the contacts of individuals and has extended many of them to a nation-wide scale. In a broad sense, America has become a national community; the minute division of labor has tied Americans together by creating a high degree of interdependence. Although there are thousands of varied groups and associations, making this one of the most heterogeneous societies in the Western world, we do share a common culture.

We have pointed out, along with other institutional changes, changes in: the economy from laissez-faire to regulated capitalism and the dominance of the corporation; government from individualism to the welfare state; the family from institutional to companionship: education from general to specialized; and religion from state church to voluntary membership and pluralism.

The consequences of this transformation are still too much a part of the present scene for the results to be clearly visible. Statements of general behavior patterns always require the formulation of an "ideal type" to which there are always exceptions. Such terms as rural society, urban society, agrarian society, and medieval society are generalizations based on specific aspects of the various societies which they purport to describe. The features of a mass society—mass production, mass consumption, mass entertainment, mass advertising—are easy to observe, but they do not tell very much about our values, beliefs, and ideologies. Our mass society is praised as the most affluent society in the world and criticized for creating alienation and conformity, for stifling individualism, de-emphasizing religion, bureaucratizing our government and our economic, educational, and religious institutions. Whether the advantages will far outweigh the disadvantages is still a problem for the future.

The community and the greater society. One of the most apparent changes resulting from the transition to a mass society has been the increasing ties of local individuals, groups, associations, and institutions to the larger, national society. Our dominant goal is greater and greater production. This is the basic underlying factor of our society; the transformation of the material base on which our institutions rest is the dominant factor in their change.

The local community—the individuals, groups, associations, and institutions, whether rural, urban, ethnic, or other—is increasingly linked with the greater society both horizontally and vertically. Community studies, such as Arthur Vidich and Joseph Bensman's *Small Town in Mass Society*, show that this is true and explain why it is true. Urbanization, industrialization, and bureaucratization are the processes which link the community to the greater society at various levels. The control of American institutions—whether economic, political, educational, or religious—has moved farther and farther away from the local community as a power center; and this has come about through the development of bureaucratic organization in which the power rests largely with those at the top who control the bureaucracies—what C. Wright Mills has called the "power elite."

This situation is easy to demonstrate. Within any local community, the policies of banks, department stores, automobile distributors, filling stations, discount houses, chain stores of all kinds, appliance distributors, commercial farm producers, labor unions, churches, and schools are in varying degrees determined by those in bureaucratic organizations somewhere outside the community. Someone who goes to a bank for a loan, for example, is usually unaware to what extent the policies of the Federal Reserve System and the fiscal policies of the United States Government influence the interest rate and the ease of securing a loan. The same is true of wages of laborers, prices of farm products, accreditation and curricula for schools, prices of gasoline, and licenses to teach and practice law or medicine. While the shift in social participation to the larger society continues, because of the vast increase in social contacts the local community serves more functions than ever before. Not only is the individual tied to the greater society as indicated above, the federal government touches him in dozens of ways. These include social security,

Medicare, guarantees of savings and loan deposits, regulation of wages, hours, working conditions, child labor, government loans of many kinds, government contracts, subsidies of many kinds, farm-price supports, and support of research and education. In 1800 there would have been none of these ties to the larger society.

Some results of this change. The processes of urbanization, industrialization, and bureaucratization shape the destinies of communities and individuals. The complexity of modern American society makes us dependent not only upon the government in dozens of ways, but also upon the output of the producers of goods and services, the effective operation of all kinds of transportation and communication facilities, and the equitable distribution of what is produced among consumers. It also places the ultimate responsibility for order and social justice increasingly at the national level.

The cohesion of a society, however, depends upon more than its social organization. Our common interests extend far beyond the economic. Peace, order, prosperity, the guarantee of civil and property rights are of vital importance. Because of wars and threats of war, the growing military establishment has, in recent times, itself become an important unifying agent. We also have common values resulting in part from standardized education and religious training, technology, and communication.

THE RESHAPING OF AMERICAN INSTITUTIONS AND VALUES

Our new way of life has, of course, radically changed the roles which individuals must perform. As individuals are called upon to perform these new roles—women working outside the home, almost everyone working for someone else, the members of the family working separately instead of together, everyone cooperating with strangers in nearly all areas of life—they are required to readjust their behavior patterns. Considering the radical change in the way people live—in their work, their entertainment, their family life, their associations, their mobility, their interdependence—it should not be surprising to find that their attitudes, ideas, beliefs, and values have changed to accord with the needs of their environment. Changes in ideology are the bases for changes in the institutional structure of our social organization.

Economic and political integration. The present concept of property rights is not as absolute as it once was; managements accept a greater degree of responsibility for the welfare of their workers, their products, and for consumers than formerly; the economy is no longer looked upon as automatically self-regulating; and the Federal Reserve System and the fiscal policies of the government are accepted as important means of regulating the economy. The former economy was almost entirely free from government influence. Today the two are so entwined that almost any action of government affects in some way some segment of the economy. The result is that all segments of the economy, including labor, have their lobbyists at both the state and national capitals to protect their interests and to secure as much of the government largess as possible.

Industrialization of America has resulted in such an absolute interdependence that the government is expected to intervene to protect the public interest. Governments at the state and local levels also take responsibiilty for industrial development, social insurance, health and welfare services, housing, education, and scientific research. There is increasing government intervention in the regulation of economic enterprises, industrial disputes, cases for the protection of the consumer, and so on.

Science and education. Because of the high degree to which scientific knowledge and activity have developed into an indispensable part of American culture, science has become a major institution in American society. The scientific method has also tended to rationalize our way of thinking, even in the field of religion. Science has, in fact, become the great American religion, and every conceivable effort is made to use the term as a stamp of authenticity. Even though science is the bedrock of our industrial society, there are many areas of life to which science is not applicable. Science cannot tell one which occupation to choose, which boy or girl to marry, which college to attend, which church to join, whether to run for political office, or whom to trust. Most of the areas of human behavior lie outside the realm of science, and education in these areas is just as important for the health of our social system as is education in science. During this century, general education, the best hope for the solution to many of the problems which confront our modern industrial society, has been neglected.

If education is to safeguard democracy, it must fulfill the hopes and aspirations of the majority as well as promote a social environment in which democracy can thrive. With the great growth in population and complexity of society, the level of American education must be raised. The most expensive single function of any community is its educational system. The proper financial support of education in our rapidly growing mass society constitutes a major problem. It is still questionable whether increasing federal aid to education is the correct answer, or whether adequate financial support can otherwise be obtained. Most large cities, where the great population is located, are facing financial disaster. The welfare of a given area is in proportion to the level of its education, and education must keep pace with its rapidly changing social environment.

The urban crisis and federalism. American cities today are faced with many problems, but the most important one is inadequacy of revenue sources. Before cities with their exploding populations can meet the demands for better schools, fire departments, police departments, streets, low-income housing, and all other services, they must somehow find sources of revenue. But unfortunately state and federal taxation have pre-empted all but the most unproductive sources, leaving mainly the ad valorem or property tax as the chief source of funds. The states have done little to help their cities. Mayor Kenneth A. Schmied of Louisville, Kentucky, said in Houston in July, 1966, that "the states have almost without exception failed to do anything for their cities except feed on their revenue and ignore their problems."[1]

The Advisory Committee on Inter-Government Relations, a 26-member bipartisan commission established by Congress, said in its eighth annual report early in 1967 that the "tremendous task of financing, servicing, and governing metropolitan America clearly poses the greatest challenge to federalism since the Civil War."[2] The states lack either the willingness or the ability to deal with major urban problems. One of the chief reasons for state inaction is their antiquated government machinery, too frequently dominated by rural legislators. The report further indicated that only eleven states had offices of urban affairs, only a half dozen were participating in urban renewal, public housing, and mass transportation programs, and only eight were assisting in construction of local sewage treatment plants despite the serious problems of water pollution. Unless the states modernize their machinery for dealing with urban problems and channel greater amounts of revenue into urban areas, the federal government will be compelled to come to the aid of the cities, by-passing the states entirely. This is already being done. Roscoe Drummond in his column on April 5, 1967, said, "If the states fail to do their part, their demise will be suicide, not murder."[3]

There is probably nothing that the states can do to keep the federal government from continuing to expand its influence into the lives of Americans. The big problems of today know no state boundaries, and it is probable that urbanization and industrialization will make still more problems national in scope. This is no reason, however, for states and cities to fail to do all in their power to meet their own problems. County governments, as administrative subdivisions of the states, ought to be

---

[1] Beaumont Enterprise, Beaumont, Texas, July 26, 1966.
[2] New York Times News Service, *ibid.* (March 30, 1967).
[3] *Beaumont Journal,* Beaumont, Texas (April 5, 1967).

made into effective administrative units for the states. Unfortunately,
however, they remain as anachronisms of an isolated agrarian society
whose powers are almost uniformly restricted to housekeeping chores.
Half of the states do not even permit their cities to have home rule. It
is incredible that the mayor of New York City should have to go to
Albany and plead with the state legislature, most of whom are not from
New York City, for taxes which he believes the city needs. Considering
the long years of neglect by rurally dominated state legislatures, and the
fact that all but a small portion of the American people are either urban
dwellers or depend upon the cities for their livelihood, it is no wonder
that cities are increasingly by-passing the state and going directly to
Washington for help. The states have already slipped from being the
dominant partner in the federal system to a subordinate position and
are in danger of further loss of status. To quote *Time* magazine of May
27, 1966, "It is therefore possible to foresee a time when the states,
through locally elected governments, will serve chiefly to give a regional
accent and interpretation to programs initiated by Washington for the
nation as a whole." Practically all problems of importance touch all three
levels of government—federal, state, and local—and the well-being of
Americans depends upon the effective operation at all three levels. The
increasing participation of the federal government in the daily lives of
all of us does not settle the problems of urban living. The administration
of all functions of government has to be carried out at the state and local
levels, and there are many reasons to believe that the democratic process,
as well as the well-being of individuals, will be better served if this is
done through efficient, democratically elected state and local officials
instead of an all-pervading federal bureaucracy.

Foreign observers since de Tocqueville observed materialistic values
in Americans. This has been in part due, no doubt, to the unusual opportunities for economic success and to success itself. As the standard of
living has increased, the attainment of a higher plane of material com-
forts has come to be the accepted birthright of all. Whether it is a
compliment or a criticism, Americans throughout most of our history
must plead guilty to the excessive pursuit of material success. While materialism is not the only significant value, it is predominant.

The impact of materialism has made American education a means to
the end of improved social status through financial achievement. Material success is not, however, the only value which Americans have or
which education should promote. The preservation of our democratic
way of life in no small way depends upon the degree to which education
also promotes other values. Extreme individualism is a selfish ideology
which must be considered in the light of social responsibility. The complexity of present-day society makes the necessity of an adequate understanding of social responsibility a vital concern.

THE INDIVIDUAL AND COLLECTIVE SECURITY

Historical crises and collective security. The growth of the United States into a national community and a great world power, the involvement in World War I and the post-war reconstruction, the Great Depression, and the rise of totalitarian movements presented an imminent threat to the traditional concepts of individualistic American democracy. The problems created under industrial capitalism were threatening the extinction of democracy and even capitalism in the traditional sense. Thoughtful Americans were alarmed at the spread of facism in Europe, and such fascist societies as the German-American Bund, William Dudley Pelley's Silver Shirts of America, and the demagogy of Father Coughlin and the Rev. Gerald L. K. Smith. Sinclair Lewis' novel, *It Can't Happen Here,* spread an alarm at the growing tendencies toward totalitarianism in America. In 1932, James Truslow Adams, author of the best-selling *Epic of America,* wrote that the lesson of the century was that in every crisis democracy had been forced to give way to autocracy or dictatorship. With the deepening of the Depression, traditional individualism was face to face with disaster. It was soon recognized that frontier individualism, localism, and laissez-faire, while values suitable for an agrarian society, were inadequate to meet the threats to both democracy and the capitalistic system. While democracy was being rejected on all sides as hopelessly inefficient and gradually dying, America chose what Harold Laski called a "positive state," what we have described as the "welfare state." In the past three or four decades, our two major social problems have been the completion of political democracy and the achievement of social justice. That traditional individualism has given way to collective security in all avenues of American life has been pointed out repeatedly. That the average American has been, and still is, able to achieve greater fulfillment under colective security than he would have been otherwise is now generally accepted as fact.

Although collective security is now the American way of life, there are many areas in which it impinges upon the democratic tradition and the individual. The involvement in Vietnam is of particular importance. America had been basically a non-military nation until about 1946. At the end of World War II, the United States did a fantastic job of demobilizing its "citizen army," discharging 1.5 million service men in the single month of December 1945. Everyone is familiar with succeeding events: the beginning of the cold war, the atomic energy race, the McCarthy episode, the development of a permanent war economy, the race in space, and America's assumption of leadership of the free world against totalitarianism. The cold war competition with its potential for destruction has frightening implications. In times of crisis—the McCarthy era, for example—private employees, college teachers, and ministers were dismissed from their positions on the grounds of alleged disloyalty, and even Congressmen dared not speak up for the traditional American doctrine of the right of dissent. What had happened to American individualism? Such are the conditions out of which totalitarianism takes over.

The postwar loyalty oath and the costly military preparedness programs made the final shift in the emphasis in American democracy from individualism to collective security. Increasingly the individual has become dependent upon social-welfare programs, government contracts to private industry and colleges, G. I. Bills of Rights, government subsidies and loans—the joint operation of our economic and political institutions at the national level. This is not an argument that collective security is bad, or that it can be avoided, only that it is different and has potential destructiveness to the American ideal of a democratic society. In this respect it is up to Americans to keep collective security which seems necessary always subject to the democratic process. Basic to this process is education: but not just any education. If education is to play its expected role in the fuller realization of American democracy, it must do more than meet the demands of the present which are so heavily weighted with purposes of material gain. It must shape those demands, if necessary, to keep them consonant with our democratic ideals. The President's Commission on Higher Education in 1948 pointed out the need for a common core of general education for this purpose. It stated that the members of a society must have a body of common experience and common knowledge—a community of values, ideas, and attitudes—to offset the results of the minute division of labor and the conflict of special interest groups.

The cold war and militarism. Since the 1930's there have been high military officials in all kinds of government policy-making positions. The spirit of the American democratic tradition has always been hostile to military influence in political life. It should be emphasized, however, that militarism is less an attitude of military men toward civilians than an attitude of civilians toward the military. Many of our oustanding military leaders have held to the idea of civilian supremacy; among the most recent are General George C. Marshall and former President Dwight D. Eisenhower. It is a legitimate question to ask why the government must rely on professional military men rather than civilians. The answer must be one of two alternatives: either Americans have repudiated a basic doctrine of the democratic ideology, or the bankruptcy of individualism finds qualified civilians so preoccupied with their own interests that they no longer accept the responsibility for serving their government. The present danger arises from the merging of the economy and the government into a war economy or garrison state. President Eisenhower warned against this "military-industrial complex" in his Farewell Message in 1961.

Change and institutional adjustment. The foundations of the mass society lie within the institutions of the local community. The traditional community with its local values is rapidly being eclipsed. The present social milieu requires institutions that are suited to the national community as well as to the local community, and this spells radical change in both social organization and social values. But radical change is always fraught with danger. There are always people who fear that change, certainly radical change, will do violence to our treasured institutions. These are usually the groups who have the most to lose.

Whatever the criticism of mass society, it should be recognized that it is not an institution and it was not planned. It has developed as a concomitant of scientific and technological advancement. That many serious problems have developed from the rapid social change of the past half century is an accepted fact. The processes of urbanization, industrialization, and bureaucratization created a social milieu in which social institutions of the rural past were inadequate, and their adjustment is still incomplete.

Institutions and values are abstractions and do not of themselves adjust to problems: it is the individuals involved who do or do not adjust. The relationships of individuals have been greatly altered by the transformation from a rural to a mass society. Critics are justified in saying that the relationships of individuals are more transitory, specialized, superficial, utilitarian, competitive, and anonymous than formerly, but the degree to which this is true is debatable, as is the question as to whether the negative side of the picture outweighs the positive. The traditional community was narrow, restrictive, and socially demanding. In contrast the individual in American mass society today is for the first time free to have his own private life free from neighborly gossip and party-line telephone eavesdropping, his choice of friends and occupations, the opportunity to achieve whatever status is whithin his capability, and, in general, a greater opportunity for individual fulfillment. Such critics, as Professor Jules Henry in his book, *Culture Against Man,* have painted some unsavory pictures of American society today. These are no doubt true and could be duplicated many times. This does not, however, prove that the average American is more degenerate today than in the past. The reverse is obviously true as any comparison of the status of all individuals of a hundred years ago and of all Americans today would show.

It is widely contended that modern art has been debauched by concessions to popular taste. It is true of course that the printing press, television, and radio have bombarded the individual with all kinds of literature, art, and music, ranging from the childish and obnoxious to passably entertaining in much larger quantities than they have with materials suitable for intellectual appetites. This does not mean that the taste of most people is lower than it used to be. The fact is that it is only recently that we have had access to any of these things. As education has advanced, there has been an impressive increase in the appreciation of culture. There are over one thousand symphony orchestras in this country and rapidly increasing numbers of museums and art schools, libraries, dramatic groups, and adult education courses and lectures. Statistics show skyrocketing figures on museum, concert, and lecture attendance, on purchases of classical records and literary and scientific books. Those who see the present as anti-intellectual and lacking in appreciation of classical art, literature and music are, in fact, defenders of the aristocratic cultural tradition. It is no doubt true, as the critics contend, that the aristocratic cultural tradition which was characteristic of an earlier period in England and France, and the Eastern seaboard of the United States until the time of the Jacksonian Era, has been sacrificed by the the rise of mass culture. This was inevitable since such a tradition was incompatible with the mass society as well as with the American democratic ideal. On the other hand, America has developed a "middle brow" culture which far exceeds in popular participation that of any preceding period of her history.

The individual. American values center on the individual, and any evaluation of their change must be measured by what they do to enhance or detract from his freedom of personal development. This is the basis of our political strength, our economic growth, and our social progress. There are certain values in American society which are necessary to the fullest self-satisfaction. Among the most important of these is freedom: not only freedom of speech, the press, and religion, but also freedom to choose a career, to move where and when one pleases; to live the kind of life one pleases; to achieve status on the basis of one's ability. Another value essential to individual fulfillment is equality: not only equality before the law, but equality of educational opportunity, and of economic, social, and political achievements. There are many other positive values, but the mass society has also been criticized for creating conformity, alienation and disengagement, insecurity, cynicism, mediocrity, and anti-intellectualism. It can hardly be denied that the dominance of large corporations and large bureaucracies do impose limitations upon the individual, but it is doubtful that these are greater limitations on the development of the individual than that they are collective and cooperative means to his personal fulfillment. The picture is neither black nor white. For a people who spend billions of dollars on foreign aid, more billions on ostentatious display of homes, cars, and other symbols of success, and whose standard of living is the envy of the world, it is a shocking contrast and indictment to find the appalling degree of poverty, of poor mental and physical health, illiteracy, juvenile delinquency, and degrading housing conditions that are permitted to blight the picture of the American dream. All of these things are remediable, given enough money and effort. Despite all the criticisms of conformity, insecurity, alienation, and loneliness, the evidence indicates an increasing devotion to social justice, concern for the general welfare, respect for the opinion of others, and increasing general welfare. These are manifestations of individual personality. The voluntary participation of Americans in the Peace Corps and other such organizations, generous foreign aid, the civil rights marches, college student protests, the seriousness of youth in the pursuit of education, the behavior of our young men in Vietnam and elsewhere, and the humanitarian efforts of Americans in general do not indicate a self-indulgent, bigoted, conforming, decadent society. The idea of returning to some simpler form of society to escape the problems that confront us is sheer wishful thinking. Given the broad education which is increasingly available to everyone, the variety of careers open to the individual are greater than ever, and the individual with a little initiative can find many avenues for self-improvement. There have always been critics of change and critics of youth. Those of today are probably no more serious than those of the past.

THE RE-INSTITUTIONALIZATION OF THE INDIVIDUAL

The discussion of social change should not obscure the person who is the center of social concern. Institutional changes are changes in role behavior of individuals. There was little place for individualism in the feudal system of the Middle Ages. The status and rights of the individual were accorded on the basis of his social class, not individually. Beginning with the fourteenth century, the individual was gradually emancipated from the regimentation of feudal restrictions, and individualism found expression in art, vernacular languages, religion, and economic and political life. In Western societies the growth of capitalism and the rise of the middle classes saw the individual increasingly freed from mercantilistic restrictions, the rule of an hereditary aristocracy, the monopoly of the ecclesiastical hierarchy, and even the family. The movement culminated in America in the nineteenth century in what was called "rugged individualism," the supremacy of the individual and freedom from external restraints. Under the impact of social Darwinism, spelled out by Herbert Spencer, preached by William Graham Sumner, and practiced by American capitalists, it reached its peak during the last quarter of last century.

The direction of change in social relationships in modern times has been pointed out by many social scientists: Sir Henry Maine's conceptualization of change from status to contract; Ferdinand Tönnies' from Gemeinschaft to Geselleschaft; Emile Durkheim's from mechanical to organized solidarity; Robert Redfield's folk to urban; Howard Becker's from sacred to secular; and Charles H. Cooley's from primary to secondary groups. All of these approaches try to establish standards by which the processes of social change can be understood. While these are ideal formulations, they are intended to describe the actual social relationships of individuals as they go about their daily affairs. It is important to distinguish, however, between individualism as a theory and as what the individual actually does. It is the latter which leads us to conclude that individualism in economic and political affairs in America has declined greatly in the twentieth century. The theory itself has also been drastically modified. The major part of the individual's behavior is tied to or conditioned by the major institutions of his society, either by choice or necessity, and hence changes in the social environment eventually impinge upon his values. This is as simple as saying that the way people live and make their living has much to do with what they believe.

The excessive individualism of the Robber Baron era brought to light the serious conflict in the two most cherished of American values—freedom and equality. The freedom of the individual to exploit not only the natural resources but also other human beings proved to be the road to monopoly and the creation of greater inequality. Theories of equality do not make equality a reality. The solution to the problem was the establishment of institutional norms defining the limits of individual behavior in terms of the rights of other members of society. Some of these norms are legal or political, but many of them are not. The great complexity and interdependence in the relationships of individuals in our mass society have led to the institutionalization of great areas of our lives. The government regulates some of the relationships between management and labor, but the great bulk of institutional arrangements are worked out by mutual agreement, or by choice. Nobody is forced to work for a corporation or for the government; but because they offer opportunities for employment, people prefer to do so. The professions become increasingly important in our society, and their activities are controlled largely by their own institutional norms and in more limited respects by government regulations.

The great growth of education in recent times has led to the institutionalization of a vast new area of life. Not too long ago most Americans spent only a few months of a few years in school. Today education dominates the lives of most individuals under 18 years of age, and many much older. It involves them in all kinds of activities which were originally only remotely related to the aims of education. The school itself is increasingly subject to new institutional norms at the local, state, and national levels. Some of these are legal, but many have to do with such things as accreditation and professional organizations. In the same way the church has attempted to involve itself increasingly in the daily lives of its members through the addition of numerous activities which at an earlier time would have been considered out of place.

The increase in political norms at local, state, and national levels is well known. The great growth in institutional participation by individuals is in keeping with the growth in size and complexity of American society. The family is the one institution whose number of traditional functions has been considerably reduced. This is because the other institutions have taken over many of the functions which the family previously performed, and not because the family is a decaying institution. The fact is that it is more concerned with its major responsibility of socialization than at any time in the past.

At first glance this great increase in institutional participation would appear to overwhelm the individual and drastically reduce his prospects of self-fulfillment. Critics are no doubt right in saying that there is greater conformity than formerly in some areas, and it may also be true that initiative in the economic area has been stifled to some extent. But individualism is a matter of relationships between the individual and other individuals and groups, and it is difficult to see that the present-day individual is seriously hampered in making personal choices in any area other than that of his job. Furthermore, it must be recognized that, in a complex society, the freedom of the individual requires regulation somewhat in proportion to the size and degree of complexity. It is also true that social participation outside the institutional sectors has increased and that by selective participation the possibility for variation in individual experiences is almost infinite. It is even doubtful that the individual in his present job is any more forced to conformity than were the majority of industrial workers in the heyday of laissez-faire. The possibility for variety in his social life is infinitely greater. With the improvement in the standard of living, the rise in the educational level, and the proliferation of opportunities for selective participation, it is possible that conformity as a way of life is considerably less than it was in the past.

BIBLIOGRAPHY

American Round Table, *The Common Good,* Digest Report. New York, The Advertising Council, 1962.

Arieli, Hehoshua, *Individualism and Nationalism in American Ideology.* Cambridge, Mass., Harvard, 1964.

Bell, Daniel, *The End of Ideology.* New York, Collier, 1962.

Dewey, John, *Individualism, Old and New.* New York, Capricorn, 1929.

Ekirch, Arthur A., Jr., *The American Democratic Tradition: A History.* New York, Macmillan, 1963.

Mills, Gordon, *Innocence and Power: Individualism in the Twentieth Century.* Austin, University of Texas Press, 1965.

President's Commission on Higher Education, *Higher Education for American Democracy.* New York, Harper, 1948.

Snyder, Richard Carlton, and H. Hubert Wilson, *The Roots of Political Behavior: Introduction to Government and Politics.* New York, American Book, 1949.

Warren, Roland L., *The Community in America.* Chicago, Rand McNally, 1963.

Williams, Robin M., Jr., *American Society: A Sociological Interpretation.* New York, Knopf, 1960.

INDEX